I0555334

Christian Posture

Volume I

Christian Posture

Walk Tall, Stand Straight in a Crooked World—
Eight Core Doctrines

David Parker Mitchell

Christian Posture

Walk Tall, Stand Straight in a Crooked World—

Eight Core Doctrines

Copyright © David Parker Mitchell 2025

All rights reserved. No part of this book may be reproduced or transmitted in any form or by any means without written permission from the author (Contact: info@christianposture.com).

ISBN 978-1-966903-28-4

Library of Congress Catalog Card Number : xx-xxxxx

Revised May 22, 2026

Scripture quotations are from Logos Legacy Edition 44.2.10 software, the KJV Pure Cambridge Edition, first published around 1900, and have been carefully typeset to remove any typographical errors and accurately reflect the original text.

BARNES & NOBLE
PUBLISHING

Dedication

I dedicate this book to my high school sweetheart and wife of 50 years, Charlotte Mitchell, who is my greatest earthly gift from the Lord.

Acknowledgments

I am eternally grateful to my wife and lifelong partner, Charlotte, for being my perpetually positive encourager, my best friend, and the only love of my life.

I am thankful for my five children and their spouses (listed chronologically):

- Jenny Calvert and the new son God gave me, Colin

- Katie Huber and the new son God gave me, Dave

- Paul Mitchell and the new daughter God gave me, Julia

- Ben Mitchell and the new daughter God gave me, Ashton

- Matthew Mitchell and the new daughter God gave me, Emily

These all work with me in our three family businesses and are the hardest working people I know. Because of them, I now have the time to write—something I have wanted to do all my life. And, because of them, I get to see my sixteen grandchildren (so far) every week. Life doesn't get better than this.

I extend my gratitude to CEO, Katie Huber; Chief Sales and Brand Officer, Dave Huber II; CFO, Colin Calvert; Chief Compliance Officer and Team Manager, Ben Mitchell; YouTube and Podcast Production Manager and Personal Strategist, Paul Mitchell; Copywriter and Marketing Specialist, Julia Mitchell;

Video Production Manager and Personal Strategist, Matt Mitchell; Style and Content Advisors, Jenny Calvert and Ashton Mitchell; Executive Director of AMPT, Geoffrey Nance, and all who make up the wonderful TRADEway team.

Also to CEO John Quinn and COO Neil Milburn and the Exos Aerospace team; Field Superintendent Preston Locke and the E. G. Hall Oil Co. team; and Ben Mitchell, Elder and Associate Pastor; Paul Davis, Elder and Director of Park Meadows Academy; Dave Huber II and Raymond Bland, Deacons of the Park Meadows Church team. I'm also grateful to our accountant for all the companies, Kyle Ballard. Thank all of you for your diligence and expertise and for joining our family in these world-changing companies. The diligent work of this team allows me the time to write.

I am so grateful for the biblical idea of the "Family Business"— working every day with our children, their spouses, and one of our grandchildren, Tyler (and soon more). My family, the amazing team members who are part of our family as well, and our country church family at Park Meadows Church have brought Charlotte and me more joy than anything on this earth.

Lastly, to Bonita Jewel for her amazing professional editorial work and final polish; and to Ronald Grayson and Michelle Mourton for their indispensable publishing expertise and encouragement. To Katie Huber, Ben Mitchell, and Ashton Mitchell for proofing and polishing in the early stages. Little is accomplished well without a team, and I'm grateful for all of you!

About the Author

David Mitchell is a businessman-pastor. He owns three companies and has delegated their day-to-day management to brilliant people who operate them. David has never taken a salary from the church during his 45 years in the ministry and 33 years as Sr. Pastor of Park Meadows Church in Corsicana, Texas.

He was a businessman with two degrees in business, including an M.B.A., fresh out of college and running his oldest family business, before he became a Christian. While David was still in high school, his father had taught him how to manage the office. This first business was the oil company David's great-grandfather, Captain C. L. Brown, purchased in the 1920s. Captain Brown was a nineteen-year-old junk dealer from Baltimore, Maryland, who travelled to Mexia, Texas, to find his fortune in the world's largest oil boom. After forty-five years working in the oil field, he bought the field and moved the family from poverty to wealth. Five generations later, everyone in the family still knows his name.

David and his wife, Charlotte, founded two companies other than the inherited oil company—an aerospace company called Exos Aerospace Systems & Technologies, Inc., which builds and launches reusable rockets, and a mid-sized FINRA-registered Investment Advisory Firm and educational company called TRADEway. David and Charlotte have five grown children, and all five of them and their spouses work with them in these companies.

David was saved at the age of 24 and called to preach five years later, at which time he began to study theology. He saw business principles in many places in the Bible and immediately realized that it was a practical book.

Through TRADEway, the family teaches their clients a system of trading and investing in the U.S. stock and options markets, developed over five generations in the family. They also share the biblical idea of the family business and entrepreneurship, teaching families how to build their own lasting legacies.

David and his wife, Charlotte, co-founded what is now known as Park Meadows Church in 1980, and Park Meadows Academy in 1981. David served as Youth Pastor and then Associate Pastor under three other pastors before he became the Sr. Pastor in 1992. His greatest love is preaching and teaching the Word of God.

Contents

Volume 1

Introduction

NO SEPARATION OF SECULAR AND SACRED

I was speaking at a large two-day TRADEway event in Dallas, Texas, with my lifelong friend, Dr. Myron Golden. I asked the crowd early the first morning, "Who knows the oldest book on the planet that contains economic and financial principles?" None of the first-time attendees raised a hand, which is the usual result when I ask this question. A look of surprise fell over the crowd of about 300 people when I answered my own question with, "The Bible!"

Dr. Golden and I spent most of the day talking about Business Principles found in the Bible. The large screens in the front of the room reflected Scripture references citing economic principles, like the law of supply and demand; financial principles, including the risk/return trade-off; stock-trading principles, such as the law of proper diversification; industry groups worthy of investments found in the Bible; God's greatest principle of wealth creation—the law of financial leverage—and other economic laws God flung into the universe after the fall of man from the garden. (I point out "after the fall" because had man NOT fallen, there would be no law of risk/return, because there would be no risk.)

On the first day of the event, Dr. Golden and I also focused on the great doctrines of the Bible that strengthen the entrepreneurial spirit, such as the doctrine of the Sovereignty of God. This is the indispensable doctrine behind the Protestant Ethic, which was responsible for the formation and expansion of the great economies of the Western world.

In the MBA program at Baylor University, I studied a major work by German sociologist Max Weber, *The Protestant Ethic and the Spirit of Capitalism* (German: *Die Protestantische Ethik und der Geist des Kapitalismus*).[1] His book was translated into English for the first time in 1930. It is considered a founding text in university studies of both *economics* and *sociology*. The Protestant Ethic, which Weber attributed to John Calvin and his followers, stressed individualism, hard work, and a strong moral center.

Weber observed that people lived according to these ethics:

- hard work, as a duty, carries its own reward;
- work is virtuous and satisfying;
- wasting time is sinful;
- tireless labor is part of God's will;
- Calvinism[2] is important because it teaches that God is in control.

These underlying ethics led to belief in personal responsibility, personal freedom, individual action, hard work, self-reliance,

---

[1] Max Weber, **The Protestant Ethic and the Spirit of Capitalism,** (New York: Scribner, 1930).

[2] Note: Calvinism is a theological system that emphasizes God's Sovereignty in tandem with man's responsibility. This is a biblical concept. The Reformer, John Calvin, was a gifted Bible teacher and theologian who espoused this viewpoint.

ambient, and thrift.[3]

People who lived according to this ethic were <u>inner-directed,</u> and the individual (i.e., individualism) was the emphasis, rather than collectivism (socialism or communism).

The *Encyclopaedia Britannica* states:

> Calvin's formulation of the doctrine of predestination stated that sinful humanity could know neither why nor to whom God had extended the grace of salvation. Weber inferred that the psychological insecurity that this doctrine imposed on Calvin's followers, stern believers in hellfire, was such that they began to look for signs indicating the direction of God's will in daily life. *The consequence was an ethic of unceasing commitment to one's worldly calling*....[4] [emphasis added]

The Protestant Ethic was primarily responsible for the economic success of the Western world. (Weber was demonstrably correct on this point.)

Isn't it interesting that one of the greatest pastors and Bible scholars of all time, John Calvin, was responsible for the most remarkable economic renaissance of all human history, which took place in the late 1800s and early 1900s? Sacred crossed the line into secular; it should be that way in the life of every Christian—if you

---

[3] Ibid.

[4] Arthur Mitzman, *Max Weber German sociologist*, Encyclopaedia Britannica, (Updated 2/11/25), (Emphasis added by the author.),
https://www.britannica.com/biography/Max–Weber–German–sociologist

can't do business, have fun, go to church, have a marriage, raise children, etc., WITH Jesus, then don't do it at all.

If you run an entrepreneurial business, then understand that it is Christ who owns it. It is also His money, not yours, but you are a steward of it. In fact, you are in HIS family business, and Jesus is in HIS Father's business. So, it is not a matter of sacred or secular life—it is just LIFE with Christ.

The Father in heaven, and His Son Jesus, were the first family business. Jesus said that He didn't do anything or say anything He had not seen His Father do. So, the Father sent the Son into the world to carry out His business.

John 5:17
17 But Jesus answered them, My Father worketh hitherto, and I work.

John 5:36
36 For the works which the Father hath given me to finish, the same works that I do, bear witness of me, that the Father hath sent me.

John 8:38
38 I speak that which I have seen with my Father….

But, then Jesus sent us!

John 20:21
21 Then said Jesus to them again, Peace be unto you: *as my Father hath sent me, even so send I you.*

At the TRADEway event that first morning, the room was filled with people from many different Christian denominations, as well as those who may not have been Christians at all, yet the atmosphere at this business meeting was like a lively church service. The group received these biblical teachings and saw that the Bible was the origin of so many business principles found in university textbooks across the country. Everyone seemed energized about what they were learning.

God has blessed these TRADEway meetings. Through the years I have received many emails saying things like: "I love the stock market stuff, but I come for the rabbit trails." The rabbit trails, to them, were times I would move from stock trading strategies, to business in the Bible, and then to deeper Bible themes such as the Sovereignty of God. I would put Scriptures on the screen and explain how understanding a particular doctrine had the power to move entrepreneurs, soldiers, generals, and presidents to a higher plane of success.

People have been saved at TRADEway meetings. We have seen people called to preach. Marketplace evangelism is perhaps reaching more people for Christ (and for growth in Christ and personal revival) than a traditional church.

In 1974, Evangelist Billy Graham organized a conference of international evangelists in Lausanne, Switzerland. It was called "The First International Congress on World Evangelization."[5] The conference was designed to coalesce worldwide resources toward

---

[5] Mark Whitaker, *Billy Graham: Messenger Of Hope*, TwoTen Magazine, (Issue 5, 4th Quarter, 2013), https://twotenmag.com/magazine/issue–5/features/billy–graham–messenger–of–hope/

Christian outreach. The Lausanne Covenant was an important outcome of the conference. One white paper produced by the Lausanne Committee for World Evangelization was "Marketplace Ministry." It called for Christian business owners to "bridge the Sunday-Monday, faith-work" gap. At this meeting, Billy Graham made a couple of important statements that, with hindsight, seem almost prophetic. First, he said:

"Christians at work in the world are the only real spiritual light in the midst of great spiritual darkness."[6]

Here is a second, more famous quote:

"I believe that one of the next great moves of God is going to be through the believers in the workplace."[7]

We have found these predictions of Billy Graham to be true. TRADEway is perhaps the largest nationwide proponent of the biblical idea of the family business (passing skill sets and finances down from one generation to the next, providing potential for generational legacy wealth creation, and promoting the entrepreneurial spirit) in America. We teach stock trading skill sets, which have been used for five generations in our family, to families across the country. Within this great platform God has given us, the

---

[6] Ibid.
[7] Ibid.

Bible is the highest authority for the laws of economics, finance, investing, and family business that we teach.

We always hope to be a blessing to God's people, but really, the most profound blessing is on us because we get to meet so many new Christian friends through TRADEway.

Near the end of the first day of the two-day event, a sharp, confident, well-dressed young man walked up to me at the back table. He introduced himself as Devyn and said, "Sir, your words moved me today."

I said, "Thanks."

He added, "I noticed while you were speaking that you could use some help with your posture."

As I stood there with my slightly hunched back and tucked in English posterior, I thought, *You're bold, and you sure got to that fast.*

Devyn then said, "I can help you with that. I'm a posture coach."

I smiled in my mind for two reasons: first, he was bold enough to say something so straightforward (and honest), and second, I instantly liked the young man's spirit and countenance. As we conversed, the smile went from my mind to my face, and I shook his hand and took his card.

Now, all these months later, Devyn drives (one hour each way) to my ranch twice a week and works out with me, with an emphasis on my posture. He didn't want to get paid. He wanted to swap educational information. I assumed he would want TRADEway educational material on how to properly trade in the stock market, worth tens of thousands of dollars, so I offered that. But that wasn't what he wanted. It was theological training he was interested in.

Devyn and his fiancé Tina drove a couple of hours to Park Meadows Church for services each Sunday. Then they moved closer just to be with us. On June 20, 2025, I officiated at their beautiful wedding. Life doesn't get better than this!

Now, I'm taking my posture guru through a study of systematic theology like I went through as a young man. What a blessing! … And my posture is already straighter!

Speaking of POSTURE, this book is about how to walk tall and stand straight as a Christian living in a crooked world. When Adam and Eve chose to go their own way in the garden, the entire cosmos was affected in a very negative way. Our parents were cast out of the garden, and that beautiful setting was replaced with thorns and thistles—the whole earth and the immeasurable universe fell with us. The Bible says:

Romans 8:22
22 For we know that the whole creation groaneth and travaileth in pain together until now.

This is why Jesus Christ died on the cross.

John 3:16

16 For God so loved the world [Gk. Kosmos],[8] that he gave his only begotten Son, that whosoever believeth in him should not perish, but have everlasting life.

Kosmos means God's orderly creation. Jesus died to bring the order back, which man destroyed when he sinned against the Holy, Loving Creator of that orderly universe.

Now man found himself in chaos also, and so Jesus died for him as well, to put *HIM* back in order—not just for him, but for the entire *kosmos*.

The same passage wherein we find the groaning *kosmos* (due to man's fall), we find this a few verses down:

Romans 8:30–39

30 Moreover whom he did predestinate, them he also called: and whom he called, them he also justified: and whom he justified, them he also glorified.

32 He that spared not his own Son, but delivered him up for us all, how shall he not with him also freely give us all things?

35 Who shall separate us from the love of Christ? shall tribulation, or distress, or persecution, or famine, or nakedness, or peril, or sword?

---

[8] Throughout this book the author will use brackets within Scripture when adding words or phrases for clarification only, usually adding colors of meaning from the Greek (Gk.) or Hebrew (Hbr.) to hopefully add clarity to translations from the original languages into English.

37 Nay, in all these things we are more than conquerors through him that loved us.

38 For I am persuaded, that neither death, nor life, nor angels, nor principalities, nor powers, nor things present, nor things to come,

39 Nor height, nor depth, nor any other creature, shall be able to separate us from the love of God, which is in Christ Jesus our Lord.

I wrote this book with two kinds of people in mind:

(1) The person who knows *about* the Lord, but does <u>not</u> *know the Lord personally*, and is not *certain* that he or she would go to heaven and...

(2) The person who is a Christian and has walked away from the Lord, but *wishes to experience renewal and revival*, and a closer, more powerful relationship with the Saviour, and who wants to *learn more about having a greater understanding of the Bible.*

To those in the *FIRST category*, if you care about your soul, and think about eternity, but you do not yet know Jesus Christ personally, then IF you find within your heart the *DESIRE* to do it, open the door of your heart and invite Jesus in. Look at His promise:

John 1:11, 12

11 He came unto his own, and his own received him not.

12 *But as many as received him, to them gave he power to become the sons of God,* even to them that believe on his name.

1 John 5:12, 13
12 He that hath the Son *hath life*; *and* he that hath not the Son of God hath not life.
13 These things have I written unto you that believe on the name of the Son of God; that ye may *know* that ye have eternal life….

Receive Him as your personal Lord and Saviour, and He will come in and save your soul and give you assurance of your salvation. (He did NOT say "You can *hope* you have life." He said, "Ye may *KNOW* that ye *HAVE* eternal life!")

And now your eternal relationship has begun.

This book will prove to be very *helpful to the new Christian* because it is all about what the Bible says are the *core doctrines* that must be mastered first.

If you are in the *SECOND category*, a Christian who has recently experienced renewal in your life (or wishes to) and who *wants to get serious about personal Bible study and learning to have a deeper walk with the Saviour, then this book is for you.* Why? Because it not only *covers the core doctrines*, but it also goes into depth on the *rules of proper Bible interpretation* which are indispensable for growing in the truth.

Look at Jesus's promise to the Christian who walks away, but then experiences revival and desires to come back to God:

"Behold, I stand at the door, and knock: if any man hear my voice, and open the door, *I **will*** *come in to him*, and will sup with him, and he with me."—**Revelation 3:20**

He has been waiting for you, so come back to your Lord and He will come in and have fellowship with you. (He did NOT say, "I *might* come in." He said, "I *WILL* come into you….")

And now your fellowship has been restored.

This two-volume book is about Spiritual Growth; we will study the *Eight Core Bible Doctrines* that you need to master in order to take on the correct Christian Posture in the often-chaotic world around us. All eight of these doctrines are found in the first twenty verses of Hebrews Chapter six. All twenty-four chapter titles come straight from this beautiful passage.

Allow me to speak a little about the format of this book. Many theological authors will write about a biblical concept, such as Jesus being the only way to heaven, for example, and then cite the reference of the verse which the idea came from, like this: (John 14:6). Because my curiosity leads me to need to look up the verse and see it before I can keep reading, this approach annoys me and retards my progress through the book.

I prefer to write this way: Jesus claims to be the only way to heaven. We find this in the N.T. book of John:

> **John 14:6** Jesus saith unto him, I am the way, the truth, and the life: no man cometh unto the Father but by me.

This way, you SEE the Scripture and are blessed by it without having to pause and chase it down. The large amount of Scripture printed word-for-word in this book is on purpose. I like you to see the Scripture and know that it is God talking to you. Hopefully, my words will fall in line with His. That is always my goal.

My prayer is that with this book, the Lord will bless these Scriptures in your life in a way that will move you to **stand tall and walk straight with the Lord**, holding His hand throughout more and more moments of every day. This is what it means to be Spirit-filled. This is the only way to carry oneself properly, with good stature, as a Christian.

The core muscles must be strong to support good posture. A Christian must understand that the **core doctrines** are the "spiritual muscles" needed to live a powerful, effective life, as a witness for Christ in this world. These doctrines must be learned and mastered before you can "go on unto perfection" (i.e., doctrinal maturity) in the Lord (Hebrews 6:1). I also pray for you, that...

"...Ye might walk worthy of the Lord unto all pleasing, being fruitful in every good work, and increasing in the knowledge of God."

—Colossians 1:10

—David Parker Mitchell
Sr. Pastor Park Meadows Church
Founder, President TRADEway
Co-founder, President Exos Aerospace
President, Owner E. G. Hall Oil Company

Chapter 1

The Doctrine of Christ—

Introduction

"Therefore leaving the principles of
the doctrine of Christ,
let us go on unto perfection; not laying again the foundation
of repentance from dead works,
and of faith toward God.
Of the doctrine of baptisms, and of laying on of hands, and
of resurrection of the dead, and of eternal judgement.... But,
beloved, we are persuaded
better things of you, and
things that accompany salvation...."
—Hebrews 6:1–2, 9

Every chapter in this book springs from just three amazing verses in the New Testament book of Hebrews chapter 6 (verses 1, 2, and 9). Hebrews is one of the richest books in the entire Bible. The book's grandeur lies in its detailed revelation of the new dispensation of grace, brought to the world by Jesus Christ, as contrasted from the old law of Moses. The beggarly law pales in comparison with grace, and the book of Hebrews makes it far easier for us "to comprehend...the breadth, and length, and depth, and height" of "...the love of Christ, which passeth knowledge, that ye might be filled with all the fulness of God" (Ephesians 3:18–19). This magnificent book also slays legalism! The word "better" is used many times as the author contrasts grace and law.

Chapter 6 of Hebrews begins by naming eight *core doctrines* in which all Christians need to be secure. We discover these doctrines by noticing that the writer exhorts his parishioners to learn these great Bible themes, master them, but then leave them and move on to even deeper things of God.

Hebrews was originally written to mostly Jewish believers who had been Christians long enough that they should have been beyond these foundational principles, but they were not. Nevertheless, it is *good for us* that they weren't because it allows us to see these *core principles* that the author was exhorting them to master.

The passage begins:

Hebrews 6:1–3, 9
1 Therefore leaving the principles of *the doctrine of Christ,* let us go on unto *perfection*; not laying again the foundation of repentance from dead works, and of faith toward God,
2 Of the doctrine of baptisms, and of laying on of hands, and of resurrection of the dead, and of eternal judgment.
3 And this will we do, if God permit.

9 But, beloved, we are persuaded better things of you, and things that accompany salvation, though we thus speak.

The word "perfection" in the first verse means "maturity." It is the Greek word, *tĕlĕiŏtēs,* which means *"completeness."* The author of Hebrews wanted this church to move on toward maturity, but here, he names the doctrines they needed to understand and master first. (The word "doctrine" just means important Bible themes we should all learn in a systematic study of God's Word.)

The first of these is "THE DOCTRINE OF CHRIST."

We immediately see from the first topic that these first doctrines are not spiritual "baby food" or "milk" but rather a list of the most important things for the *new believer* to learn first and the *revived believer* to master. It is like exercising your core when you work out. A strong core promotes good posture.

This first one may be the most important doctrine of all—**it answers the question, *WHO IS CHRIST?***

Was He just a good man and teacher, as the Mohammedans are taught in their Quran? Was He a rebel, even a false prophet, as many of the Jews believed in the first century, and many still believe? Was He the King of the Jews, as the Romans believed He claimed to be? Was He a created, angelic being, as the Jehovah's Witnesses and Mormons (The Church of Jesus Christ of Latter-day Saints [LDS]) teach?

Was He just a spirit who only appeared to be physical, as Docetism taught? Or was Jesus Christ two separate beings (Jesus being one, physical; and Christ being another, the Eternal Son) as the first century Gnostics believed? (Note: The Apostle John seemed to be fighting both these first-century heresies when he was inspired by the Holy Spirit to say: "Hereby know ye the Spirit of God: Every spirit that confesseth that Jesus Christ is come in the flesh is of God."—1 John 4:2)

Or is He, in fact, fully man and fully God as Biblical Christianity—both Protestant and Catholic—teaches?

Let's pause a moment and discuss what this first topic, which we will cover in the first ten chapters of this book, is NOT. The scope of this book does not allow us to go into a study of the times, places, and traditions of the world Jesus was born into, though books like *The Life of Christ Visualized* by Ray Baughman, can be very interesting.[9]

Nor can we go into detail about the life and times of Jesus Christ, as did the magnificently written work from the 1800s, *Jesus the Messiah*, by Alfred Edersheim.[10]

Nor can we discuss the history of Christology (what theologians call the study of Christ); thoughts of early church fathers such as Justin Martyr, Irenaeus, or Origen; thoughts of heretics such as the Arians; considerations of the different Councils of the church[11]—all this is far beyond the scope of these chapters because this doctrine alone would need to be covered in several books!

Although I believe it is important to understand what our brothers and sisters have believed about certain passages over the

---

[9] Ray E. Baughman, **The Life of Christ Visualized**, (Chicago: The Moody Bible Institute, 1968).
[10] Alfred Edersheim, Ray E. Baughman, ed., **Jesus The Messiah**, (Grand Rapids, Michigan: Eerdman's Publishing Company, 1889).
[11] Richard A. Norris, Jr, **The Christological Controversy**, (Philadelphia: Fortress Press, 1980).

past two millennia, the Bible is the highest standard, and so here, we will take a purely biblical view rather than a philosophical view of "the doctrine of Christ." What does the **BIBLE** say about Him?

We hold the Bible to be the verbally inspired Word of God, with God as its author and forty different humans as its penmen. The concept of HOW God transmitted His eternal Word into space and time, from a place that is not a place and where there is no time, is thought provoking. Yet the way God brought His Word to us, really, is as simple as this:

"Men *and* brethren, this scripture must needs have been fulfilled, *which the Holy Ghost by the mouth of David spake*...."[12]—**Acts 1:16**[13]

God used David—his personality, his mind, his experience, and his voice—and spoke through him to us. But make no mistake; *it was God talking.*

It is my conviction that when you study the Bible with the understanding that **GOD wrote it,** preserved it to this time, and will preserve it until the last generation, you come away with a heart that burns and a turned-on mind that gains knowledge, understanding, and wisdom.

The Bible says of itself:

---

[12] Throughout this book any emphasis added to the Scriptures is mine.
[13] All Scripture References in this book are from: **KJV 1900 from Logos**; or C.I. Scofield, D.D, **The Scofield Reference Bible, KJV**, (New York: Oxford University Press, 1945).

"All scripture *is* given by inspiration of God [i.e., God-breathed], and *is* profitable for doctrine, for reproof, for correction, for instruction in righteousness: That the man of God may be perfect, thoroughly furnished unto all good works."—**2 Timothy 3:16–17**

The Bible self-testifies that it is *breathed* by God (the Greek word for "inspired," ***thĕŏpnĕustŏs***, literally means "God-breathed") and is sufficient for the furnishing of all Christians. It is the highest authority for the Christian. All reason and tradition must be placed below it and must answer to it.

What, then, does the Bible say about Jesus Christ?

There are 300+ specific prophecies in the Old Testament concerning the Messiah. The historic man Jesus Christ has Fulfilled most of these already in his birth, life, ministry, death, resurrection, and ascension.

It is safe to extrapolate that He will fulfill the rest of them in His future second coming and millennial reign on earth. So, the majority of these have already been fulfilled by Jesus Christ in his birth and life 2000+ years ago.

In the next chapters, we will look at just a few of these remarkable, specific, prophetic predictions of the Messiah, made hundreds of years, and in some cases thousands of years, before Jesus Christ was born and fulfilled perfectly in the life of this one man. These prophecies also reveal important information about who Jesus Christ really is.

The Most Sublime of these is—JESUS IS THE ONLY MAN BORN OF A VIRGIN BIRTH! Now, let's dive into this glorious reality together.

Chapter 2

The Doctrine of Christ—

THE MAN BORN OF A VIRGIN

**"Therefore leaving the principles of
the <u>doctrine of Christ</u>,
let us go on unto perfection...."
—Hebrews 6:1**

From time to time, I have had the opportunity to talk to atheists and agnostics about my Lord Jesus Christ. This is never an easy task, but one thing I always do is challenge them to read the Bible to prove it wrong. I explain to them that over 300 specific prophecies in the O.T. were fulfilled in the life of one historical figure, the man Jesus Christ. I discuss the mathematical probability of that happening if God does not exist (it approaches zero). Then, I tell them the story of one of the most influential people in my young Christian life, Sue Riddle (who, as all my mentors are, is in heaven now).

Ms. Riddle was a published professional fashion artist by trade. (I always called her Ms. Riddle because she was my elder but also a prodigious Bible scholar and teacher).

Before I knew her, she was a professed atheist. She had two young daughters, Rebecca and Rachel. Rachel, the youngest, was found to have brain cancer. A Christian in Ms. Riddle's circle of life said she would pray for her daughter. Ms. Riddle said, "I don't believe in God because if God were there and God were good, He would not allow this to happen." The Christian friend said:

> Sue, God IS there, and He IS good, and His ways are higher than our ways, and His thoughts are higher than our thoughts. He sees the whole picture of the entire universe from the beginning of time to the end and His Will, His Plan, is perfect, and He is pleased with it.
>
> Yes, He allowed man to exert his will, and this brought sin and sorrow into the world, but God is all-knowing and good. I challenge you to read the Bible through and prove it wrong while I pray for your daughter.

A few months went by, the malignant tumor was successfully removed, and Rachel was healed. Ms. Riddle finished reading the last page of the Holy Bible and received Jesus Christ as her Lord and Saviour. She led scores to Christ and discipled multiple hundreds, and taught them the great doctrines of the Bible.

Many years later, doctors found another tumor in Rachel's brain. Rachel was grown, married, with children, and Ms. Riddle, in her old age, prayed for her beautiful daughter. This second tumor was removed successfully. Ms. Riddle shined as a bright light for the Lord and taught His Word to many until she went to heaven on July 29, 2020.

Rachel is well to this day. Both of Ms. Riddle's beautiful daughters (inside and out), Rachel and Rebecca, serve the Lord faithfully.

The Word of God is more powerful than a two-edged sword, and never returns void (Hebrews 4:12; Isaiah 55:11).

Let's look at a few of these remarkable, specific prophetic predictions of the Messiah, fulfilled in the life of the man Jesus Christ. These are the very things that speak to the intellectual mind—minds that want faith to be built upon facts—to beautiful minds like that of Sue Riddle.

The first fulfilled prophecy we will examine is the virgin birth of the Messiah.

1. **First Old Testament prophecy: The Messiah would be born of a virgin. He would be fully God and fully man.**

   Isaiah 7:14–15
   14 Therefore the Lord himself shall give you a sign; Behold, a virgin shall conceive, and bear a son, And shall call his name Immanuel.
   15 Butter and honey shall he eat, That he may know to refuse the evil, and choose the good.

The prophet Isaiah wrote this in 758 B.C.[14] This prediction was fulfilled perfectly in the life of one man in history, the Lord Jesus Christ, 758 years later when He was born in the manger.

The passage reveals four things about the Messiah: (1). He would be born of a virgin (FULLY MAN); (2). His title would be Immanuel—which means "God with us" (FULLY GOD). (3). Christ would be of low estate, not a person of high esteem or popularity with people of status. He will "eat butter and honey," as common people do (Fully Man); (4). He would be the only human to ever keep the law perfectly and never sin, and "he will know to refuse the evil and choose the good" (Fully God). Much information is packed into this prophecy when we look beyond the surface.

We will discuss His title more later, but let's look a little deeper into the virgin birth.

This is more than a Christmas theme. Yes, he was of low estate, and was born in a manger and raised by a carpenter, but have you ever considered the fact that without the virgin birth, Christ could not be our Saviour? The Messiah had to be without sin to save others (otherwise, he would have been constrained to dying only for His own sins).

As all the Old Testament sacrifices pictured, He had to be the perfect Lamb, without blemish. Therefore, this is about more than the fact that a virgin birth happened as a sign or a miracle (perhaps the greatest miracle of all time). It explains how it is that JESUS

---

[14] Archbishop James Ussher, *The Annals of the World,* 1650. In his book, Ussher predicted the dates of the chapters in the Bible. C.I. Scofield used Ussher's dates in *The Scofield Reference Bible, KJV,* (New York: Oxford University Press, 1945). I used these estimated dates for purposes of dating the prophecies of the Messiah.

CHRIST IS the Messiah, the only begotten Son of God (the only man born of a virgin); the only man who never sinned and who fulfilled the Law perfectly; the only man Who COULD die for our sins, satisfy God the Father's holiness and justice, and pay our sin debt (the wages of sin is death) so that He might extend His love and mercy to us, righteously. Jesus could die in our place because He lived a righteous life, never sinning, even though He lived in this sinful world. JESUS'S SPIRITUAL POSTURE WAS PERFECT— He walked a straight path all the days of His life on this earth because of Who He was inside and out!

What did the Law say about the required sacrifice?

"Your lamb shall be <u>without blemish,</u> a male of the first year: ye shall take *it* out from the sheep...."—**Exodus 12:5**

What does the historical record say about Jesus Christ?

"And ye know that he was manifested to take away our sins; and ***<u>in him is no sin</u>***."—**1 John 3:5**

"Forasmuch as ye know that ye were not redeemed with corruptible things, *as* silver and gold, from your vain conversation [lifestyle] *received* by tradition from your fathers; "But with the precious blood of Christ, as of ***<u>a lamb without blemish and without spot</u>***: Who verily was foreordained before the foundation of the world, but was manifest in these last times for you."— **1 Peter 1:18–20**

"Though he were a Son, yet *learned he obedience* by the things which he suffered;

"And being *made perfect*, he became the author of eternal salvation unto all them that obey him."— **Hebrews 5:8–9**

"Made perfect" in Greek is in the **aorist** tense, **passive, participle**. This means that someone greater than He made Him this way without regard to time (aorist). Jesus proceeded forth and came out from God perfect when He spiraled from eternity into time (Proverbs 8:22–24).

The resurrection of Jesus Christ declared Him to be the Messiah, the Son of God with power. He had the power to live a sinless life in a sinful world. (He can give YOU the power to *walk tall and stand straight in a crooked world* because He lives in you once you receive Him as your personal Lord and Saviour.)

"And declared *to be* the Son of God with power, according to the *spirit of holiness*, by the resurrection from the dead."—*Romans 1:4*

The writer of Hebrews testifies that Jesus lived a sinless life.

Hebrews 4:15 says, "For we have not a high priest which cannot be touched with the feeling of our infirmities; but was in all points tempted like as *we are, yet* without sin."

So, again, He lived a sinless life. He WAS the perfect Lamb of God, without blemish.

Jesus was always kind, always meek when He was with His people. However, when He was with religious hypocrites or false teachers, such as the Pharisees, it was as if He were purging the temple with a whip! He displayed righteous anger.

Who were these Pharisees?

Allow me the privilege of a small "rabbit trail," as my TRADEway students affectionately call them. (This will help explain how the Pharisees caused the Jewish nation to miss her Messiah.)

There were 400 years between the last book of the O.T., Malachi, and the appearance of John the Baptist in the early chapters of the N.T. gospels. During this time, especially toward the end, the priests of Israel stopped reading and teaching straight from the O.T. Scriptures, but rather taught from the *targums*.

Targums were *paraphrases* of the Scriptures. In other words, they taught the people what *THEY* thought the Scriptures meant, rather than teaching the actual Scriptures. This is similar to the Good *News for Modern Man* "Bible" of modern times, which are not translations, but rather paraphrases. This marked the downfall of Bible knowledge among the masses of Jews, and the uprising of the leadership called the Pharisees, which had literally become false teachers of Israel by the time Jesus was born in the manger.

An example of what they taught is this passage from the O.T. book of Isaiah:

Isaiah 53:5

5 But he was wounded for our transgressions, He was bruised for our iniquities: The chastisement of our peace was upon him; And with his stripes we are healed.

This is an excellent place to go if you wish to witness to a Jewish person, because they may not accept the N.T., but this is the gospel in the O.T., THEIR book! However, for at least three hundred years before the birth of Jesus, the Pharisees began to teach from the targums. I have a portion of a targum which includes Isaiah, Ch. 53, verse 5 in my study.

Where the Bible says, "He was wounded for our transgressions…" the *targum* says, "Our nation was wounded for our transgressions…" They eliminated the truth that their Messiah would suffer for the sins of God's people! They accomplished this by changing one word, "He," to "Our nation." They made many changes like this throughout Chapter 53 of Isaiah, always removing the ideas of the substitutionary death of Christ, propitiation, and justification by the blood of Christ. So, this is THE predominant reason the masses of Jews rejected their Messiah, Jesus, because they had never seen this passage in the Scriptures taught correctly.

They did not know about a *"suffering servant"* coming to *die for their sins.* They only expected a military leader who would free them from Rome, as the Pharisees had been teaching for years. So, the Pharisees were the worst of the worst false teachers. They taught

90% truth, but the 10% error caused the nation of Israel, from the human viewpoint, to miss their messiah (except for those like Simeon and Anna, John the Baptist and his parents, Joseph and Mary, and a few others who actually read the Scriptures rather than the targums).

Of Simeon, the Scriptures say:

Luke 2:25–32
25 And, behold, there was a man in Jerusalem, whose name was Simeon; and the same man was just and devout, *waiting for the consolation of Israel: and the Holy Ghost was upon him.*
26 And it was revealed unto him by the Holy Ghost, that he should not see death, before he had seen the Lord's Christ.
27 And he came by the Spirit into the temple: and when the parents brought in the child Jesus, to do for him after the custom of the law,
28 Then took he him up in his arms, and blessed God, and said,
29 Lord, now lettest thou thy servant depart In peace, according to thy word:
30 *For mine eyes have seen thy salvation,*
31 Which thou hast prepared before the face of all people;
32 *A light to lighten the Gentiles, and the glory of thy people Israel.*

Simeon knew exactly who the Christ was, because he had rejected the "fake Bibles" of the day, the targums.

The Pharisees, claiming to be God's spokesmen, eventually crucified Jesus, for they hated Him.

We learn much about Jesus when we contrast Him with the false religious leaders of His day. Look how Light and dark cannot co-exist.

Matthew 23:15, 27–28

15 Woe unto you, scribes and Pharisees, hypocrites! for ye compass sea and land to make one proselyte, and when he is made, ye make him twofold more the child of hell than yourselves.

27 Woe unto you, scribes and Pharisees, hypocrites! for ye are like unto whited sepulchres, which indeed appear beautiful outward, but are within full of dead men's bones, and of all uncleanness.

28 Even so ye also outwardly appear righteous unto men, but within ye are full of hypocrisy and iniquity.

Imagine if preachers spoke like that today? Mega-churches might become mini-churches! However, these false teachers were not sheep but goats. They were not wheat but tares. Look at the stern, powerful rebuke of the Light to the darkness as Jesus spoke to the same group of Pharisees in John Chapter 8.

John 8:21, 23–24

21 Then said Jesus again unto them, I go my way, and ye shall seek me, and shall die in your sins: whither I go, <u>ye cannot come</u>. (Note: Jesus did NOT say, you won't choose to come, He said you CANNOT come.)

23 And he said unto them, Ye are from beneath; I am from above: ye are of this world; I am not of this world. **24** I said therefore unto you, that ye shall die in your sins: for if ye believe not that I am he, ye shall die in your sins.

John 8:42–47

42 Jesus said unto them, If God were your Father, ye would love me: for I proceeded forth and came from God; neither came I of myself, but he sent me.
43 Why do ye not understand my speech? even because ye cannot hear my word.
44 Ye are of your father the devil, and the lusts of your father ye will do. He was a murderer from the beginning, and abode not in the truth, because there is no truth in him. When he speaketh a lie, he speaketh of his own: for he is a liar, and the father of it.
45 And because I tell you the truth, ye believe me not.
46 *Which of you convinceth me of sin?* And if I say the truth, why do ye not believe me?
47 He that is of God heareth God's words: ye therefore hear them not, because ye are not of God.

Please remember that learning from *paraphrased* Scripture, even today—which is the same mistake the Jews made while learning from the targums—can be devastating to your understanding of the truth of God's Word. Look at how Jesus treated these false teachers who paraphrased Scripture! That tells us a lot!

Read an accurate version of the Bible (my personal study of manuscript evidence has convinced me that the KJV is the most accurate English Bible).[15] Also, learn to interpret Scripture correctly. Remember, false teachers subtly change words as they cite Scriptures, and thus they bring forth false interpretations. This is tantamount to paraphrasing.

But here is what I want you to notice in the remarkable passage above. In John 8:46, 47 Jesus asked the Pharisees (who hated Him), *"Which of you convinceth [convicts] me of sin?* He that is of God heareth God's words: *ye therefore hear them not, because ye are not of God."*

Jesus claimed He had __no sin__ in His life by asking them if they could name a single sin He had committed. They could not because the people were standing around watching, and they knew the holy life of Jesus, so the Pharisees used the ad hominem fallacious argument—"You are a Samaritan and have a demon."

Jesus responded:

John 8:54–55
54 Jesus answered, If I honour myself, my honour is nothing: it is my Father that honoureth me; of whom ye say, that he is your God:
55 Yet ye have not known him; but I know him: and if I should say, I know him not, I shall be a liar like unto you: but I know him, and keep his saying.

Jesus, no doubt, lived a holy life. He was tempted in all points, as we, and yet without sinning.

---

[15] Please see Appendix 1 for my suggestions of Bibles and Bible helps.

However, the requirement for the Lamb of God to be without a spot not only meant that Jesus had to LIVE a sinless life…

…It also meant that he could not partake in Adam's ORIGINAL SIN.

Living a sinless life was not enough, even as wonderful as this perfect life was.

This is perhaps the foremost reason the virgin birth was more than a sign. *The virgin birth also ensured that Jesus had not inherited a sin nature from Mary or Joseph.* This is of paramount importance, for without this truth, we all die in our sins.

Few people, however, ask the question, "What about original sin?" If Jesus had human parents, wouldn't He be guilty of original sin, being in Adam? Wouldn't He have a sin nature, being fully man?

Now, this would be a major problem without the virgin birth.

Let's talk about what *original sin* is and why the virgin birth is of profound importance regarding Jesus's ability to die in our place—to pay our sin debt for us.

I wish to give a vignette first, concerning why Jesus MUST have been totally without sin in order to die for OUR sins (this is called the substitutionary death of Christ).

All through the O.T., especially books like Leviticus, we see the establishment of animal sacrifices in the true and godly worship of Israel. Even before this, all the way back in the first chapters of Genesis, we see the first blood sacrifices. The first one was actually performed by God Himself.

After Adam and Eve sinned and fell and were cast out of the garden, God killed an animal (this was the first death Adam and Eve had ever seen). God took the skins and made proper clothing to hide the nakedness of Adam and Eve, now that they knew they were naked and were no longer innocent. But to do this, God had to shed blood.

He must have taught them that this blood pictured the precious blood of the coming Messiah out in the future, who would die for Adam and Eve and all God's people down through time, and whose blood would remove their sins because it was a perfect sacrifice, which propitiated (satisfied) God's justice.

Why was this necessary? Because the first law, and the law that echoed all through the Bible, stated, "In the day that you eat the fruit thereof, ye shall surely die."—**Genesis 2:17**

Echoed again in **Ezekiel 18:4**, "The soul that sinneth it shall die."

And again in the **N.T. Romans 6:23**, "For the wages of sin is death…."

But **Romans 6:23** continues, "…But the gift of God *is* eternal life through Jesus Christ our Lord."

The O.T. picture of Jesus, the true Lamb of God, looks like this:

Numbers 28:3

3 And thou shalt say unto them, This is the offering made by fire which ye shall offer unto the Lord; two lambs of the first year **_without spot_** day by day, for a continual burnt offering.

Leviticus 5:18

18 And he shall bring a ram **_without blemish_** out of the flock, with thy estimation, for a trespass offering, unto the priest: and the priest shall make an atonement…and it shall be forgiven him.

The *"spot and blemish" pictures sin.* The sacrificial animals must be without spot or blemish so that their blood can atone for the sins of the people. This was done for thousands of years, rolling the sins of God's people forward, year after year, until the Messiah would come and be the *TRUE, PERFECT LAMB OF GOD*, who would ultimately remove the sins of God's people through His own sacrificial death. How? By paying their sin debt on their behalf.

So, this Messiah, Jesus, must also be without spot or blemish, and He was! And He died in the place of God's people, paying THEIR sin debt in full. This is what Jesus did 2,000 years ago, on the cross.

1 Peter 1:18–19

18 Forasmuch as ye know that ye were not redeemed with corruptible things, as silver and gold, from your vain conversation received by tradition from your fathers;

19 But ***with the precious blood of Christ, as of a lamb without blemish and without spot.***

In the O.T. it was prophesied that the Messiah would be the perfect Lamb who would die as a substitute for God's people that they may be saved, and God's justice and wrath against sin could at the same time be satisfied by His death, in the place of those who owed the sin debt—*US*.

Isaiah 53:8, 11
8 He was taken from prison and from judgment: And who shall declare his generation? For he was cut off out of the land of the living: For the transgression of my people was he stricken.
11 He shall see of the travail of his soul, and <u>shall be satisfied:</u> By his knowledge shall my righteous servant justify many; For he shall bear their iniquities.

Now that we understand why the Son of God had to live a perfect life, being tempted as we are but without sin, and then die in our place to satisfy Holy God's justice, we can discuss WHY Jesus had to not only be free from Sin, but also ***free from the nature of sin*** that had been passed down to all the children of Adam and Eve.

So, NOW let's discuss ***original sin*** and why the virgin birth is of profound importance regarding Jesus's ability to die in our place—to pay our sin debt for us.

The Bible teaches that all men are born in sin. They have inherited a sin nature from their parents, their grandparents, etc., going all the way back to Adam and Eve. In fact, the Bible teaches that from God's viewpoint, since Adam is guilty because of his original sin, we are all guilty because we were in Adam when he sinned.

I imagine you are scratching your head and thinking, HUH???

Yet, we know that we are all part of a fallen race, bound for hell. "The wages of sin is death" (Romans 6:23), and we have all sinned because we all have a sin nature (Romans 3:23).

But what does it mean that "we were in Adam?"

Fortunately, the Apostle Paul was inspired by the Holy Spirit to explain this fact and help us understand. Please read these verses carefully.

Romans 5:12, 15, 19
12 Wherefore, as by one man [Adam] sin entered into the world, *and death by sin; and so death passed upon all men*, for that all have sinned:
15 …For if through the offence of one [Adam] *many be dead, much more the grace of God*, and the gift by grace, which is by one man, Jesus Christ, hath abounded unto many.
19 For as by one man's [Adam's] disobedience many were made sinners, so by the obedience of one [Jesus Christ] shall many be made righteous.

The Holy Spirit teaches us, here, through the penman Paul, that sin entered the world through Adam and passed upon all men; therefore, all men have a sin nature and are sinners.

All men are made sinners by Adam's disobedience.

The Old Testament bears this principle out. King David says:

Psalm 51:4–5
4 Against thee, thee only, have I sinned, And done this evil in thy sight: That thou mightiest be justified when thou speakest, And be clear when thou judgest.
5 Behold, I was shapen in iniquity; And *in sin did my mother conceive me.*

David understood the idea of original sin 3,000 years ago! He was considering the truth that "My mother was a sinner when I was conceived, and therefore I am a sinner."

Psalm 58:3
3 The wicked are estranged from the womb: They go astray as soon as they be born, speaking lies.

Have you ever noticed that a newborn will be screaming, and when you run in, he looks up and smiles at you? He just lied. Pretty funny, but pretty true. And anyone who has raised children (and is still rational) will agree that you do not have to teach children to be bad; however, you must teach them to be good.

Jeremiah, in the O.T., understood the nature of sin.

Jeremiah 17:9

9 The heart is deceitful above all things, and desperately wicked: who can know it?

The Apostle Paul was the greatest Christian who ever lived. He, of all men, perhaps understood the sin nature best because, before his conversion, he persecuted and even killed Christians! He wrote:

1 Timothy 1:13–15
13 [I, Paul] Who was before a blasphemer, and a persecutor, and injurious: but I obtained mercy, because I did it ignorantly in unbelief.
14 And the grace of our Lord was exceeding abundant with faith and love which is in Christ Jesus.
15 This is a faithful saying, and worthy of all acceptation, that Christ Jesus came into the world to save sinners; of whom I am chief.

Paul spoke most definitely and profoundly about the sin nature of all human beings.

Romans 3:23
23 For all have sinned, and come short of the glory of God;

Romans 6:23
23 For the wages of sin *is* death; but the gift of God *is* eternal life through Jesus Christ our Lord.

Romans 3:10–18

10 As it is written, There is none righteous, no, not one:

11 There is none that understandeth, there is none that seeketh after God.

12 They are all gone out of the way, they are together become unprofitable; there is none that doeth good, no, not one.

13 Their throat *is* an open sepulchre; with their tongues they have used deceit; the poison of asps *is* under their lips:

14 Whose mouth *is* full of cursing and bitterness:

15 Their feet *are* swift to shed blood:

16 Destruction and misery *are* in their ways:

17 And the way of peace have they not known:

18 There is no fear of God before their eyes.

In this passage, Paul was quoting from the book of Psalms in the O.T. The Holy Spirit saw fit to put these truths in the O.T. and N.T., emphasizing the importance of understanding *the depravity of man*, i.e., man is born in sin without the ability or desire to seek God.

Without the calling of the Holy Spirit (by the grace of God), no one ever would seek Him—we are our own god! But God is great in His mercy and can reach lost, blind, deaf, walking-dead men and women and raise them from the dead! However, to do this, Jesus had to live a perfect life on this earth, fulfill the O.T. law perfectly, and die in our place, paying our sin debt in full—He had to be without sin of His own.

The O.T. passage Paul quoted from is here:

Psalm 14:2–4

2 The Lord looked down from heaven upon the children of men, To see if there were any that did understand, and seek God.

3 They are all gone aside, they are all together become filthy: There is none that doeth good, no, not one.

4 Have all the workers of iniquity no knowledge? Who eat up my people as they eat bread, And call not upon the Lord.

The topic here is original sin, but I do not want to leave you hanging with the depravity of man alone. This doctrine is not often taught in churches today and can be shocking to discover. However, this biblical information, while true, must be accompanied by this *beautiful* gospel information:

And then, while we were yet sinners, ***Christ died for the ungodly***.

Romans Ch. 3 and Psalm 14, written 1,000 years earlier, both state clearly that men and women do not seek God naturally. But when Jesus Christ came and died for His people and then sent His Holy Spirit to awaken us, we were no longer "having no hope and without God in the world."

Ephesians 2:12–14

12 That at that time ye were without Christ, being aliens from the commonwealth of Israel, and strangers from the covenants of promise, having no hope, and without God in the world:

13 But now in Christ Jesus ye who sometimes were far off are made nigh by the blood of Christ.

14 For he is our peace, who hath... broken down the middle wall of partition *between us*.

Romans 5:6–8

6 For when we were yet without strength, in due time Christ died *for* the ungodly.

8 But God commendeth his love toward us, in that, while we were yet sinners, Christ died for us.

These passages make it clear that men are born with a sinful nature and are in a depraved state. They need a loving Saviour!

Jesus brought reconciliation between God and God's people, and the Holy Spirit, Whom Jesus sent into the world, makes it possible for depraved humans to feel conviction about a need for Christ.

However, for Jesus to bring reconciliation to us, it was necessary for Him to be without sin. Again, the virgin birth becomes of the utmost importance.

There is another passage that sheds light on the principle of original sin and helps us understand that because Adam was guilty, we are born with a sinful nature and are, therefore, guilty before our Holy God.

In the N.T. book of Hebrews, there is a fascinating teaching about how Jesus is a priest after the order of Melchisedec (who was NOT from the priestly line of Levi). The writer of Hebrews uses this to prove that Jesus is a higher priest than the O.T. Levitical priests.

Their father Levi tithed to Melchisedec, and the lesser tithes to the greater. How is this so? Levi paid tithes to Melchisedec because *he was "in the loins of his father, Abraham,"* when ***Abraham*** paid tithes to Melchisedec. Melchisedec is greater than Abraham and, therefore, greater than Levi. The ultimate conclusion is that Jesus is a priest on a higher plane than the Levitical priests of the Old Testament.

Hebrews 7:9–10
9 And as I may so say, Levi also, who receiveth tithes [because he was a priest], payed tithes in Abraham.
10 For he was yet in the loins of his father, when Melchisedec met him.

This biblical concept of us being "in the loins of our forefathers as they lived their lives" indicates that since we were "in the loins of Adam" when he sinned, we took part in the original sin. This is what Paul was speaking of in Romans 5:12–19, above.

Now that we have some understanding of the principle of original sin, if Jesus were born of human parents, wouldn't He also have inherited original sin?

If Jesus inherited original sin, would He have been worthy to die for the sins of others?

This is the problem we are addressing! The answer would be "no" because He had to be the sinless Lamb of God to pay the ransom price for the sins of His people.

Part of the problem we see here is solved merely by the fact of the virgin birth. Since Mary was with a child but a virgin, then that child's father was NOT Joseph. She had not been with Joseph.

Joseph, of all people, knew this, and the angel of the Lord had to calm him down!

Matthew 1:19–20

19 Then Joseph her husband, being a just man, and not willing to make her a public example, was minded to put her away privily.

20 But while he thought on these things, behold, the angel of the Lord appeared unto him in a dream, saying, Joseph, thou son of David, fear not to take unto thee Mary thy wife: for that which is conceived in her is of the Holy Ghost.

So, Joseph did not pass his sin nature to Jesus.

But what about Mary?
Wouldn't she have passed her sin nature to Jesus?

This is where the history of the church gets interesting. Roman Catholics and the Protestants agree that Jesus did not inherit the sin nature. However, their reasons for how, are different.

I think it important to say, first, that I have many close, dear friends and business associates who are Roman Catholics, and I have many who are Protestants. I love them all. We do not have to agree on everything to be friends, or even to be brothers and sisters in Christ. In fact, in this life, we most likely never will fully agree on every little detail of the Bible.

As I have become an older Christian (and pastor), I now breathe the fresh air of not having to feel everyone must believe exactly as I do. However, at the same time I believe (and have tested in my life and friendships) that:

If two or more people will pledge to keep the rules of proper Bible interpretation, and not cheat on any of them just to win an argument, then over time their beliefs will merge closer and closer together.

Everywhere I have the opportunity to speak to crowds across the country, I attempt to persuade people to *give the God-inspired Scriptures a higher level of authority* than the ideas of men, no matter how devout or scholarly the men may be. I suggest that adults should come to a place where they recognize that the teachings of the denominations they were raised in are not perfect, and therefore we should use the rules of proper Bible interpretation, relying upon the Holy Spirit as we study, and eliminate everything we were taught that is not in line with clear Scripture, especially if it contradicts the Bible. My wife and I have spent a lifetime eliminating things that we were taught that were wrong and allowing the Bible to teach us what it plainly says. It is refreshing and freeing.

I do not believe *"Sola Scriptura"* means we should not consider the thoughts and ideas of our brothers and sisters who lived before us concerning passages of the Bible. We must. However, at the same time, I believe it dangerous to consider the traditions, beliefs, interpretations, etc., of sinful men to be on the same level as Scripture. The Bible must be on the highest plane.

As far as I can tell (by both a half century of Bible study and observation of human beings), everyone—including myself—besides Jesus Christ, has been less than perfect and thus capable of introducing false ideas into our understanding of the Bible, and of God and His ways.

It is best to let the Scripture interpret the Scripture, and let the Bible inform us rather than piously thinking we can inform or critique Scripture. (This is what liberal theologians call "higher criticism" of the Bible—it is nonsense and dangerous but appears very scholarly so if one has spiritual pride, it is alluring.) As we listen to the thoughts of men, we must hold them up to some objective authority, and I believe that authority is the Bible. Where men contradict that authority, we cast their ideas aside, and where they do not, then we pray and think about what we can learn from them.

My job in this book is not to promote either Protestant or Roman Catholic theology, but at the same time, I personally would listen very critically to any person from either side who believes he can "improve" the Scriptures by changing the clear meanings of passages taken in context, and in the light of the whole Bible; or to any person who would teach a man-made idea which contradicts clear teachings throughout the Bible. I would also listen with a very critical ear to anyone who adds any idea to our world of Systematic Theology that is not clearly taught somewhere in the Holy Bible, the only inspired Word of God.

Anything other than Scripture is subjective. Scripture is objective and judges us all and judges all things which claim to be truth.

Both the Protestants and Roman Catholics agree that Jesus Christ is fully God and fully man. They also agree that He could not have inherited the sin nature. However, they have different explanations for why Jesus did not inherit the sin nature.

Roman Catholic Stories

The Roman Catholics created three stories to deal with this problem of the possibility of Mary passing down the human sin nature to Jesus. (And, this is a conundrum that must be considered!)

- **The First Catholic Story—the Immaculate Conception:**

In 1854, Pope Pius IX, with the papal bull "Ineffabilis Deus,"[16] enunciated the idea that Mary, the mother of Jesus, was sinless and that she was free from sin from the moment of her conception until her death. This is called the "Immaculate Conception."

- **The Second Catholic Story—the Assumption of Mary into Heaven:**

Catholics also believe that Mary was miraculously "assumed" into heaven and never died a physical death. "In 1950, Pope Pius

---

[16] Pope BI. Pius IX, *Ineffabilis Deus, The Immaculate Conception*–1854, PAPAL ENCYCLICALS ONLINE, Your guide to online Papal and other official documents of the Catholic Church, https://www.papalencyclicals.net/pius09/p9ineff.htm.

XII declared the Assumption of Mary the official dogma of the Roman Catholic Church. The Catholic Church teaches that the Virgin Mary 'having completed the course of her earthly life, was assumed body and soul into heavenly glory.'"[17] This may have been believed long before 1950 by some Catholics, possibly back to the fourth century A.D.; however, it was not formally defined by their church until 1950, at least 1,800 years after the N.T. was inspired by God and penned by holy men in the first century A.D.

Father Kenneth Doyle gives a fair rendition of what Catholic tradition is on this matter: "But other evidence seems to show that under the protection of the apostle John, Mary went to a place near Ephesus (modern-day Turkey) and stayed there *until she was assumed into heaven.* This tradition is linked to the 19th-century visions of Anne Catherine Emmerich, a bedridden Augustinian nun in Germany."[18]

Neither of these two stories are found in the Bible. For example, the Bible does NOT teach that Mary was free from sin. Nor does the Bible teach that she was assumed into the clouds of heaven. As Father Doyle said, "This tradition is linked to a 19th century vision...."[19] These stories are not biblical but rather are the traditions of men.

True, the Bible clearly teaches that Jesus Christ, as He was dying on the cross, placed Mary into the care of John. However, it does

---

[17] Renee Barouxis, **Origins and Practices of the Assumption of Mary**, (Boston Public Library, August 14, 2019), https://www.bpl.org/blogs/post/origins–and–practices–of–the–assumption–of–mary/.

[18] Father Kenneth Doyle, **Did the Virgin Mary die and, if so, where?**, (The Catholic Courier, August 3, 2020), https://catholiccourier.com/articles/did-the-virgin-mary-die-and-if-so-where/.

[19] Ibid.

NOT say that he took her to Turkey or that God took her bodily into heaven, never having died. The former is from tradition dating back to Irenaeus. The latter (her ascension), according to Father Doyle, is also from tradition, not from the Bible. (Doyle's statement is kind of like quotes with no authoritative footnotes.) The Bible, on the other hand not only lacks any statement that Mary was assumed into heaven, but on the contrary, Jesus said:

"And no man hath ascended up to heaven, but he that came down from heaven, *even* the Son of man which is in heaven."—John 3:13

Some Roman Catholics teach that this does not prove Mary wasn't assumed into heaven. They argue that the verse is speaking of a time period moving back in time from when Jesus stated this, and therefore would not preclude Mary from ascending in the future, after Christ. This is just a game to attempt to win an argument. "Well, Jesus may have said no man had ever in the past ascended into heaven but the Son of man, but he didn't say a person couldn't do it in the future!" Nonsense. Of course you cannot prove a negative. But the point is that the Bible certainly does not say anywhere that Mary was assumed into heaven.

Or, they sometimes play semantics and argue that Mary did not "ascend" but was "assumed into heaven." They argue, "Jesus did not say that no one would be 'assumed.'" I understand the difference—one is active (ascend) and the other is passive (be assumed) —but I don't consider it important in this discussion. To me, this kind of argument is designed to get you to take your eye off the ball. None of this has any Scriptural authority.

With regard to whether Jesus's statement would be valid moving forward into the future, in John 3:13, "hath ascended" in the Greek is in the *perfect tense*, *active voice*, and *indicative mood*. This means that the action happens in the present time (not the past, as the English seems to infer), that the subject (Jesus) carries out the action, and that it is a true statement.

Perhaps a closer English translation would be:

"And no man ascends up to heaven, but...the Son of man which is in heaven."

That changes everything. First, the statement Jesus made is for all time, not just the past.

Second, we know from Scripture that after the first resurrection at the end of the church age, there will be a gathering of the church (1 Thessalonians 4:16, 17). Mary, in the first century, could not have been part of the rapture.

Third, you can see that this whole verse transcends time, because Jesus is speaking to a man on the earth, face to face (Nicodemus) and says, "...even the Son of man which IS in heaven." Was Jesus on the earth with Nicodemus, or in heaven? Both! (Because He is God.) At any rate, this is not past tense. It is a statement that only Jesus ascends into heaven, and the Bible certainly nowhere says Mary ascended or was assumed into heaven. So, this is a story made up by men, and introduced recently into the Catholic Church as dogma.

I convey this not to denigrate the Catholic scholars; I merely say I would be critical of these arguments, if not skeptical. My reason for bringing this up is to ask the question WHY did they make up this story?

Regarding the idea that Mary was sinless, I would ask, why do we need her to be sinless? The fact is, she was not sinless. She was a sinner who had to be saved by the substitutionary death of Jesus on the cross, as all who will be saved must be.

The fact is, the Bible indicates that she and all women in the line of the Messiah, from Eve to Mary, must be "saved through childbearing." In other words, only through bearing the child Jesus Christ could Mary be saved from her sins because He would be HER Saviour, too! He would bear HER sins on the cross. And this is true for all women (and men) from Eve down through the lineage of the Messiah ending with Mary!

1 Timothy 2:13–15
13 For Adam was first formed, then Eve.
14 And Adam was not deceived, but the woman being deceived was in the transgression.
15 Notwithstanding, <u>she shall be saved in childbearing,</u> if they continue in faith and charity and holiness with sobriety.

How do we know this applies not only to Eve but to Mary? We go back to the beginning of time when sin first came into the world.

Genesis 3:15–16

15 And I will put enmity between thee and the woman, and between thy seed and her seed; it shall bruise thy head, and thou shalt bruise his heel.

16 Unto the woman he said, I will greatly multiply thy sorrow and thy conception; in sorrow thou shalt bring forth children; and thy desire shall be to thy husband, and he shall rule over thee.

God told Eve that through childbearing, someday the Messiah would be born, and He would crush the head of Satan, and Satan would bruise the heel of Jesus. This happened 4,000 years later when Jesus died on the cross and rose again on the third day, having ransomed all God's children, including Mary, from the slave market of sin and Satan. Thus four thousand years of childbearing down through the lineage of the Messiah, Jesus Christ, saved everyone for whom He died. Mary was no exception. Being the last woman in the lineage of the Messiah, Jesus had to take her sins upon Himself also, in order for her to be saved.

- **The Third Catholic Story: Mary lived her whole life as a virgin never having other children.**

The Catholics also say that Mary never knew a man, but Jesus spoke of his brothers, so she DID know a man, Joseph, and bore other children. (Not that sexual intercourse in marriage is a sin, or that childbearing is a sin, but it IS demonstratively incorrect to say that Mary lived her whole life as a virgin and never had other children). The Bible clearly speaks of Jesus's siblings.

Matthew 12:47–50

47 Then one said unto him, Behold, thy mother and <u>thy brethren</u> stand without, desiring to speak with thee.

48 But he answered and said unto him that told him, Who is my mother? and who are my brethren?

49 And he stretched forth his hand toward his disciples, and said, Behold my mother and my brethren!

50 For whosoever shall do the will of my Father which is in heaven, the same is my brother, and sister, and mother.

Jesus had two kinds of brothers: physical brothers, born of His mother Mary after Jesus (who were outside the room in this story), and spiritual brothers, who were His followers (inside the room).

The Bible does not teach the immaculate conception; this was invented by man, given authority by a pope in 1854, and is not in the Bible. Nor does the Bible teach the assumption of Mary—it originated from a vision of a dying woman. The Bible DOES teach that Mary had other children. Though very important traditions to Roman Catholics, all three of these are man-made stories—but WHY?

The Roman Catholics understood that if Jesus were born of a woman who was part of the sinful human race, He would have inherited the sin nature. They invented this story to attempt to solve this problem.

I commend them for recognizing the problem! However, it is not permissible to add to the Word of God in order to attempt to solve it.

The Protestant Story

The Protestants teach that sin is passed down only by the man, not the woman. Therefore, Jesus did not inherit the sin nature because Joseph was not His father; the Holy Spirit came upon Mary, and she conceived a child. They teach, "Since the woman does not relay the sin nature, but only the man, Jesus did not have a sin nature."

Again, I commend the Protestants for recognizing the problem of Mary potentially passing her sin nature to Jesus, which cannot happen.

This idea is elegant because it also fits well with the idea of the federal headship of Adam. The idea of federal headship is certainly a valid theological concept. Not only is the man the spiritual head of the home, but the theological idea is broadened by verses like these:

Romans 5:14–15

14 Nevertheless death reigned from Adam to Moses, even over them that had not sinned after the similitude of Adam's transgression, who is the figure of him that was to come.

15 But not as the offence, so also is the free gift. For if through the offence of one many be dead, much more the grace of God, and the gift by grace, which is by one man, Jesus Christ, hath abounded unto many.

19 For as by one man's disobedience many were made sinners, so by the obedience of one shall many be made righteous.

1 Corinthians 15:21–22

21 For since by man came death, by man came also the resurrection of the dead.

22 For as in Adam all die, even so in Christ shall all be made alive.

The Protestant answer, "Since the woman does not relay the sin nature, but only the man, Jesus did not have a sin nature," combined with the truth of the virgin birth, and the idea of the federal headship of Adam, is a better answer. The bottom line is that Jesus was not born with the sin nature that the rest of us have. He was fully God, and fully man yet without inheriting the sin nature from Adam. Thus, He is the second Adam (1 Cor. 15:45), without sin.

How did the virgin birth happen?

When Joseph saw that Mary was with child, he was concerned that she had been with another man and was thinking of putting her away quietly for her own protection. We pick up the story in Matthew Chapter One, while he was contemplating this.

Matthew 1:20–21

20 But while he thought on these things, behold, the angel of the Lord appeared unto him in a dream, saying, Joseph, thou son of David, fear not to take unto thee Mary thy wife: for that which is conceived in her (or as Luke 1:35 says, that which is "born of her") is of the Holy Ghost.
21 And she shall bring forth a son, and thou shalt call his name JESUS: for he shall save his people from their sins.

We see the gospel penman, Matthew, quoting Isaiah 7:14–15. Matthew confirms that Jesus's name means the one "who would save his people from their sins." A literal translation of the Greek here would be, "For He shall save the people of him, from the sins of them."

Matthew spoke of Mary, the mother of Jesus, who gave birth to Jesus in Bethlehem 758 years after Isaiah wrote that a sign would be given by God—a virgin would conceive, and 720 years after Micah wrote that the Messiah would be a child born in Bethlehem Ephratah. Only the man Jesus Christ fulfilled these prophecies!

This child was conceived OF THE HOLY GHOST. This is HOW the miracle of the virgin birth took place. We also see the angel speaking with Mary.

Luke 1:26–38
26 And in the sixth month the angel Gabriel was sent from God unto a city of Galilee, named Nazareth,

27 To a virgin espoused to a man whose name was Joseph, of the house of David; and the virgin's name was Mary.

28 And the angel came in unto her, and said, Hail, thou that art highly favoured, the Lord is with thee: blessed art thou among women.

29 And when she saw him, she was troubled at his saying, and cast in her mind what manner of salutation this should be.

30 And the angel said unto her, Fear not, Mary: for thou hast found favour with God.

31 And, behold, thou shalt conceive in thy womb, and bring forth a son, and shalt call his name JESUS.

32 He shall be great, and shall be called the Son of the Highest: and the Lord God shall give unto him the throne of his father David:

33 And he shall reign over the house of Jacob for ever; and of his kingdom there shall be no end.

Mary asked the same question we are asking—how could the virgin birth happen?

34 Then said Mary unto the angel, How shall this be, seeing I know not a man? [i.e., have not had intercourse with a man—I'm a virgin!]

35 And the angel answered and said unto her, *The Holy Ghost shall come upon thee*, and the *power of the Highest shall overshadow thee:* therefore, also that holy thing which shall be born of thee shall be *called the Son of God.*

36 And, behold, thy cousin Elisabeth, she hath also *conceived* a son in her old age: and this is the sixth month with her, who was called barren.

37 For with God nothing shall be impossible.

38 And Mary said, Behold the handmaid of the Lord; be it unto me according to thy word. And the angel departed from her.

I always love to read Mary's response to this astounding information, that she, a virgin, would be overshadowed by the power of God, and the Holy Ghost would come upon her, and she would carry a child; she simply accepts that this is possible with God, as the angel said, and she replies: *"Behold the handmaid of the Lord; be it unto me according to thy word."*

How lovely is that statement! It is powerful in its humility.

And the holy child was called "The Son of God." This child was none other than the ONE MAN born in Bethlehem to a Jewish virgin at exactly the right time to fulfill the 300 prophecies written hundreds and thousands of years earlier—the Lord Jesus Christ!

Chapter 3

The Doctrine of Christ—

THE MAN BORN
IN BETHLEHEM
AT EXACTLY THE RIGHT TIME

The prophets not only wrote that the Messiah would be born of a virgin but also that this would be for a sign. They also predicted other "signs," such as exactly WHERE the Messiah would be born (720 years before it happened) and exactly WHEN he would be born (538 years before). These are the second and third fulfilled prophecies we will discuss.

2. **Second Old Testament prophecy: The Messiah would be born in a specific town. It implies once again that He would be fully God and fully man.**

The prophet Micah predicted in 720 B.C. that the Saviour would be a man born in Bethlehem Ephratah.

Micah 5:2

2 But thou, Beth-lehem Ephratah, Though thou be little among the thousands of Judah, Yet out of thee shall he come forth unto me that is to be ruler in Israel….

There are two Bethlehems in the Middle East: Bethlehem Ephratah on the West Bank near Jerusalem (where Jesus was born) and Bethlehem of Galilee, located further north near Nazareth. Micah specifically called out the city in which the Messiah would be born 720 years in the future!

Exactly 720 years after Micah wrote, the man Jesus Christ was born in Bethlehem Ephratah, and Micah's prophecy was fulfilled perfectly ONLY in this ONE man's birth—the Lord Jesus Christ.

3. Third Old Testament prophecy: The Messiah would be born at a specific time.

Daniel 9:23–26

23 At the beginning of thy supplications the commandment came forth, and I am come to shew thee; for thou art greatly beloved: therefore understand the matter, and consider the vision.
24 Seventy weeks are determined upon thy people and upon thy holy city, to finish the transgression, and to make an end of sins, and to make reconciliation for iniquity, and to bring in everlasting righteousness, and to seal up the vision and prophecy, and to anoint the most Holy.

25 Know therefore and understand, that from the going forth of the commandment to restore and to build Jerusalem unto the Messiah the Prince shall be seven weeks, and threescore and two weeks: the street shall be built again, and the wall, even in troublous times.
26 And after threescore and two weeks shall Messiah be cut off, but not for himself: and the people of the prince that shall come shall destroy the city and the sanctuary; and the end thereof shall be with a flood, and unto the end of the war desolations are determined.

It is beyond the scope of this book to discuss this in detail, but Daniel is talking about weeks of years. The Hebrew word for "weeks" in v. 25 above is *sh^ebû 'âh*, literally meaning *"sevened."* Daniel is talking about seventy-sevens of years, or 70 x 7 years, or 490 years from the decree of Artaxerxes to restore Jerusalem until the Messiah.

As such, Daniel predicted the first advent and death of the Messiah and the destruction of Solomon's temple in A.D. 70 by the Romans. Daniel prophesied this in 538 B.C. Jesus Christ is the ONE man in history who fulfilled this in His birth, life, ministry, and death, exactly 538 years after the prophecy.

You can also read about this in detail in Josh McDowell's *Evidence that Demands a Verdict*, which I highly recommend.[20]

---

[20] Josh McDowell, *Evidence that Demands a Verdict*, (Campus Crusade for Christ, Inc., 1972).

We find facts like this in McDowell's book:

- Daniel's prophecy in Daniel 9:26 states that the Messiah would be "cut off" after 483 years (seven and three score and two weeks of years). The math: three score or 20 (a score = 20 years) x 3 = 60, plus 2 = 62 weeks; 7 + 62 = 69 weeks of years; 69 x 7 = 483 years.
- The 483 years are calculated from the decree to rebuild Jerusalem in 444 B.C. by King Artaxerxes I of Persia.
- Using the 360-day year used by the ancient Jews, 483 years becomes 476 years on our solar calendar.
- Adjusting for the switch from B.C. to A.D., 476 years after 444 B.C. is A.D. 33. This is the year Jesus Christ rode into Jerusalem.
- The prophecy in Daniel 9:25 states that 483 years after the decree, "the Anointed One will be cut off." This prophecy is considered to have been fulfilled when Jesus Christ was crucified.
- The prophecy also states that after the Messiah is killed, the people of the ruler who will come will destroy Jerusalem. This was fulfilled in A.D. 70 when the Romans under Titus destroyed Jerusalem.

Skeptics among higher critics of the Bible, in an attempt to disregard this ancient prediction of the life of Christ, claimed that Daniel was written possibly AFTER Christ was born.

However, fragments of the Book of Daniel were found in the Dead Sea Scrolls, which were discovered in 1952. The Book of Daniel was then dated well before 200 B.C., proving the skeptics wrong. An article titled "The Shiloh Excavations," from the Associates for Biblical Research, states:

Hebrew and Aramaic texts of the book of Daniel were published from among the Dead Sea scroll textual finds made originally in 1952 in Cave 4 at Qumran. [21]

The publication by Professor Eugene Ulrich, "Daniel Manuscripts from Qumran" (1989), gives us full insight into these pivotal textual finds and follows the one published two years earlier on other parts of these finds (Ulrich 1987).... 4QDane [when published] is to have a few words of various parts of Daniel 9."[22]

This fulfilled prophecy by Daniel, written some 2,600 years ago, between 200 and 530 years before Jesus Christ was born in Bethlehem, is perhaps the most astounding proof that the Bible is a miraculous book written by the ONLY Person Who could have known WHEN the Messiah would come into the world—GOD!

This should draw any skeptic to at least read the Bible once and be amazed by the fact that 66 books were written by 40 different people, separated by thousands of years and hundreds of miles. People from different backgrounds—fishermen, tax collectors, scholars, holy men, kings, carpenters, and wealthy businessmen— penned the Bible, and yet it is just ONE book with ONE unified theme: God's solution for man's sin problem. The solution is Jesus Christ, the Saviour of the world!

---

[21] Dr. Gerhard F. Hasel, *New Light on the Book of Daniel from the Dead Sea Scrolls*, (The Shiloh Excavations, Associates for Biblical Research, 1992). Reproduced in *Bible and Spade* with permission. https://biblearchaeology.org/research/divided-kingdom/3193-new-light-on-the-book-of-daniel-from-the-dead-sea-scrolls.
[22] Ibid.

The first mention of God's promise of a Messiah, a Saviour coming to take away the sins of the world and defeat Satan, was found in Genesis 3:15, called the ***proto-evangelium***. God Himself spoke it 6,004 years ago, and it was recorded by Moses 3,491 years ago when he penned the first five books of the Bible. This is the first gospel message.

Genesis 3:15

15 And I will put enmity between thee [Satan] and the woman [Eve], and between thy seed and her seed; it shall bruise thy head, and thou shalt bruise his heel.

The Messiah would come through the childbearing of Eve and every woman in the lineage of the Messiah down through Mary, and He would bruise the head of Satan, i.e., destroy the power of Satan.

Daniel's prophecy proves beyond doubt that Jesus Christ IS the long-awaited Messiah of the Jews (and the Gentiles). He is the only man who was crucified in A.D. 33, 483 years (476 years on the solar calendar) after King Artaxerxes I of Persia's decree to rebuild Jerusalem in 444 B.C., the only man who also fulfilled over 300 other specific prophecies of the Messiah.

Chapter 4

The Doctrine of Christ—

THE GOD-MAN

We saw that the Messiah would be virgin born in Chapter 2, but the prophet Isaiah predicted something else—something very important. Seven hundred fifty-eight years before Jesus Christ was born of a virgin in the manger in Bethlehem, he said they *"shall call his name Immanuel." WHO is this Messiah?*

4. **Fourth Old Testament prophecy: Tells WHO the Messiah IS—the .God-man. The New Testament Confirms He is fully God and fully man, and His name is Jesus Christ.**

Isaiah 7:14

14 Therefore the Lord himself shall give you a sign; Behold, a virgin shall conceive, and bear a son, And shall *call his name Immanuel.*

The Hebrew word for *"name"* in the verse is **shêm**, a primary word which comes from the root word **sîym**, to *put* or appoint. So, it carries the idea of a definite and conspicuous *position*.

Immanuel is a title, not the Messiah's name.

The title is *'Immânûw'êl*, which means, *with us* (is) *God; or "God with us."*

Isaiah claimed the Messiah would be *a man* (born of a virgin) but also **God** *with us*. This is an early reference to **the Messiah as the God-man**. He would exist as FULLY GOD and FULLY MAN.

This prophecy was fulfilled perfectly over 758 years later, as recorded by the New Testament penman, Matthew. It is ONLY fulfilled by one man in history, JESUS CHRIST.

Matthew 1:20–23

20 But while he thought on these things, behold, the angel of the Lord appeared unto him in a dream, saying, Joseph, thou son of David, fear not to take unto thee Mary thy wife: for that which is conceived in her is of the Holy Ghost.

21 And she shall bring forth a son, and thou shalt call his name JESUS: for he shall save his people from their sins.

22 Now all this was done, that it might be fulfilled which was spoken of the Lord by the prophet, saying,

23 Behold, a virgin shall be with child, and shall bring forth a son, and they shall call his name Emmanuel, **which being interpreted is, God with us.**

We see Matthew quoting Isaiah 7:14–15 and confirming that Jesus's *name* means the one "who would save his people from their sins." A literal translation of the Greek here is, "For He shall save the people of him, from the sins of them."

Matthew also confirmed that the Messiah's *title* would be Emmanuel (slightly different spelling than in the O.T.), which is interpreted as "God with us," just as Isaiah prophesied. *Matthew espoused the truth that JESUS was the God-man—He is "God with us."*

In the passage quoted earlier in Micah Ch. 5, we saw WHERE Messiah would be born, but there is MORE information there—astounding information!

Micah 5:2

2 But thou, Beth-lehem Ephratah, *Though* thou be little among the thousands of Judah, *Yet* out of thee shall he come forth unto me *that is* to be ruler in Israel; **Whose goings forth *have been* from of old, from everlasting.**

The Hebrew word "everlasting" is:

ʻôwlâm, or

ʻôlâm, concealed, the vanishing point; time out of mind, i.e., eternity.

Micah not only predicted WHERE the Messiah would be born, but he also said that the Messiah would be a ruler of Israel *(fully man)* and that he would be a person whose "goings forth have been from of old, from everlasting" *(fully God)*.

There is only ONE who is from eternity past, from beyond the vanishing point, from time out of mind— and that is God!

When you place these prophecies together, they predict **WHERE** *the* Messiah would be born and **WHO** He would be— FULLY MAN (a ruler born of a virgin in Bethlehem Ephratah) and FULLY GOD (from eternity past).

The theological term for this *"God-man"* existence of Jesus Christ is the *"hypostatic union."* The word comes from the Greek word *"hypostasis,"* which means "subsistence" or "individual existence." So, Jesus Christ exists as both fully God and fully man.

You must believe this to be a Biblical Christian. It is the first step in *standing straight* **with Christ**—knowing WHO Jesus is, but this information is confirmed throughout the Bible, the God-breathed Word of God.

For example, the Holy Spirit inspired the Apostle John, in the N.T., to write:

1 John 1:1–2
1 That which was from the beginning, which we have heard, which we have seen with our eyes, which we have looked upon, and our hands have handled, of the Word of life;

2 (For the life was manifested, and we have seen *it*, and bear witness, and shew unto you that eternal life, which was with the Father, and was manifested unto us.)

John testifies that Jesus Christ was "from the beginning," yet we have seen and handled Him. He is the "Word of Life." He is the "LIFE manifested." He is "eternal life." He was "with the Father" in eternity past.

We see it again in the O.T. book of Isaiah.

When I was a young pastor in my 30s, two Mormon "elders" (I put it in quotes because they were 18 years young) in white shirts and skinny black ties with nice haircuts walked into my church office and wanted to speak with me. I pulled up a couple of chairs, and they sat across my desk from me.

They began to attempt to prove to me that the Book of Mormon was spoken of in the Bible (and at the same time I was waiting for them to school me on the fact that Mormons do not believe Jesus is God)!

I said, "Oh, really? Show me where the Bible speaks of the Book of Mormon." They then turned to this verse and read:

Zechariah 5:1–2
1 Then I turned, and lifted up mine eyes, and looked, and behold a flying roll.
2 And he said unto me, What seest thou? And I answered, I see a flying roll; the length thereof *is* twenty cubits, and the breadth thereof ten cubits.

They said, "See there, the flying roll is the Book of Mormon."

Now, I knew the book of Mormon was published in 1830. I said, "Would you mind if we read more of this passage to see the context?"

They said, "Sure."

So, I read from Ch. 5, v. 1, all the way through Ch. 6, v. 15.

(I want you to learn from this example the value of requiring people who wish to debate doctrine to consider the immediate context of the proof text they are attempting to use to prove their point.)

Immediately after the verse, which they had taken out of context, the Bible began to indicate what the rolls actually signified.

Zechariah 5:2–3
2 And he said unto me, What seest thou? And I answered, I see a flying roll; the length thereof *is* twenty cubits, and the breadth thereof ten cubits.
3 Then said he unto me, ***This is the curse that goeth forth over the face of the whole earth:*** For every one that stealeth shall be cut off *as* on this side according to it; And every one that sweareth shall be cut off *as* on that side according to it.

First, the rolls symbolized a terrible curse over the face of the earth. Then the Scripture asks, "What is this, what do the rolls signify?"

Zechariah 5:6–8

6 And I said, ***What is it?*** And he said, This *is* ***an ephah*** that goeth forth. He said moreover, This *is* their resemblance through all the earth.
7 And, behold, there was lifted up ***a talent of lead***: and this *is* a woman that sitteth in the midst of the ephah.
8 And he said, ***This is wickedness***. And he cast it into the midst of the ephah; and he cast the weight of lead upon the mouth thereof.

The size of the rolls was a symbol of the size of the devastation of Israel and Babylon in a coming war. The ephah and talent of lead are signs of judgment (as these, along with rolls, symbolize the coming judgment of God in Jeremiah 36 and Ezekiel 2). Verse 8 SAYS these things symbolize the WICKEDNESS they would be judged for.

Then, when we arrived at Zechariah 6:15, God gave us the exact TIME this was referring to, and it was NOT the year 1830!

Zechariah 6:15
15 And they *that are* far off shall come and build in the temple of the Lord, and ye shall know that the Lord of hosts hath sent me unto you. And *this* shall come to pass, if ye will diligently obey the voice of the Lord your God.

This is the refurbishing of the Temple in Jerusalem, which happened in the sixth year of Darius, around 516 B.C.

It is NOT the writing of the Book of Mormon by Joseph Smith in 1828–29, in Manchester, New York.

I simply used the context to prove they were misinterpreting the Scriptures.

Then, I said, "Do you guys believe that Jesus is God?"

They said, "No, we do not." And I asked them to turn to Isaiah 9:6.

I read part of it to them, "For unto us a child is born, unto us a son is given...And his name shall be called Wonderful, Counseller...The Prince of Peace." I said, "Who is this speaking of?"

They said, "Jesus Christ."

Then, I said: "Well, I didn't read the whole verse, let me re-read it." And I read this aloud to them:

> "For unto us a child is born, unto us a son is given: And the government shall be upon his shoulder: And his name shall be called Wonderful, Counselor, ***The mighty God***, ***The everlasting Father***, *The Prince of Peace.*"—**Isaiah 9:6**

Now, I pointed to the words: ***"The mighty God, the Everlasting Father,"*** and said, ***"This is the same person as the Prince of Peace,*** clearly, in the context, ***so Jesus is God."***

They said, "We've never seen this; we'll have to study this further."

Then I said, "Listen, you teach that people are saved through doing good works. None of these works save anyone; people are saved by the BLOOD OF JESUS, and His blood only."

At the mention of the blood of Christ, one of them leaned over my desk and tried to grab my neck; the other took hold of his waist and pulled him back down into the chair. I said, "I think it's time you leave."

A few weeks later, I was knocking on doors in my city witnessing and a lady was walking by. She said, "I'm glad to see you doing this; usually, it's only the Mormons. Two of them were living in my upstairs apartment over there, and they were calling phone numbers to hear women talk dirty to them (they were too stupid to know I got the phone bills), and then one night, they went into a frenzy and broke my furniture and threw some out the upstairs window. I had to call the local mission president, and they came and took them away, and I never saw them again."

These were the same two who were attempting to instruct me in the ways of God.

This passage has proven useful many times in my ministry in definitively proving that Jesus, the Messiah, is God.

Isaiah 9:6–7

6 For unto us a child is born, unto us a son is given: And the government shall be upon his shoulder: And his name shall be called Wonderful, Counseller, The mighty God, The everlasting Father, The Prince of Peace.

7 Of the increase of his government and peace there shall be no end, Upon the throne of David, and upon his kingdom, To order it, and to establish it with judgment and with justice From henceforth even for ever. The zeal of the LORD of hosts will perform this.

This one who is called "The Prince of Peace" in this wonderful passage quoted so often at Christmas **is also called** *"The mighty God, The everlasting Father…."*

Therefore, Jesus is the "Prince of Peace" *(man), AND* Jesus is "The Everlasting Father" *(God).*

Once again, *Jesus is the God-man,* fully God and fully man.

Isaiah predicted in 740 B.C. that the Messiah would be born and would be called the prince of peace. Only one man has fulfilled this in His birth, life, and ministry—the man born 740 years later in Bethlehem: Jesus Christ.

The New Testament, like the Old Testament, tells WHO Jesus is.

He is "God with us."

Matthew 1:23

23 Behold, a virgin shall be with child, and shall bring forth a son, and they shall call his name Emmanuel, which being interpreted is, *God with us*.

He is the one "by whom are all things"—the Creator of the universe, Maker of all that exists.

Hebrews 2:9–11

9 But we see Jesus, who was made a little lower than the angels for the suffering of death, crowned with glory and honour; that he by the grace of God should taste death for every man.

10 For it became him, **for whom** *are* **all things, and by whom** *are* **all things**, in bringing many sons unto glory, to make the captain of their salvation perfect through sufferings.

11 For both he that sanctifieth and they who are sanctified *are* all of one: for which cause he is not ashamed to call them brethren.

Jesus is God. He is the one **BY WHOM** and **FOR WHOM** all things were made.

The Apostle John confirmed this in the New Testament, saying Jesus is the Creator of all things and the life and light of the world.

John 1:1–4, 14

1 In the beginning was the Word, and the Word was with God, and the Word was God.

2 The same was in the beginning with God.

3 All things were made by him; and without him was not any thing made that was made.
4 In him was life; and the life was the light of men.

This is speaking of Jesus Christ, as the context shows later in verse 14.

14 And the Word was made flesh, and dwelt among us, (and we beheld his glory, the glory as of the only begotten of the Father,) full of grace and truth.

I will always remember, as brand-new Christians, my wife Charlotte and I learned that Jesus was God while studying this amazing passage in John Ch. 1, together with John and Charlotte Posey, a young deacon and his wife, and life-long friends of ours who discipled us when we were new Christians. This set the tone for our ability to continue to grow in Christ through the years that followed.

We learned early on that all things were made BY Jesus and FOR Jesus, but we were amazed to see this goes deeper. God is not a God who flung everything into existence and then folded His arms and said, "Let's see how this turns out." He is a God who is *immanent*, i.e., with us, here in this universe, in this world, in our lives, even living in our bodies side-by-side with our New Man once we are born again. We know this because the Bible says that ***all things in the created universe are held together by Him.***

Colossians 1:15–17
15 Who is the image of the invisible God, the firstborn of every creature:

16 For by him were all things created, that are in heaven, and that are in earth, visible and invisible, whether *they be* thrones, or dominions, or principalities, or powers: all things were created by him, and for him:

17 And he is before all things, and *by him all things consist.*

"Consist," in Greek, is *sunistēmi,* to stand together. Therefore, the Colossians passage above reveals that the Lord Jesus Christ is…

- "God-seen."
- He is the first to rise from the grave (i.e., the firstborn of every creature).
- All things in heaven, in earth, visible and invisible, were created BY Him and FOR Him.
- He holds everything together—all the molecules and atoms and electrons, protons, and neutrons, down to the tiniest particles observed and unobserved by man.
- Without His direct and unfaltering energy, nothing could continue to exist.

When Jesus said, "For without me you can do nothing" (John 15.5), He meant this literally.

As **Creat-*OR*, Jesus cannot be a creat-*ED* thing** such as an angel, or a "firstborn spirit child of the Heavenly Father," as some false cults, such as Jehovah's Witness and Mormons, teach. The book of Hebrews destroys these false teachings and clearly reveals who Jesus really is.

Hebrews 1:3–10

3 Who being the brightness of *his* glory, and the express image of his person, and upholding all things by the word of his power, when he had by himself purged our sins, sat down on the right hand of the Majesty on high;

4 Being made so much better than the angels, as he hath by inheritance obtained a more excellent name than they.

5 For unto which of the angels said he at any time, Thou art my Son, this day have I begotten thee? And again, I will be to him a Father, and he shall be to me a Son?

6 And again, when he bringeth in the first begotten into the world, he saith, And let all the angels of God worship him.

7 And of the angels he saith, Who maketh his angels spirits, and his ministers a flame of fire.

8 But unto the Son *he saith*, Thy throne, O God, *is* for ever and ever: a sceptre of righteousness *is* the sceptre of thy kingdom.

9 Thou hast loved righteousness, and hated iniquity; therefore God, *even* thy God, hath anointed thee with the oil of gladness above thy fellows.

10 And, Thou, Lord, in the beginning hast laid the foundation of the earth; and the heavens are the works of thine hands:

- Jesus is the brightness of God's glory!
- Jesus is the express image of God's person.
- He upholds all things by His powerful Word.
- Jesus took our sins away (only God could do that).

- He is "so much better than the angels." (One cannot be both an angel and better than the angels at the same time, so Jesus is NOT an angelic being.)
- He has obtained by inheritance a more excellent NAME than the angels.
- God said to Jesus, "Thou art my Son, this day have I begotten thee; I will be your Father, and you will be my Son." He did NOT say that to the angels.
- When He brought the first begotten into the world, He said, **"Let all the angels of God worship Him" (Hebrews 1:6).**
- **God the Father called Jesus "God!" (Hebrews 1:8).** "But unto **the Son** *he saith,* **Thy throne, O God,** *is* **for ever and ever**: a scepter of righteousness *is* the scepter of thy kingdom."

Jesus Christ, who was called God by God the Father, deserves our worship!

Men have attempted to worship angels, but angels never allow it. Jesus, on the other hand, DID allow men to worship Him, which is another proof that He is not an angel.

Matthew 28:9–10
9 And as they went to tell his disciples, behold, Jesus met them, saying, All hail. And they came and *held him by the feet, and worshipped him.*
10 Then said Jesus unto them, Be not afraid: go tell my brethren that they go into Galilee, and there shall they see me.

Notice that Jesus did not rebuke them for worshipping Him. He accepted the worship. Later when the eleven saw Him, they also worshipped Him:

Matthew 28:16–17
16 Then the eleven disciples went away into Galilee, into a mountain where Jesus had appointed them.
17 And when they saw him, they worshipped him....

He also received worship in many other places in the N.T. (John 9:38; Revelation 5:11–14; Revelation 7:9–12).

But, we see below, that angels absolutely will NOT accept worship from men.

Revelation 22:8–9
8 And I John saw these things, and heard *them*. And when I had heard and seen, I fell down to worship before the feet of the angel which shewed me these things.
9 Then saith he unto me, ***See thou do it not***: for I am thy fellowservant, and of thy brethren the prophets, and of them which keep the sayings of this book: ***worship God.***

The angels will not accept worship, and *they* worship God alone.

Psalm 148:1–2

1 Praise ye the Lord. Praise ye the Lord from the heavens: Praise him in the heights.
2 Praise ye him, all his angels: Praise ye him, all his hosts.

God said, "Let the angels worship Jesus." The angels don't accept worship, and do not worship anything but God; therefore, again, Jesus is God, not an angelic being.

Matthew 4:11
11 Then the devil leaveth him, and, behold, angels came and ministered unto him.

Matthew 25:31
31 When the Son of man shall come in his glory, and all the holy angels with him, then shall he sit upon the throne of his glory:

1 Peter 3:22
22 Who is gone into heaven, and is on the right hand of God; angels and authorities and powers being made subject unto him.

If the angels are made subject to Jesus, then Jesus is not an angel—He is higher than the angels.

Isaiah 6:1–3

1 In the year that king Uzziah died I saw also the Lord sitting upon a throne, high and lifted up, and his train filled the temple.

2 Above it stood the seraphims….

3 And one cried unto another, and said, Holy, holy, holy, *is* the Lord of hosts: The whole earth *is* full of his glory.

The Lamb of God, Jesus Christ, is worshipped in heaven because He is the Creator of all things.

Revelation 4:8–11

8 And the four beasts had each of them six wings about *him*; and *they were* full of eyes within: and they rest not day and night, saying, Holy, holy, holy, Lord God Almighty, which was, and is, and is to come.

9 And when those beasts give glory and honour and thanks to him that sat on the throne, who liveth for ever and ever,

10 The four and twenty elders fall down before him that sat on the throne, and worship him that liveth for ever and ever, and cast their crowns before the throne, saying,

11 Thou art worthy, O Lord, to receive glory and honour and power: for thou hast created all things, and for thy pleasure they are and were created.

Revelation 21:22–24

22 And I saw no temple therein: for the Lord God Almighty and the Lamb are the temple of it.

23 And the city had no need of the sun, neither of the moon, to shine in it: for the glory of God did lighten it, and the Lamb *is* the light thereof.

24 And the nations of them which are saved shall walk in the light of it: and the kings of the earth do bring their glory and honour into it.

Revelation 22:1–4

1 And he shewed me a pure river of water of life, clear as crystal, proceeding out of the throne of God and of the Lamb.

3 And there shall be no more curse: but the throne of God and of the Lamb shall be in it; and his servants shall serve him:

4 And they shall see his face; and his name *shall be* in their foreheads.

Revelation 7:9–12

9 After this I beheld, and, lo, a great multitude, which no man could number, of all nations, and kindreds, and people, and tongues, stood before the throne, and before the Lamb, clothed with white robes, and palms in their hands;

10 And cried with a loud voice, saying, Salvation to our God which sitteth upon the throne, and unto the Lamb.

11 And all the angels stood round about the throne, and *about* the elders and the four beasts, and fell before the throne on their faces, and worshipped God,

12 Saying, Amen: Blessing, and glory, and wisdom, and thanksgiving, and honour, and power, and might, *be* unto our God for ever and ever. Amen.

The passage in Hebrews 1:9 says that Jesus was anointed with the oil of gladness above His fellows, and God said of Him in v. 10, *"Thou, Lord, in the beginning hast laid the foundation of the earth; and the heavens are the works of thine hands."*

The penman of Hebrews quoted the Psalms:

Psalm 45:6–7
6 Thy throne, O God, *is* for ever and ever: The sceptre of thy kingdom *is* a right sceptre.
7 Thou lovest righteousness, and hatest wickedness: Therefore God, thy God, hath anointed thee With the oil of gladness above thy fellows.

This man, Jesus Christ, is not a created angel. He is the Creator OF the angels and of all things visible and invisible in heaven and on earth.
He is God the Eternal Son.
He is the God-man.

Chapter 5

The Doctrine of Christ—

THE MAN WHO WAS CRUCIFIED

The O.T. book of Psalms includes a prophecy of the crucifixion of the Messiah, some 440 years before crucifixion existed in the world.

The act of crucifixion was instituted by the Babylonians around 600 B.C. We know that, "In 519 BC Darius I, king of Persia, crucified 3,000 political opponents in Babylon; in 88 BC Alexander Jannaeus, the Judaean king and high priest, crucified 800 Pharisaic opponents."[23]

The Roman form of crucifixion was grim. It was designed to be both horribly painful to the one crucified, and a lesson and warning to others who observed it to obey the Emperor of Rome.

The criminal would be beaten and whipped almost to death before his crucifixion, and then forced to carry his heavy wooden cross to the hill, and then up the hill that looked like a skull—

---

[23] The editors of Encyclopaedia_Britannica, *Crucifixion, capital punishment*, (Encyclopaedia Britannica, 2/25/2025), https://www.britannica.com/topic/crucifixion-capital-punishment.

Golgotha. (I have been to Israel twice and seen this hill—it literally looks like a skull).

The perpetrator would be laid on the cross, on the ground, and his feet and hands would be nailed through and into the wood of the cross. The nails, about the size of railroad nails, were driven in with sledgehammers by stout Roman guards. Then the cross would be stood up and dropped into a hole in the ground, dislocating every bone in the person's body.

The weight of the body could not be held up long, due to the heavy loss of blood, the disjointed arms and legs, and the pain of the feet in particular. This put extreme pressure on the lungs and the diaphragm, making it increasingly difficult to breathe. The person would have to try to push up with his swollen, throbbing feet just to get a breath, and the breath was hardly worth the pain. The loss of blood caused incredible thirst, and a mouth so dry and swollen that air could hardly pass through.

If you were the crucified one, passersby would spit on you and mock you with all the hatred of Satan himself.

Our Lord Jesus Christ was crucified between two criminals. As God the Father turned His head, OUR sins were placed upon the body of Jesus. Jesus said, "My God, my God, why hast thou forsaken me?" This was unusual for Jesus to call Him "My God," because His normal name for His Father in Heaven was Abba, which means "Daddy." But now it was "God," because all of God's wrath was poured out upon His Son, as He bore our sins in His body on the tree.

No one will ever know the depth of the spiritual agony felt by Jesus, as He was separated from His Father for the first time in all eternity. This is the larger part of what hell is—the absence of God.

This is what caused Christ to sweat blood from His forehead in the garden just before His arrest. Not the physical pain, not the physical death, but the spiritual death, i.e., separation from His Father with Whom He had been ONE for all eternity past. There is no clearer passage of Scripture describing the pain of crucifixion which our Lord faced than this O.T. passage written some 600 years before His birth into the Roman Empire at the focal point of history.

Isaiah 53:2–12

2 For he shall grow up before him as a tender plant, And as a root out of a dry ground: He hath no form nor comeliness; And when we shall see him, *there is* no beauty that we should desire him.

He had been beaten and whipped so badly, before He was crucified, that no one could recognize Him as a human being. He had no form or beauty at this point; no man desired Him, everyone poured out their hatred upon Him.

3 He is despised and rejected of men; A man of sorrows, and acquainted with grief: And we hid as it were *our* faces from him; He was despised, and we esteemed him not.

Yet, HE died for US, bearing our sorrows and trouble, and still we esteemed Him not.

4 Surely he hath borne our griefs, And carried our sorrows: Yet we did esteem him stricken, Smitten of God, and afflicted.

We counted Him as if He deserved the punishment we could SEE God pouring out upon Him. Little did we know it was OUR sins that brought God's wrath upon Jesus! WE put Him on that cross, WE hammered the nails into His hands and feet! WE spat upon Him, yet He could not avoid the cross *because He loved us so much!*

As David Crowder says in his magnificent song, "Forgiven," I am the one who held the hammer and the nails, denied Christ, and slew Christ, but He looked at me with His arms wide from the cross, and said, "You are forgiven!" Crowder points out that Jesus loves us even when we don't deserve it, and His blood, and His blood alone makes us innocent![24]

So, Jesus died in our place. He was wounded for our transgressions and bruised for our iniquities. The little word *"for"* is interesting because it means both that *He died in our place* and that *He died BECAUSE* of us.

We came into the world depraved and not seeking God. He died for us even while He knew we were this way! Why?

Because…We are HIS sheep.

---

[24] Ed Cash/David Crowder, *Forgiven*, Musixmatch, Forgiven lyrics © Worshiptogether.com Songs, Sixsteps Music, Capitol Cmg Paragon, Inot Music, 2016.

Isaiah 53:5–6

5 But he *was* wounded *for* our transgressions, *He was* bruised *for* our iniquities: The chastisement of our peace *was* upon him; And with his stripes we are healed.

6 All *we like sheep* have gone astray; We have turned every one to his own way; And the Lord hath laid on him *the iniquity of us*....

...And HE is OUR Sacrificial Lamb!

7 He was oppressed, and he was afflicted, Yet he opened not his mouth: He is brought as a *lamb to the slaughter*, And as a *sheep* before her shearers is dumb, So he openeth not his mouth.

8 He was taken from prison and from judgment: And who shall declare his generation? For he was cut off out of the land of the living: *For* the transgression of my people was he stricken.

Isa. 53:9 And he made his grave with the wicked, And with the rich in his death; Because he had done no violence, Neither *was any* deceit in his mouth.

This makes it clear that He had no sin of His own!

10 Yet it pleased the Lord to bruise him; he hath put *him* to grief: When thou shalt make his soul an offering

for sin, He shall see *his* seed, he shall prolong *his* days,
And the pleasure of the Lord shall prosper in his hand.
11 He shall see of the travail of his soul, *and* ***shall be
satisfied*...*.

This is ***propitiation,*** something Jesus did ***FOR*** the Father. He died to ***satisfy*** (propitiate) His justice and wrath against sin so that He then could exercise His great mercy and grace and save us without breaking His own law—"the wages of sin is death."

11b...By his knowledge shall my righteous servant justify many; For ***he shall bear their iniquities***.

We are saved by "knowledge of Jesus Christ"—by knowing Jesus Christ. He bears OUR iniquities, so that we can bear His righteousness. (This is the doctrine of ***imputation,*** which we will discuss in detail later in this chapter.)

12b ...Because he hath poured out his soul unto death: And he was numbered with the transgressors; And he bare the sin of many, And made intercession for the transgressors.

This last verse teaches the doctrine of ***limited atonement*** (He bare the sin of "many," not all) and the ***advocacy of Christ*** (He is as our attorney, always proclaiming our innocence against the accusations of Satan). All of these doctrines are N.T. doctrines, but prophesied in the O.T. (This is a tremendous passage for witnessing to Jewish people.)

This was prophesied 712 years before Jesus was born. Now you know a little about the dreadful act of crucifixion of the Romans, who had perfected it. And, you know a little, a very little drop of what Jesus did for you and me that day, 2,000 years ago.

5. Fifth Old Testament prophecy: The Messiah would be crucified (predicted 440 years before crucifixion was invented).

The following passage in the Psalms was written in approximately 1040 B.C.[25] King David of Israel would have been around 30 years old. It is clearly a prophecy of the coming Messiah who would someday rule from the throne of David.

Psalm 22:1–2, 6–8, 14–17, 27–31
1 *My God, my God, why hast thou forsaken me?* Why art thou so far from helping me, and from the words of my roaring?
2 O my God, I cry in the daytime, but thou hearest not; And in the night season, and am not silent.
6 But I am a worm, and no man; A reproach of men, and despised of the people.
7 All they that see me laugh me to scorn: They shoot out the lip, they shake the head, *saying,*
8 He trusted on the LORD that he would deliver him: Let him deliver him, seeing he delighted in him.

---

[25] Ussher, op. cit.

14 I am poured out like water, And all my ***bones are out of joint***: My heart is like wax; It is melted in the midst of my bowels.

15 My strength is dried up like a potsherd; And ***my tongue cleaveth to my jaws***; And thou hast brought me into the dust of death.

16 For dogs have compassed me: The assembly of the wicked have inclosed me: ***They pierced my hands and my feet***.

17 I may tell all my bones: They look *and* stare upon me.

18 They part my garments among them, And ***cast lots upon my vesture***.

The following verses fit all the Bible prophesies concerning the Messiah, Jesus Christ. It is clear Who this is speaking of.

27 All the ends of the world shall remember and turn unto the LORD: And all the kindreds of the nations shall worship before thee.

28 For the kingdom is the LORD's: And he is the governor among the nations.

29 All they that be fat upon earth shall eat and worship: All they that go down to the dust shall bow before him: And none can keep alive his own soul.

30 A seed shall serve him; It shall be accounted to the Lord for a generation.

31 They shall come, and shall declare his righteousness Unto a people that shall be born, that he hath done this.

One thousand and forty years after this was written, the New Testament confirms this prediction, line by line (as with all the prophecies)! This proves without a doubt that Jesus Christ is the Messiah.

- **Jesus said the very words that the Psalms predicted the Messiah would say while on the cross.**

Matthew 27:45–46
45 Now from the sixth hour there was darkness over all the land unto the ninth hour.
46 And about the ninth hour Jesus cried with a loud voice, saying, Eli, Eli, lama sabachthani? that is to say, *My God, my God, why hast thou forsaken me?*

- **The people around the cross despised Him and He was a reproach of men. They laughed at him, and said, "He trusted on the Lord *that* he would deliver him: Let him deliver him, seeing he delighted in him."**

Matthew 27:49
49 The rest said, Let be, let us see whether Elias will come to save him.

Mark 15:29–32
29 And they that passed by railed on him, wagging their heads, and saying, Ah, thou that destroyest the temple, and buildest *it* in three days,
30 Save thyself, and come down from the cross.

31 Likewise also the chief priests mocking said among themselves with the scribes, He saved others; himself he cannot save.

32 Let Christ the King of Israel descend now from the cross, that we may see and believe. And they that were crucified with him reviled him.

Luke 23:11, 35–39, 44–47

11 And Herod with his men of war set him at nought, and mocked *him*, and arrayed him in a gorgeous robe, and sent him again to Pilate.

35 And the people stood beholding. And the rulers also with them derided *him*, saying, He saved others; let him save himself, if he be Christ, the chosen of God.

36 And the soldiers also mocked him, coming to him, and offering him vinegar,

37 And saying, If thou be the king of the Jews, save thyself.

38 And a superscription also was written over him in letters of Greek, and Latin, and Hebrew, THIS IS THE KING OF THE JEWS.

39 And one of the malefactors which were hanged railed on him, saying, If thou be Christ, save thyself and us.

44 And it was about the sixth hour, and there was a darkness over all the earth until the ninth hour.

45 And the sun was darkened, and the veil of the temple was rent in the midst.

46 And when Jesus had cried with a loud voice, he said, Father, into thy hands I commend my spirit: and having said thus, he gave up the ghost.

47 Now when the centurion saw what was done, he glorified God, saying, Certainly this was a righteous man.

- **It was prophesied that the Messiah's "strength is dried up like a potsherd; And my tongue cleaveth to my jaws, And thou hast brought me into the dust of death" (Psalm 22:15).**

John 19:28–30
28 After this, Jesus knowing that all things were now accomplished, that **the scripture might be fulfilled, saith, I thirst.**
29 Now there was set a vessel full of vinegar: and they filled a spunge with vinegar, and put *it* upon hyssop, and put *it* to his mouth.
30 When Jesus therefore had received the vinegar, he said, It is finished: and he bowed his head, and gave up the ghost.

- **It was prophesied, "For dogs have compassed me: The assembly of the wicked have inclosed me: They pierced my hands and my feet" (Psalm 22:16).**

Matthew 27:33–35
33 And when they were come unto a place called Golgotha, that is to say, a place of a skull,
34 They gave him vinegar to drink mingled with gall: and when he had tasted *thereof*, he would not drink.

35 And they crucified him….

John 20:25–28

25 The other disciples therefore said unto him, We have seen the Lord. But he said unto them, Except *I shall see in his hands the print of the nails, and put my finger into the print of the nails,* and thrust my hand into his side, I will not believe.

27 Then saith he to Thomas, *Reach hither thy finger, and behold my hands;* and reach hither thy hand, and thrust *it* into my side: and be not faithless, but believing.

28 And Thomas answered and said unto him, My Lord and my God.

- **It was prophesied, "They look *and* stare upon me" (Psalm 22:17b).**

Matthew 27:36

36 And sitting down they watched him there.

John 19:34–37

36 For these things were done, that the scripture should be fulfilled….

37 And again another scripture saith, They shall look on him whom they pierced.

There are multiple prophesies occurring all at once during the hours of the crucifixion described in Psalm 22, all fulfilled only in the life of one man, Jesus Christ.

6. Sixth Old Testament prophecy: The Roman guards would cast lots for Jesus's clothing. Also, the concept of the Finished Work of Christ.

Psalm 22:18 They part my garments among them, And cast lots upon my vesture.

This was fulfilled a thousand years later in only ONE man at exactly the right time in history, the man Jesus Christ, who gave His life as a ransom to set His people free from sin and from Satan.

Matthew 27:35
35 And they crucified him, and parted his garments, casting lots: that it might be fulfilled which was spoken by the prophet, They parted my garments among them, and upon my vesture did they cast lots.

Jesus's blood was the ransom price, and it even paid for the sins of one of the soldiers who nailed His hands and feet to the cross and one of the thieves who died beside Him. The blood of Jesus saves everyone for whom it is given! Everyone for whom the ransom is paid is set free!

The centurion, who may have driven the nails into Jesus' hands and feet, was saved by grace through faith.

Matthew 27:54

54 Now when the centurion, and they that were with him, watching Jesus, saw the earthquake, and those things that were done, they feared greatly, saying, Truly this was the Son of God.

The thief beside Jesus on the cross was saved by faith in Christ alone. (He had no time to do good works.)

Luke 23:42–47

42 And he said unto Jesus, Lord, remember me when thou comest into thy kingdom.

43 And Jesus said unto him, Verily I say unto thee, To day shalt thou be with me in paradise.

44 And it was about the sixth hour, and there was a darkness over all the earth until the ninth hour.

45 And the sun was darkened, and the veil of the temple was rent in the midst.

46 And when Jesus had cried with a loud voice, he said, Father, into thy hands I commend my spirit: and having said thus, he gave up the ghost.

47 Now when the centurion saw what was done, he glorified God, saying, Certainly this was a righteous man.

John 19:30

30 When Jesus therefore had received the vinegar, he said, *It is finished*: and he bowed his head, and gave up the ghost.

At this darkest of scenes where men gambled for His clothes, mocked Him, and spat upon Him, let us contemplate exactly what Jesus did for us on that cross two thousand years ago, at the focal point of history.

When Jesus said, "It is finished," He meant that His ***redemptive work*** was ***complete (finished) and replete (abundantly and sufficiently supplied with grace).*** Redemption means to "set free by paying a price." God gave the blood of His only begotten Son as the price that set us free! To say that Jesus's finished work of redemption for the souls of His people is complete and replete means that NOTHING can be added to it, nor needs to be added to it.

A good summary of the sentiment of the reformers would be, "We are saved by the blood of Jesus plus nothing."

John 19:30 is the announcement of the "finished work of Christ." It is by His blood and His blood alone that we are justified.

Many Christians who say they are "saved" really mean they have been "justified," i.e., made right with God. Justification is part of the "past tense" of our salvation. However, salvation is a much larger set of doctrinal truths, which includes the past, present, and future work of Christ in our lives, as well as many related doctrinal concepts. Sometimes, in this book, I will use the terms "justified" and "saved" interchangeably, speaking simply of the fact of our salvation. (For decades I have taught my children and our church family to remember what "justification" means. It means, "Just-as-if-I'd never sinned." This is how the Father sees us once we're born-again!)

We do not DO anything to be saved. Salvation is a gift we receive. It is the *"operation of God"* (Colossians 2:12)—something done by Him to us and for us. God performs a heart transplant; we are the patient, and He is the surgeon. When the Holy Spirit regenerates us, He gives us over thirty-three things as part of this "operation of God."[26] We receive a new heart and the gift of saving faith.

Ephesians 2:8–9

8 For by grace are ye saved through faith; and that not of yourselves: *it is the gift* of God:
9 Not of works, lest any man should boast.

Colossians 2:12–17

12 Buried with him in baptism [i.e., Spirit Baptism, being placed into Christ by the Holy Spirit upon regeneration], wherein also ye are risen with *him* through the *faith of the operation of God*, who hath raised him from the dead.
13 And you, being dead in your sins and the uncircumcision of your flesh, hath he *quickened [made alive]* together with him, having *forgiven* you all trespasses;

---

[26] Lewis Sperry Chafer, D.D., Litt. D., Th.D., *Chafer Systematic Theology*, (Dallas: Dallas Seminary Press, 1980), Vol 3, pg. 234.

14 Blotting out the handwriting of ordinances that was against us, which was contrary to us, and took it out of the way, nailing it to his cross;
15 *And* having spoiled principalities and powers, he made a shew of them openly, triumphing over them in it.
16 Let no man therefore judge you in meat, or in drink, or in respect of an holyday, or of the new moon, or of the sabbath *days*:
17 Which are a shadow of things to come; but the body *is* of Christ.

The Greek construct of the phrase "the faith *of* the operation of God" indicates this means **the faith which originates from the operation of God.** This is because the phrase "the operation of God" is subjective *genitive* in the Greek, which we know due to the context (i.e., v. 13) showing that prior to regeneration we were dead, then God's operation upon us brought us to life (quickened us). *In other words, this operation which God performs produces the faith, and places it within us.* Few dig deeply enough to see this, but it is an indispensable component of the fact that we are not regenerated by things *we* do but *by what God has done for us and to us*.

We are saved by grace through faith; we are placed into Christ and Christ into us; we receive His faith, His love, and 33 or more other things as gifts given by the Holy Spirit to us; we are made alive from the dead (quickened); we are forgiven ALL trespasses; we are set free from Satan and from legalism (the law was nailed to the cross with Christ) as Jesus Himself fulfilled the law on our behalf, then placed the law in our hearts! All of this is called "the operation of God."

Our salvation is not in keeping ordinances, rules, sabbath days, or anything else, but we find our rest by being IN CHRIST—"but the body is Christ" (v. 17 above).

Perhaps the greatest proof of this is the salvation of the very Roman guard who cast lots for Jesus's clothing at the foot of the cross and the salvation of the thief who never had a chance to get baptized, do good works, tithe, or be religious. These men were saved by grace through faith in the *finished work* of Jesus Christ—the God-man who was crucified—apart from the deeds of the law.

Chapter 6

The Doctrine of Christ—

THE MAN WHOSE BONES WOULD NOT BE BROKEN AND WHO WOULD COME OUT OF EGYPT

7. Seventh Old Testament prophecy: The Messiah's bones would not be broken on the cross.

Psalm 34:20
20 He keepeth all his bones: Not one of them is broken.

This Psalm was fulfilled in the New Testament, 1,000 years later by one man, Jesus Christ, whose bones were not broken upon the cross.

John 19:34–36
34 But one of the soldiers with a spear pierced his side, and forthwith came there out blood and water.
35 And he that saw *it* bare record, and his record is true: and he knoweth that he saith true, that ye might believe.

36 For these things were done, that the scripture should be fulfilled, *A bone of him shall not be broken.*

The two thieves on either side of Jesus had their legs broken so that they would die before dusk. This was a necessity because the Jews could do no work, such as taking dead bodies down from their crosses, on the special sabbath attached to the Passover, which would begin at dusk. They would have done the same to Jesus, but since He had already died, they did not break his legs. This fulfilled a prophecy written 1,000 years before Jesus was born.

8. Eighth Old Testament prophecy: The Messiah, the Son of God, would be called out of Egypt.

Hosea 11:1
1 When Israel *was* a child, then I loved him, And called my son out of Egypt.

Matthew 2:14–15
14 When he arose, he took the young child and his mother by night, and departed into Egypt:
15 And was there until the death of Herod: that it might be fulfilled which was spoken of the Lord by the prophet, saying, Out of Egypt have I called my son.

Hosea wrote 740 years before Jesus was born that God's Son would be called out of Egypt.

How could this be when we know He was to be born in Bethlehem, according to Micah?

The O.T. sages and the wise men in the N.T., together with the Jews and Pharisees of the first century, had a tough time reconciling this, but we, with hindsight, see how both were true at the same time. (This should teach us to trust the Scriptures, even when historical events in the present may tempt us to doubt.)

Jesus Christ is the one man in history who was both born in Bethlehem, according to the scriptures, and whose parents took him to Egypt to protect him from Herod, according to the scriptures.

Now, we have listed <u>eight specific prophecies (and several other smaller concurrent prophecies)</u> fulfilled in the birth, life, and death of Jesus Christ.

In fact, there are over 300 prophecies in the Old Testament predicting the birth, the place of birth, the TIME of birth, and the life and death of the Messiah. Jesus Christ fulfilled all these at exactly the right time in history.

The mathematical odds of ***just eight*** of these predictions coming true in the life of one man between A.D. 1 and 33 would be like taking silver dollars, placing them across Texas two feet deep, marking ONE and shuffling it in, blindfolding a man and telling him to find it.[27]

Professor Peter W. Stoner was chairman of the Departments of Mathematics and Astronomy at Pasadena City College in California and chairman of the science division at Westmont College in

---

[27] Josh McDowell, op. cit. p. 175.

California. In his book *Science Speaks,* Professor Stoner outlines the mathematical probability of one person in the first century fulfilling just eight of the most clear and straightforward Messianic prophecies as *1 in 10^{17} (1 in 100,000,000,000,000,000).* Josh McDowell quotes Stoner in his book *Evidence that Demands a Verdict.*[28]

Of course, since _God_ inspired the prophecies of the Old Testament, then the odds of this happening, and Jesus BEING the Messiah, were a 100% chance.

There are many more things that both the Old Testament and New Testament reveal about Jesus Christ.

In the following chapters, we will discuss not so much fulfilled prophecies, but rather truths that the Bible teaches about Jesus Christ, the Messiah.

---

[28]Ibid, p. 175.

Chapter 7

The Doctrine of Christ—

THINGS JESUS CHRIST CLAIMED CONCERNING WHO HE IS

9. In the Old Testament book of Exodus, God calls Himself "I AM." The man Jesus Christ claimed to be the "I AM."

Exodus 3:13–14

13 And Moses said unto God, Behold, *when* I come unto the children of Israel, and shall say unto them, The God of your fathers hath sent me unto you; and they shall say to me, What *is* his name? what shall I say unto them?

14 And God said unto Moses, *I AM THAT I AM*: and he said, Thus shalt thou say unto the children of Israel, I AM hath sent me unto you.

Jesus called Himself "I AM." This is another proof not only that He is God but that He <u>called</u> Himself God.

John 8:57–59

57 Then said the Jews unto him, Thou art not yet fifty
years old, and hast thou seen Abraham?
58 Jesus said unto them, Verily, verily, I say unto you,
Before Abraham was, *I AM.*

In case anyone believes He was NOT claiming to be God, look
at the reaction of the Pharisees!

59 Then took they up stones to cast at him: but Jesus
hid himself, and went out of the temple, going through
the midst of them, and so passed by.

Some say that Jesus is not necessarily claiming to be the "I AM"
here; however, the Jews would not have considered this
blasphemous unless they understood Jesus was claiming to be God,
the "I AM."

**Jesus claims to be the "I AM"
while speaking to the Pharisees.**

**Further, Jesus warned that those who
do not believe that He is the "I AM"
shall die in their sins, and the wages of sin
is death and hell for unbelievers.**

John 8:24
24 I said therefore unto you, that ye shall die in your
sins: for if ye believe not that *I AM*, ye shall die in your
sins.

Jesus provides this stark warning (but a loving warning because it is the TRUTH) when He says, "If ye believe not that **I AM**, ye shall die in your sins."

It is therefore imperative that we understand WHO Jesus Christ is—He is "all the fullness of the Godhead, in a body." He is fully God and fully man. He is Immanuel, God with us.

This is what separates biblical Christianity from the false religions and cults of the world, which admit Jesus was a good man, a wise teacher, and even a prophet but teach that He was not the Son of God.

Once, a young Islamic businessman and I had a lengthy religious discussion. He told me the Islamic people believe, "We will all spend a little time in hell, to work off our sins before entering Paradise." I thought this was interesting, and very similar to what Roman Catholics believe.

I asked him, "What do you think is the main difference between Biblical Christianity and Islam?"

He said, "Well, I attended a Catholic School in Pakistan for a while. I believe the main difference is that we (followers of Islam) do NOT have a 'Son of God'; we just have God."

I said, "So, how long did Mohammed spend in hell?"

He quickly said with an exasperated voice, "Oh, do not say that; we have a problem. Mohammed did not go to hell."

I said, "WE do not have a problem; YOU have a problem because we Christians have a Son of God who died for us so that we do not have to spend ANY time in hell, so how long did Mohammed spend in hell since he does not have a Son of God?" The subject was changed very quickly!

You must believe in the TRUE Jesus to be saved. The Apostle Paul says there are "other Jesuses."

2 Corinthians 11:3–4
3 But I fear, lest by any means, as the serpent beguiled Eve through his subtilty, so your minds should be corrupted from the simplicity that is in Christ.
4 For if he that cometh preacheth another Jesus, whom we have not preached, or if ye receive another spirit, which ye have not received, or another gospel, which ye have not accepted, ye might well bear with him.

Paul was afraid these new Christians might be led astray by false teachers. There was the danger that they might go with them away from the true gospel and the true historical Christ. That danger still exists today.

The TRUE Jesus is God in the flesh. Only HE can save you.

10. Jesus Christ claimed to be God to the Apostle Thomas.

John 20:24–29

24 But Thomas, one of the twelve, called Didymus, was not with them when Jesus came.

25 The other disciples therefore said unto him, We have seen the Lord. But he said unto them, Except I shall see in his hands the print of the nails, and put my finger into the print of the nails, and thrust my hand into his side, I will not believe.

26 And after eight days again his disciples were within, and Thomas with them: *then* came Jesus, the doors being shut, and stood in the midst, and said, Peace *be* unto you.

27 Then saith he to Thomas, Reach hither thy finger, and behold my hands; and reach hither thy hand, and thrust *it* into my side: and be not faithless, but believing.

28 And Thomas answered and said unto him, *My Lord and my God.*

29 Jesus saith unto him, Thomas, because thou hast seen me, thou hast believed: blessed *are* they that have not seen, and *yet* have believed.

Not only did Jesus claim to be God, but here, He demonstrated His deity by entering the room with the apostles without opening the door—He simply passed through the walls without disturbing the molecules.

John 20:30–31

30 And many other signs truly did Jesus in the presence of his disciples, which are not written in this book:

31 But these are written, that ye might believe that Jesus is the Christ, the Son of God; and that believing ye might have life through his name.

The passage continues, saying Jesus did "many other signs." A "sign" is a miraculous event that God empowers His apostles, prophets, and Christ to do, to authenticate their message (especially when the message is new information on how God deals with His people).

In this case, the change was HUGE from the O.T. economy (the way God dealt with man then) to the N.T. gospel of salvation by faith in the finished work of Christ, apart from the works of the law. This was a very difficult thing for Jews, especially, to accept; therefore, signs and wonders were given to them as proofs of the message at the dawning of Christianity.

Verse 31 above says the **signs** have been recorded for us in the N.T. *that we "might believe* that Jesus is the Christ, the Son of God; and that believing ye might have life through his name." So, we see that the biblical Christian faith is based upon facts of history. It is not a blind faith. We also see definitively that the sign gifts were given in order to authenticate the new message of a new dispensation, and that we might believe that message (MUCH more on this truth later, in Chapter 9 and other chapters).

11. Jesus claimed to be God to Philip, the apostle.

John 14:8–10
8 Philip saith unto him, Lord, shew us the Father, and it sufficeth us.

9 Jesus saith unto him, Have I been so long time with you, and *yet hast thou not known me, Philip*? *he that hath seen me hath seen the Father;* and how sayest thou *then*, Shew us the Father?

10 Believest thou not that I am in the Father, and the Father in me? the words that I speak unto you I speak not of myself: but the Father that dwelleth in me, he doeth the works.

It is important to note that verse 10, above, clarifies that the Father and the eternal Son are distinct Persons of the Godhead, while at the same time emphasizing that the Father and Jesus are One in essence—they are deity.

The passage in John 14 continues:

John 14:11–14

11 Believe me that I *am* in the Father, and the Father in me: or else believe me for the very works' sake.

12 Verily, verily, I say unto you, He that believeth on me, the works that I do shall he do also; and greater *works* than these shall he do; because I go unto my Father.

13 And *whatsoever ye shall ask in my name, that will I do*, that the Father may be glorified in the Son.

14 If ye shall ask any thing in my name, I will do it.

Jesus clearly claimed He was God in human form. (My amazing mentor, who is in heaven now, Dr. Irwin Freeman, said, "Jesus is God seen.")[29]

In case one doubts He meant this, He ended the discussion with, *"If ye shall ask any thing in my name, I will do it."* Only God can answer prayers.

12. Jesus claimed to be the BREAD of life, who gives everlasting life to all who partake of Him by faith.

John 6:48, 50-51
48 *I am that bread of life.*
50 This is the bread which cometh down from heaven, that a man may eat thereof, and not die.
51 I am the living bread which came down from heaven: if any man eat of this bread, he shall live for ever: and the bread that I will give is my flesh, which I will give for the life of the world.

13. Jesus claimed to be the WATER of life.

John 4:13–15, 25–26
13 Jesus answered and said unto her, Whosoever drinketh of this water shall thirst again:

---

[29] You may hear sermons from Dr. Irwin Freeman, a Jewish believer who was a world–renowned revivalist, and my mentor and my "seminary," at www.ParkMeadowsChurch.com.

14 But whosoever drinketh of the water that I shall give him shall never thirst; but the water that I shall give him shall be in him a well of water springing up into everlasting life.

15 The woman saith unto him, Sir, give me this water, that I thirst not, neither come hither to draw.

25 The woman saith unto him, I know that Messias cometh, which is called Christ: when he is come, he will tell us all things.

26 Jesus saith unto her, *I that speak unto thee am he.*

All these are beautiful allegories that teach us in many ways, through many different word pictures, that Jesus Christ is the only Saviour of the World. Like bread and water, He keeps us alive. When we take Him into our lives by faith, He frees us from eternal death and from Satan. He becomes part of our very being and dwells within us. Wherever we go, He stands with us. We, as Christians can stand with perfect posture in this crooked world because Jesus stands straight, and we are connected to Him.

14. Jesus claimed to be the only DOOR to heaven. All other ways to heaven are false, and all others who claim to be the way are thieves and robbers who come only to steal and to kill and to destroy (i.e., false teachers; false Messiahs).

John 10:1–2, 4–5, 7–11

1 Verily, verily, I say unto you, He that entereth not by the door into the sheepfold, but climbeth up some other way, the same is a thief and a robber.

2 But he that entereth in by the door is the shepherd of the sheep.

4 And when he putteth forth his own sheep, he goeth before them, and the sheep follow him: for they know his voice.

5 And a stranger will they not follow, but will flee from him: for they know not the voice of strangers.

7 Then said Jesus unto them again, Verily, verily, I say unto you, I am the door of the sheep.

8 All that ever came before me are thieves and robbers: but the sheep did not hear them.

9 I am the door: by me if any man enter in, he shall be saved, and shall go in and out, and find pasture.

10 The thief cometh not, but for to steal, and to kill, and to destroy: I am come that they might have life, and that they might have *it* more abundantly.

11 I am the good shepherd: the good shepherd giveth his life for the sheep.

We learn much about our relationship with Jesus by studying a shepherd's relationship with his sheep. Sheep hear only their shepherd's voice, and when he calls, they come running because only he brings nourishment and safety to them. Jesus said He was the door into the sheepfold—the only way into the safe place where He keeps His sheep. Outside this sheepfold, Satan, as a lion, roams to and fro seeking whom he may devour.

1 Peter 5:8–9

8 Be sober, be vigilant; because your adversary the devil, as a roaring lion, walketh about, seeking whom he may devour:

9 Whom resist steadfast in the faith....

There is no other way into this safe place than through Jesus, who is the ONLY door of the sheepfold. Men who teach other "ways" to God are liars, murderers, and thieves, according to Jesus Christ.

> **15. Jesus claimed He was the ONLY way to heaven, the ONLY truth, and the ONLY life, and that _no_ man comes to the Father except by Jesus Christ. He also said, "If you've seen me, you have seen the Father."**

John 14:6–7

6 Jesus saith unto him, I am the way, the truth, and the life: no man cometh unto the Father, but by me.

7 If ye had known me, ye should have known my Father also: and from henceforth ye know him, and have seen him.

The parable of the DOOR is beautiful, but here, Jesus says He is the only way to heaven in very plain, simple, and powerful language—no parable needed to convey this truth: "I am the way, the truth, and the life: no man cometh unto the Father, but by me. Henceforth, you have seen him [the Father]."

16. Jesus said of Himself that no other had ever seen the Father except Himself, adding, "He that believes in me HAS everlasting life," and, "I am the light of the world... if you follow me you shall have the light of life."

John 6:45–47

45 It is written in the prophets, And they shall be all taught of God. Every man therefore that hath heard, and hath learned of the Father, cometh unto me.

46 Not that any man hath seen the Father, save *he which is of God, he hath seen the Father.*

47 Verily, verily, I say unto you, He that believeth on me hath everlasting life.

One of the things that makes Jesus Christ different than all other "holy men" in the religions of the world is that He is the only one who came from the Father in eternity past into this universe to save a remnant from a fallen race.

Satan's people cannot hear and understand Jesus's teachings and never will. But if His words tug at *YOUR* heart, that is a very good sign that you are one of His sheep. When you see Jesus for Who He is, your Shepherd who can fill all your spiritual pangs of hunger, then receive Him as your personal Lord and Saviour. Your life will never be the same after that because then, for the first time, YOU ARE ACTUALLY ALIVE.

John 8:42–45

42 Jesus said unto them, If God were your Father, ye would love me: for ***I proceeded forth and came from God;*** neither came I of myself, but he sent me.

43 Why do ye not understand my speech? *even* because ye cannot hear my word.

Notice Jesus did NOT say you don't *choose* to hear my word; He said you <u>CANNOT</u> hear my word. They did not have "ears to hear." How many times did Jesus say, "If any man have ears to hear, let him hear"?—**Mark 7:16**, et. al. …And, why could they not hear with understanding? Jesus continued:

John 8:44 Ye are of *your* father the devil, and the lusts of your father ye will do. He was a murderer from the beginning, and abode not in the truth, because there is no truth in him. When he speaketh a lie, he speaketh of his own: for he is a liar, and the father of it.

45 And because I tell *you* the truth, ye believe me not.

**Jesus claimed to be the only man who had seen God,
and He claimed He had
proceeded forth and come out from God.**

Leading up to this, these same men Jesus was speaking to, the Pharisees, had brought to Him a woman caught in adultery. They were trying to catch Jesus between the law and his message of truth, faith, and love, and they desired that He stone the woman. But Jesus said, "Let him who has no sin cast the first stone," and the men walked away one by one, the oldest to the youngest. In this context, we find this:

John 8:12

12 Then spake Jesus again unto them, saying, I am the light of the world: he that followeth me shall not walk in darkness, but shall *have the light of life.*

So, Jesus is the only light that brings understanding of eternal life.

17. Jesus claimed that He was the Good Shepherd who laid down His life for the sheep. He also claimed He would be resurrected. He is the risen Saviour.

John 10:14–18

14 I am the good shepherd, and know my *sheep*, and am known of mine.

15 As the Father knoweth me, even so know I the Father: and *I lay down my life for the sheep.*

16 And other sheep I have, which are not of this fold [He speaks here of the Gentiles]: them also I must bring, and they shall hear my voice; and there shall be one fold, *and* one shepherd.

17 Therefore doth my Father love me, because I lay down my life, that I might take it again.

18 No man taketh it from me, but I lay it down of myself. I have power to lay it down, and I have power to take it again. This commandment have I received of my Father.

I have said many times, to many audiences across the country, that I was saved in my car driving to work from college when I was twenty-four years old. The Holy Spirit called me with His effectual calling. It was as if He took my chin and lifted it up so that I could gaze into the face of Jesus with eyes that could see for the first time and ears that could hear, and He said, "This is your Shepherd. You're a sheep. You're hungry. He has the food. What will you do with Him?"

And I said, "Lord, I've always known about you, but for the first time, I want YOU to be my boss rather than me being my boss." I spoke as a businessman because that's what I was, and He saved me.

What happened is that the Holy Spirit brought me to repentance by God's grace, which means He helped me know that I needed to change my mind about Who God is. In that car, I came to understand Who God is—and it isn't me. I went home from work that day a different man. My wife, Charlotte, who was already a born-again Christian, was very happy.

Later in the same passage, Jesus says:

John 10:27–30

27 My sheep hear my voice, and I know them, and they follow me:

28 And I give unto them eternal life; and they shall never perish, neither shall any *man* pluck them out of my hand.

29 My Father, which gave *them* me, is greater than all; and no *man* is able to pluck *them* out of my Father's hand.

30 I and *my* Father are one.

All God's sheep hear the Master's voice when He calls; eternal life is a gift (not earned); Jesus's sheep never perish (they cannot lose their salvation because they did not earn it in the first place); nothing can pluck them from Jesus and the Father's hands; Jesus and the Father are one (once again we see the God-man truth).

From the time I was around eight years old, I worked my grandfather's cattle. This was the only job I had until I went to college. So, I was a "shepherd" of cattle, so-to-speak. My grandfather was not a sanctified man; he was a gruff, cussing oil man. I loved him because he was my grandfather.

From time to time, his prized Santa Gertrudis bull would decide to visit the "ladies" in the next pasture. Now, imagine if this happened, and I came home at the end of the day and said to my cussing grandpa, "Papa, your bull is gone. He is in the neighbor's pasture," and Papa asks, "Well, did you go get him back?" … and I say, "No, Papa, your bull, of his own free will, chose to leave, and he's gone for good."

What do you think my grandfather would say? (Let's not repeat it out loud!) So, who is *responsible* for the bull staying safe in the pasture, *the bull or the shepherd?* Think about that: this is why you cannot lose your salvation. You are not responsible for it; your heavenly Shepherd is. If you were ever lost, Jesus would answer to the Father for that … and that isn't happening!

John 10:27–30, 39, 43–44

27 My sheep hear my voice, and I know them, and they follow me:

28 And I give unto them eternal life; and they shall never perish, neither shall any *man* pluck them out of my hand.

29 My Father, which gave *them* me, is greater than all; and no *man* is able to pluck *them* out of my Father's hand.

30 I and *my* Father are one.

39 And this is the Father's will which hath sent me, that of all which he hath given me ***I should lose nothing***, but should raise it up again at the last day.

43 Jesus therefore answered and said unto them, Murmur not among yourselves.

44 No man can come to me, except the Father which hath sent me draw him: and ***I will raise him up*** at the last day.

Jesus Christ is our Great Shepherd, and HE IS RESPONSIBLE for keeping us saved, keeping us safe here on this earth, and bringing us to heaven.

Chapter 8

The Doctrine of Christ—

THINGS JESUS CHRIST CLAIMED
HE WOULD ACCOMPLISH

18. Jesus claimed that He would go to Heaven and prepare a place for us and come again (the Second Coming of Christ) to take us there.

John 14:1–3

1 Let not your heart be troubled: ye believe in God, believe also in me.

2 In my Father's house are many mansions: if *it were* not *so*, I would have told you. I go to prepare a place for you.

3 And if I go and prepare a place for you, I will come again, and receive you unto myself; that where I am, *there* ye may be also.

The Apostle Paul describes this time in our future in detail.

1 Thessalonians 4:15–18

15 For this we say unto you by the word of the Lord, that we which are alive *and* remain unto the coming of the Lord *shall not prevent [precede] them* which are asleep.

16 For the Lord himself shall descend from heaven with a shout, with the voice of the archangel, and with the trump of God: *and the dead in Christ shall rise first:*

17 Then we which are alive *and* remain shall be caught up together with them in the clouds, to meet the Lord in the air: and so shall we ever be with the Lord.

18 Wherefore comfort one another with these words.

1 Corinthians 15:51–52, 58

51 Behold, I shew you a mystery; We shall not all sleep, but we shall all be changed,

52 In a moment, in the twinkling of an eye, *at the last trump:* for the trumpet shall sound, and the dead shall be raised incorruptible, and we shall be changed.

58 Therefore, my beloved brethren, be ye steadfast, unmoveable, always abounding in the work of the Lord, forasmuch as ye know that your labor is not in vain in the Lord.

Paul speaks of the rapture of the church and tells when it will happen. It will happen AFTER the first resurrection, which will occur at the end of the church age (1 Thessalonians 4:15; 1 Corinthians 15:52). Therefore, the rapture of the church does not happen before the second coming, as so many popular books and movies incorrectly portray.

Jesus also gives a very clear chronology of the end times in Matthew Chapter 24. Shouldn't we consider Him the highest authority on the subject? We see Him describe His second coming with the rapture happening as part of it (not before it but immediately after).

Matthew 24:21–22, 27–31

21 For then shall be great tribulation, such as was not since the beginning of the world to this time, no, nor ever shall be.

22 And except those days should be shortened, there should no flesh be saved: but for the elect's sake those days shall be shortened.

27 For as the lightning cometh out of the east, and shineth even unto the west; so shall also *the coming of the Son of man be*.

28 For wheresoever the carcase is, there will the eagles be gathered together.

29 Immediately *after* the tribulation of those days shall the sun be darkened, and the moon shall not give her light, and the stars shall fall from heaven, and the powers of the heavens shall be shaken:

30 And then shall appear the sign of the Son of man in heaven: and then shall all the tribes of the earth mourn, and they shall see the Son of man coming in the clouds of heaven with power and great glory.

31 And he shall send his angels with a great sound of a trumpet, and they shall *gather together his elect* from the four winds, from one end of heaven to the other.

I didn't always have this conviction about the timing of the rapture. It came through personal study and through a conversation with a friend, who once said, "David, I don't want to argue with you, but could I ask you a couple of questions?"

I said, "Sure."

He asked, "How many 'last' trumps can there be, and would you consider letting Jesus's chronology of the end times in Matthew 24 be more authoritative than the books you've read about the rapture?"

I considered those to be fair questions, and my whole understanding of the end-times changed in the year that followed. I did my own in-depth Bible study of the topic rather than sieving the Bible through men's theories, which I had read.

We will discuss this topic more in Vol. 2, Ch. 23 concerning the resurrection, but for now, I just want you to be thinking about *what the Bible actually says*, taking everything in context—not what people believe or wish it says. Context is everything.

19. Jesus claimed that after He went to heaven, He would send the Holy Spirit to indwell every believer and be our Comforter.

John 16:5–7
5 But now I go my way to him that sent me; and none of you asketh me, Whither goest thou?
6 But because I have said these things unto you, sorrow hath filled your heart.
7 Nevertheless I tell you the truth; It is expedient for you that I go away: for if I go not away, the Comforter

will not come unto you; but if I depart, I will send him unto you.

Just before Jesus went to the cross to die for our sins, His followers were sad, but He said this.

John 14:16–18

16 And I will pray the Father, and he shall give you another Comforter, that he may abide with you for ever;
17 *Even* the Spirit of truth; whom the world cannot receive, because it seeth him not, neither knoweth him: but ye know him; for **_he dwelleth with you, and shall be in you_**.
18 I will not leave you comfortless: I will come to you.

This knowledge was something completely new, and it distinguished the church age from the Old Testament believers' walk with God. The Spirit of God had dwelt *with* you, but now He shall dwell *in* you! This is the promise of the indwelling Holy Spirit that marks the church age.

The O.T. saints experienced the Holy Spirit from time to time. He would come upon them and then perhaps move away for a season, then come back. This is why King David said…

Psalm 51:11–12

11 Cast me not away from thy presence; And take not thy holy spirit from me.

12 Restore unto me the joy of thy salvation; And uphold me *with thy* free spirit.

But now, for the Christians in the church age, the Holy Spirit never leaves us, ***He dwells within us and is sealed within us by God!*** It works like this….

2 Corinthians 1:21–22
21 Now he which stablisheth us with you in Christ, and hath anointed us, *is* God;
22 Who hath also ___sealed us,___ and given the earnest of the Spirit in our hearts.

Ephesians 1:11–14
11 In whom also we have obtained an inheritance, being predestinated according to the purpose of him who worketh all things after the counsel of his own will:
12 That we should be to the praise of his glory, who first trusted in Christ.
13 In whom ye also *trusted*, after that ye heard the word of truth, the gospel of your salvation: in whom also after that ye believed, ___ye were sealed with that holy Spirit of promise___,
14 Which is the earnest of our inheritance until the redemption of the purchased possession, unto the praise of his glory.

When the Holy Spirit calls us to Christ, He opens our eyes and ears to Who Jesus is, quickens our dead spirits, and regenerates us.

He comes to dwell in our bodies and is sealed within us. Our bodies become the temple of God! That has to change us!

1 Corinthians 6:19–20
19 What? know ye not that *your body is the temple of the Holy Ghost which is in you,* which ye have of God, and ye are not your own?
20 For ye are bought with a price: therefore glorify God in your body, and in your spirit, which are God's.

And the beautiful thing about this is that He never leaves us (this is another of hundreds of reasons a person, once truly saved, cannot lose his salvation).

Ephesians 4:30
30 And grieve not the holy Spirit of God, whereby *ye are sealed unto the day of redemption.*

From the time of Pentecost after Jesus had ascended into heaven—when the Holy Spirit was sent down into the room where the disciples met, and they were given *signs and wonders* proving that the Holy Spirit had come upon them—from that time forward, everyone who believes in Christ is indwelt instantly and forever by the Holy Spirit.

Acts 10:43–45

43 To him give all the prophets witness, that through his name whosoever believeth in him shall receive remission of sins.

44 While Peter yet spake these words, the Holy Ghost fell on all them which heard the word.

45 And they of the circumcision which believed were astonished, as many as came with Peter, because that on the Gentiles also was poured out the gift of the Holy Ghost.

This is the great difference between the O.T. and the N.T.: "Christ in us, the hope of glory!" The Holy Spirit *in* us is our hope of living right, of **standing tall and walking straight** with Christ in this world.

It is very important to note that the indwelling is completely different than the doctrinal idea of being "filled with the Spirit." The indwelling is something God DOES TO you when you are saved. He comes to live inside of you, by the Holy Spirit, until the "day of redemption," which means the second coming. So, between now and then, He will not and cannot leave you. This is the *indwelling* (which happens at the same time and is part of the **baptism of the Spirit** at the moment of your regeneration).

The *filling* of the Holy Spirit is different; it is **your** choice to make every moment of every day. Will you **choose** to be filled with the Holy Spirit, or will you choose to walk in the flesh? The key to being a better Christian is to choose to walk hand in hand with Jesus for more moments of every day!

Ephesians 5:18

18 And be not drunk with wine, wherein is excess; but be filled with the Spirit.

"Be filled with the Spirit" is an imperative in Greek—something God tells us to do. I think of it like this. My wife and I love each other and live in the same house. When I am working in my study at the back of the house, I love it when she is in the kitchen or the den at the front of the house—she doesn't have to be right next to me, but she is in the house. I love just knowing she is near. This is like the ***indwelling***; the Holy Spirit is always in the house (I believe He dwells within our brain and nervous system).

But then there are times when my wife and I are in the same room, right beside each other, intimate, and become one flesh. I like this far better than when she is in the garden, or the kitchen, or anywhere else. This oneness in the physical relationship between man and wife is a ***type***, or picture of the ***filling*** of the Holy Spirit in the Bible. The filling is a choice YOU make (as the bride of Christ). Will you just be "in the kitchen" while Christ is "in the study" or will you, during certain moments, be one with the Holy Spirit, holding Jesus's hand, walking where He walks, talking with Him, listening to Him, loving Him?

Here is the passage where we learn how the Bible relates the intimacy between a man and a woman, physically, to the spiritual concept of being filled with the Spirit—Christ's Spirit and our spirit becoming ONE spirit. The greatest of the mysteries that God revealed to mankind through the Apostle Paul for the church age is the indwelling, and also the filling of the Holy Spirit:

1 Corinthians 6:16–17

> **16** What? know ye not that he which is joined [to a woman][30]…is one body? for two, saith he, shall be one flesh.
> **17** But he that is joined unto the Lord is one spirit.

I think men especially can learn much about how we make the Lord feel sometimes. Gentlemen, ask yourself the question, who usually has to make the decision to be "in the mood" in your marriage, you or your wife? I think most men are always ready, but it's not all about that for women; romance is a large part of it. So, they often must make a ***decision*** to be in the mood, and this can be greatly helped by their man being more romantic. Am I right, ladies? Men, if you "dwell with your wife in knowledge" (1 Peter 3:7) and learn to understand these things about her, you'll both be happier.

We are the bride, and Jesus is the groom. He is always ready to be one with us, but we are not. We need to think about this and spend more time with Him, not just in the house, but hand in hand.

20. Jesus claimed He would die and raise Himself up in three days.

John 2:18–21
18 Then answered the Jews and said unto him, What sign shewest thou unto us, seeing that thou doest these things?

---

[30] The author made a slight change in wording here for discretion. In another place at another time, we will discuss why the Lord chose to write it as He did—there is a real teaching there too.

19 Jesus answered and said unto them, Destroy this temple, and in three days I will raise it up.

20 Then said the Jews, Forty and six years was this temple in building, and wilt thou rear it up in three days?

21 But he spake of the temple of his body.

Much like today, where in some church groups they wish to see a miracle every Sunday, these wanted to walk by sight, not by faith. Jesus told them the only sign He would show them would be that He would raise Himself from the dead! The Bible elsewhere teaches that the Father played a role in the resurrection (Acts 2:24), and the Holy Spirit did as well (Romans 1:4). Here Jesus claims to have raised Himself from the grave! Later the Pharisees would twist these words and take them out of context to condemn Jesus by claiming He said He would tear down the Jewish temple.

Jesus encouraged His sorrowful disciples in the next passage, with the promise that it was best for Him to leave this earth, for then He could send the indwelling Holy Spirit which would come and comfort all God's children *only* if Jesus first ascended into heaven.

John 16:4–7, 18, 20, 22

4 But these things have I told you, that when the time shall come, ye may remember that I told you of them. And these things I said not unto you at the beginning, because I was with you.

5 But now I go my way to him that sent me; and none of you asketh me, Whither goest thou?

6 But because I have said these things unto you, sorrow hath filled your heart.

7 Nevertheless I tell you the truth; It is expedient for you that I go away: for if I go not away, the Comforter will not come unto you; but if I depart, I will send him unto you.

18 They said therefore, What is this that he saith, A little while? we cannot tell what he saith.

20 Verily, verily, I say unto you, That ye shall weep and lament, but the world shall rejoice: and ye shall be sorrowful, but your sorrow shall be turned into joy.

22 And ye now therefore have sorrow: but I will see you again, and your heart shall rejoice, and your joy no man taketh from you.

Just before the crucifixion, and at the foot of the cross, all the apostles but one, along with a few women, fled in fear! What made these same apostles and disciples become heroes within just a few days? The resurrection turned their sadness and fear into joy and boldness! Jesus had overcome the world!

John 16:28–33

28 I came forth from the Father, and am come into the world: again, I leave the world, and go to the Father.

29 His disciples said unto him, Lo, now speakest thou plainly, and speakest no proverb.

30 Now are we sure that thou knowest all things, and needest not that any man should ask thee: by this we believe that thou camest forth from God.

31 Jesus answered them, Do ye now believe?

32 Behold, the hour cometh, yea, is now come, that ye shall be scattered, every man to his own, and shall leave me alone: and yet I am not alone, because the Father is with me.

33 These things I have spoken unto you, that in me ye might have peace. In the world ye shall have tribulation: but be of good cheer; *I have overcome the world*.

The only explanation for the immediate change in the character and bravery of the apostles and disciples of Christ is the verity of the resurrection!

21. Jesus claimed HE came to seek and to save that which was lost.

Luke 19:10

10 For the Son of man is come to seek and to save that which was lost.

As we understand that our Saviour said, "As I have been sent, even so send I you," then we ought to be seeking souls to witness to, but only to those whom the Holy Spirit leads us. We must not cast our pearls before the swine, lest they turn and rend us (Matthew 7:6).

22. Jesus prayed for His own sheep.

All of John Chapter 17 is a prayer of Jesus to His Father! Take a moment and read the passage, and then let's discuss what Jesus asks of His Father in heaven.

John 17:1–4, 8–24, 26

1 These words spake Jesus, and lifted up his eyes to heaven, and said, Father, the hour is come; glorify thy Son, that thy Son also may glorify thee:

2 As thou hast given him power over all flesh, that he should give eternal life to as many as thou hast given him.

3 And this is life eternal, that they might know thee the only true God, and Jesus Christ, whom thou hast sent.

4 I have glorified thee on the earth: ***I have finished the work which thou gavest me to do***.

Jesus mentions that He has ***"finished"*** the work God gave Him to do regarding the salvation of His people. Remember our discussion of the finished work of Christ in Chapters 5 and 7? When He took our sins upon Himself on the cross, and gave His blood for us, He satisfied the Father's requirements for justice, and He justified us (by giving us His own righteousness). The substitutionary death of Christ on the cross for the sins of His people is a majestic theme throughout the Scriptures. We can learn many important truths in this remarkable passage.

John 17:8 For I have given unto them the words which thou gavest me; and they have received *them*, and have known surely that I came out from thee, and they have believed that thou didst send me.

9 I pray for them: I pray not for the world, but for them which thou hast given me; for they are thine.

10 And all mine are thine, and thine are mine; and I am glorified in them.

11 And now I am no more in the world, but these are in the world, and I come to thee. Holy Father, keep through thine own name those whom thou hast given me, that they may be one, <u>as we are</u>.

13 And now come I to thee; and these things I speak in the world, that they might have my joy fulfilled in themselves.

14 I have given them thy word; and the world hath hated them, because they are not of the world, even as I am not of the world.

15 I pray not that thou shouldest take them out of the world, but that thou shouldest keep them from the evil.

16 They are not of the world, even as I am not of the world.

17 Sanctify them through thy truth: thy word is truth.

18 As thou hast sent me into the world, even so have I also sent them into the world.

19 And for their sakes I sanctify myself, that they also might be sanctified through the truth.

20 Neither pray I for these alone, but for them also which shall believe on me through their word;

21 That they all may be one; as thou, Father, *art* in me, and I in thee, that they also may be one in us: that the world may believe that thou hast sent me.

22 And the glory which thou gavest me I have given them; that they may be one, even as we are one:

23 I in them, and thou in me, that they may be made perfect in one; and that the world may know that thou hast sent me, and *hast loved them, <u>as</u> thou hast loved me.*

24 Father, I will that they also, whom thou hast given me, be with me where I am; that they may behold my glory, which thou hast given me: for thou lovedst me before the foundation of the world.

26 And I have declared unto them thy name, and will declare *it*: that the love wherewith thou hast loved me may be in them, and I in them.

John 18:1-2

1 When Jesus had spoken these words, he went forth with his disciples over the brook Cedron, where was a garden, into the which he entered, and his disciples.

2 And Judas also, which betrayed him, knew the place: for Jesus ofttimes resorted thither with his disciples.

Here is what we learn from Jesus's prayer:

(1) Jesus prayed that He would be glorified so that He could bring glory to the Father by giving eternal life to "as many as the Father had given Him" (vv. 1–4).

He prayed that He would "have power over all flesh, that he should give eternal life to as many as *thou hast given him.*" In other words, Jesus asked the Father to give Him the power over men's flesh to save those God wanted Him to save, even though they would not desire Him at first.

Many people do not yet realize that God has always known His children with love from before the foundation of the world.

Ephesians 1:3–7

3 Blessed *be* the God and Father of our Lord Jesus Christ, who hath blessed us with all spiritual blessings in heavenly *places* in Christ:

4 According as he hath chosen us in him **before the foundation of the world**, that we should be holy and without blame before him in love:

5 Having predestinated us unto the adoption of children by Jesus Christ to himself, according to the good pleasure of his will,

6 To the praise of the glory of his grace, wherein he hath made us accepted in the beloved.

7 In whom we have redemption through his blood, the forgiveness of sins, according to the riches of his grace;

Romans 8:29–31

29 For whom he did *foreknow*, he also did *predestinate to be* conformed to the image of his Son, that he might be the firstborn among many brethren.

30 Moreover whom he did predestinate, them he also **called**: and whom he called, them he also **justified**: and whom he justified, them he also **glorified**.

31 What shall we then say to these things? If God *be* for us, who *can be* against us?

The Father gave these (known as "the elect" in Scripture) to His Son Jesus Christ **as a love gift** because Jesus loved the sons of men. The whole human race had been lost in the garden of Eden, but the Father chose to save a remnant to give to His Son. Thus, Jesus said:

John 6:39–40, 44

39 And this is the Father's will which hath sent me, that of all which *he hath given me* I should lose nothing, but should raise it up again at the last day.

40 And this is the will of him that sent me, that every one which seeth [beholds] the Son, and believeth on him, may have everlasting life: and I will raise him up at the last day.

44 No man can come to me, except the Father which hath sent me draw him: and *I will raise him up* at the last day.

(2) Jesus prayed that the ones given to Him by the Father would be "kept" by the Father, in the Father's name (this is called eternal security of the believer (vv. 8–11). So, your eternal security is as certain as the likelihood Jesus would get His prayers answered!

(3) He prayed that they would be protected from the evil one while on this earth, because the world hates them because they love His Word (vv. 11–15).

(4) He prayed that His saved ones would have joy in this life (v. 13).

(5) Jesus prayed that His own would not be worldly, but would be made more like Him (sanctified) day by day (vv. 16–17).

(6) Jesus prayed that as He was sent into this world, His followers would be sent to spread the gospel message of salvation by faith apart from the works of the law throughout the world (v. 18).

(7) He prayed that His followers would be sanctified specifically by the Word of God (v. 19).

(8) Jesus prayed not only for His followers during His earthly ministry but also for those who would believe through their witness, and so on into the future (that's us!) (v. 20).

(9) Jesus asked the Father to make His followers one with each other, with Christ and with the Father, so that the world may believe that God sent Jesus into the world (v. 21).

This makes Christian unity in the local church, and in our homes, VERY important.

(10) Jesus prayed that God would give His followers the same glory that God had given Him so that we may be one with God as Jesus is one with God (v. 22).

(11) He prayed that we and the world would know that God loves us with the same love with which He loves Christ (v. 23). Don't read over this one too fast—this is profound!

(12) Jesus prayed that we would be with Christ wherever He is so that we may behold His glory, both here and in heaven, for God loved Jesus before the foundation of the world (i.e., He is eternal—v. 24).

The great Prince of Preachers, Charles Spurgeon, said that when comforting a person who has lost a loved one, we should explain that this is simply Jesus getting His prayer answered: "Father, I will that they also, whom thou hast given me, be with me where I am; that they may behold my glory, which thou hast given me: for thou lovedst me before the foundation of the world." What a beautiful thought.

These are the twelve things Jesus asked the Father for just before Judas betrayed Him, and He went to the cross! I would ask, did Jesus always get His prayers answered? So, it brings us great joy and encouragement to look at all the answered prayers He has for US!

John 13:1

1 Now before the feast of the passover, when Jesus knew that his hour was come that he should depart out of this world unto the Father, having loved his own which were in the world, *he loved them unto the end.*

23. Jesus claimed He would come again, just as He went into Heaven.

John 14:3

3 And if I go and prepare a place for you, *I will come again*, and receive you unto myself; that where I am, *there* ye may be also.

Matthew 24:27, 30

27 For as the lightning cometh out of the east, and shineth even unto the west; so shall also the coming of the Son of man be.
30 And then shall appear the sign of the Son of man in heaven: and then shall all the tribes of the earth mourn,

and they shall see the **Son of man coming in the clouds of heaven** with power and great glory.

Acts 1:9–11

9 And when he had spoken these things, while they beheld, he was taken up; and *a cloud received him out of their sight.*

10 And while they looked stedfastly toward heaven as he went up, behold, two men stood by them in white apparel;

11 Which also said, Ye men of Galilee, why stand ye gazing up into heaven? this same Jesus, which is taken up from you into heaven, *shall so come in like manner as ye have seen him go into heaven.*

Jesus's second coming and the rapture which follows are just as literal as His ascension after His first advent. As He went up into the clouds, so shall He return in like manner.

24. Jesus claimed He would raise the dead at the first resurrection.

John 11:25–26

25 Jesus said unto her, I am the resurrection, and the life: he that believeth in me, though he were dead, yet shall he live:

26 And whosoever liveth and believeth in me shall never die. Believest thou this?

Revelation 20:4

4 And I saw thrones, and they sat upon them, and judgment was given unto them: and *I saw* the souls of them that were beheaded for the witness of Jesus, and for the word of God, and which had not worshipped the beast, neither his image, neither had received *his* mark upon their foreheads, or in their hands; and **they *lived and reigned with Christ a thousand years.***

Luke 20:35–36

35 But they which shall be accounted worthy to obtain that world, and the resurrection from the dead…

36 Neither can they die any more: for they are equal unto the angels; and are the children of God, being the children of the resurrection.

(Note: This does not mean we die and become angels, but rather we are like them in the sense that we are then immortal.)

Matthew 22:31–33

31 But as touching the resurrection of the dead, have ye not read that which was spoken unto you by God, saying,

32 I am the God of Abraham, and the God of Isaac, and the God of Jacob? God is not the God of the dead, but of the living.

33 And when the multitude heard *this*, they were astonished at his doctrine.

25. Jesus claimed He would separate the sheep from the goats, the wheat from the tares; that He would send the wheat/sheep (believers) to heaven; and bind the tares into bundles and burn them, i.e., send the tares/goats (unbelievers) to hell.

Matthew 25:31–34, 40–41

31 When the Son of man shall come in his glory, and all the holy angels with him, then shall he sit upon the throne of his glory:

32 And before him shall be gathered all nations: and he shall separate them one from another, as a shepherd divideth *his* sheep from the goats:

33 And he shall set the sheep on his right hand, but the goats on the left.

34 Then shall the King say unto them on his right hand, Come, ye blessed of my Father, *inherit the kingdom prepared for you from the foundation of the world:*

40 And the King shall answer and say unto them, Verily I say unto you, Inasmuch as ye have done *it* unto one of the least of these my brethren, ye have done *it* unto me.

41 Then shall he say also unto them on the left hand, Depart from me, ye cursed, into everlasting fire, prepared for the devil and his angels:

Matthew 13:29–30

29 But he said, Nay; lest while ye gather up the tares, ye root up also the wheat with them.

30 Let both grow together until the harvest: and in the time of harvest I will say to the reapers, Gather ye together first the tares, and bind them in bundles to burn them: but gather the wheat into my barn.

There can be no doubt that Jesus taught a literal heaven and a literal hell. Jesus explained to His disciples that He did not plant the tares in the earth; the devil did. Jesus planted the good seed, the wheat, which represent the elect, whom God knew before the foundation of the world as His own.

Satan cannot create human beings, only God can, but the devil "planted" the tares by tempting Eve to sin. When she sinned, her "conception" was multiplied (Genesis 3:16), thus making it possible for non-elect people to be brought into the world after the fall. Jesus did not consider Himself to be the Father of the non-elect; rather, He said that they were of their father the devil (John 8:44). They were from below (John 8:23, 24), while Jesus and His elect were from above.

Matthew 13:38–40

38 The field is the world; the good seed are the children of the kingdom; but the tares are the children of the wicked *one*;

39 The enemy that sowed them is the devil; the harvest is the end of the world; and the reapers are the angels.

40 As therefore the tares are gathered and burned in the fire; so shall it be in the end of this world.

**Jesus left us the Great Commission,
to witness to the lost.**

Matthew 28:16–20

16 Then the eleven disciples went away into Galilee, into a mountain where Jesus had appointed them.

17 And when they saw him, they worshipped him: but some doubted.

18 And Jesus came and spake unto them, saying, All power is given unto me in heaven and in earth.

19 Go ye therefore, and teach all nations, baptizing them in the name of the Father, and of the Son, and of the Holy Ghost:

20 Teaching them to observe all things whatsoever I have commanded you: and, lo, I am with you alway, *even* unto the end of the world. Amen.

Acts 1:7–12

7 And he said unto them, It is not for you to know the times or the seasons, which the Father hath put in his own power.

8 But ye shall receive power, after that the Holy Ghost is come upon you: and ye shall be witnesses unto me both in Jerusalem, and in all Judaea, and in Samaria, and unto the uttermost part of the earth.

9 And when he had spoken these things, while they beheld, he was taken up; and a cloud received him out of their sight.

10 And while they looked stedfastly toward heaven as he went up, behold, two men stood by them in white apparel;

11 Which also said, Ye men of Galilee, why stand ye gazing up into heaven? this same Jesus, which is taken up from you into heaven, shall so come in like manner as ye have seen him go into heaven.

12 Then returned they unto Jerusalem from the mount called Olivet, which is from Jerusalem a sabbath day's journey.

...and they turned the world upside down!

Chapter 9

The Doctrine of Christ—

THINGS OTHER N.T.
PERSONAGES
SAID ABOUT JESUS CHRIST

26. John the Baptist testified that Jesus Christ was the Son of God, the Lamb of God who would die for the sins of God's people.

John 1:32–36

32 And John bare record, saying, I saw the Spirit descending from heaven like a dove, and it abode upon him.

33 And I knew him not: but he that sent me to baptize with water, the same said unto me, Upon whom thou shalt see the Spirit descending, and remaining on him, the same is he which baptizeth with the Holy Ghost.

34 And I saw, and bare record that ***this is the Son of God.***

35 Again the next day after John stood, and two of his disciples;

36 And looking upon Jesus as he walked, he saith, ***Behold the Lamb of God!***

John the Baptist, according to Jesus, was the greatest man born of women. He had the high privilege of being the forerunner of the Messiah, announcing the Jesus Christ WAS the Lamb of God.

Matthew 11:11

11 Verily I say unto you, Among them that are born of women there hath not risen a greater than John the Baptist....

John was the great witness that Jesus Christ was the predicted Messiah, the Lamb of God. John said that Jesus would baptize with the Spirit. Later in our chapter on baptisms, we will see that baptism does not always mean "in water." It is a transliteration of the Greek word ***baptizō***, "to make whelmed." Webster says "whelmed" means to be engulfed. It can mean being engulfed or surrounded by anything, not just water.

The English mind thinks "water" when it reads the word "baptized." However, there are many forms of baptism, and here, in John 1:33, the Bible speaks of Spirit Baptism, not water baptism.

We will learn later that water baptism is a picture of Spirit Baptism, which occurs when we are saved. We are placed into Christ, and Christ is placed into us by the Holy Spirit. This Spirit Baptism is the indwelling, or "baptism" of the Holy Spirit.

When we are baptized in water, it is a beautiful picture and testimony to the world that we have already been placed into Christ and indwelt by the Holy Spirit at the moment of our regeneration. It is our first step of obedience after salvation. It is our confession that John the Baptist was correct when he said, "Behold the Lamb of God," and that we believe that Jesus, our sacrificial lamb, died for us and has become our personal Saviour.

27. The Apostle Paul says Jesus Christ is "all of the fullness of the Godhead in a body." He is God in the flesh.

Colossians 2:8–10

8 Beware lest any man spoil you through philosophy and vain deceit, after the tradition of men, after the rudiments of the world, and not after Christ.
9 For in him *dwelleth all the fulness of the Godhead bodily.*
10 And ye are complete in him, which is the head of all principality and power:

Paul warned that the world system would not accept that Jesus is God. Man's vain philosophy would teach that He was just a man, or a good teacher, or even a prophet, but not God.

Paul rebukes the world's doubt, and confirms that Jesus Christ is all the fullness of the Godhead in a human body.

"Godhead" is an interesting English word which means all of God, i.e., The Father, The Son, The Holy Spirit. The Greek word for this is *thĕŏtēs,* which means "divinity."

This literally means that Jesus is all of God in a human body; thus, He is divine.

The great theologian, B.B. Warfield, once said this in regard to the word *thĕŏtēs* (Godhead) in the above passage:

> The very Deity of God, that which makes God God, in all its completeness, has its permanent home in Our Lord, and that in a "bodily fashion," that is, it is in Him clothed with a body.[31]

28. Jesus is the Author and Finisher of our Faith, according to the penman of Hebrews (most likely Paul).

Hebrews 12:2

2 Looking unto Jesus the **author** and **finisher** of *our faith*; who for the joy that was set before him endured the cross, despising the shame, and is set down at the right hand of the throne of God.

Webster's Dictionary defines "author" as: "One that originates or creates something." I am about to show you, in Scripture, how Jesus Christ is the originator of your faith in a way you may have never seen before. But first, here is a well-known doctrine. Jesus Christ is the Author of our faith, in that He died in our place, and we

---

[31] B. B. Warfield, *The Works of Benjamin B. Warfield*, *"The Person of Christ,"* (Grand Rapids: Baker Book House, 1981), II: p. 184.

were in Him (spiritually and positionally) when He died and was buried; and when He arose, our new man arose with Him. (This makes the doctrine of imputation possible; we will discuss this in more detail below.)

We are saved by the "blood of Christ plus nothing," as the Puritans taught. He is the ONLY Author of our faith.

Please remember that *we* are not the _co_-author of our own faith. There are no co-authors of our faith. Jesus is THE Author. He creates the faith within us, and He is the origin of our faith, if we have saving faith. Now, it might be instructive to realize that there are two kinds of faith people can have—(1). A mere mental assent of a fact (the demons have that, and are not saved, [James 2:19]), and (2). Saving faith.

If we are truly born-again, then we are not of those who have mere human belief of the mind, but of them who believe to the saving of the soul. So, there is a human belief, and there is a faith which results in the eternal security of the soul. Keeping this in mind will open your eyes to the truths you are about to contemplate.

> **Hebrews 10:38, 39**
> **38** Now the just shall live by faith: but if *any man* draw back, my soul shall have no pleasure in him.
> **39** But we are not of them who draw back unto perdition [hell]; but of them that believe to the saving of the soul.

One of the things the Holy Spirit does for us at the moment of our regeneration, when He calls us to see Jesus for the first time, is that He **gives us the very faith _OF_ Christ as a gift**. This is worthy of more study, so we will re-visit this later, as we discuss the fact that Jesus Himself is THE Author (and only author) of faith.

First, please notice that the word "our" in Hebrews 12:2, above, is not in the Greek, it was added in the English translation (therefore it is in italics in the English).

> **Hebrews 12:2**
> **2** Looking unto Jesus the **author** and **finisher** of *our* **faith**....

In the Greek, it reads, literally, "…Jesus the author and finisher of faith…." So, clearly, Jesus is the author, or originator of the faith that He gives us as a free gift the moment we are called and regenerated by the Holy Spirit (Eph. 2:8-9).

Here is one example of a verse that speaks of us receiving the faith *of* Christ as a gift upon our regeneration (and you will see others below)...

> **Galatians 2:20**
> **20** I am crucified with Christ: nevertheless I live; yet not I, but Christ liveth in me: and the life which I now live in the flesh I live by the faith **of** the Son of God, who loved me, and gave himself for me.

Please notice the word *"of"* in the phrase "faith **of** the Son of God." It is different from the word "in" in both English and Greek.

The Bible speaks of faith *IN* Christ in many, many places, and no one will enter heaven without believing *in* the Lord Jesus Christ as their personal Saviour. This means trusting Him with your soul (not trusting yourself), and receiving Him as your own (John 1:12). The word "receive" in the Greek, *paralambanō*, comes from two smaller Greek words:

para, *near, or beside.*

+

Lambanō to *take*, to *get hold* of.

Thus, "To hold Jesus near, or beside you."

So, believing *in* Christ is the main theme of salvation in the N.T., provided you understand what this means, as we see above. It is a choice of the will that the believer makes.

But at the same time, in verses like the one above (Gal. 2:20), and there are many, the Bible also speaks of the faith *OF* Christ that is placed inside us, or given to us (as a free gift) by the Holy Spirit when we are saved. In other words, the Bible speaks of *both* Jesus's faith within us (the source of our faith), and our belief in Him (the object of our faith), as you will see below.

Many have never noticed this, and this is often due to the fact that all popular modern versions of the English Bible mistranslate these verses and put the word "in" where the word "of" should be (as it would also read in the Greek). The KJV, however, gets this right every time, and the Geneva bible gets it right some of the time.)

Now, where you see "in" in the English, it is most often "*en*" in the Greek (used about 2,700 times in the N.T.). However, where you see "of" in English (in Gal. 2:20, above) there is no Greek word there. The word "of" is implied in the Greek and added in English for accuracy. This is because the phrase "the Son of God," in Gal. 2:20 above, and other verses where this construct is found, is in the subjective genitive case in the Greek. It would best read, "I live by the Son of God's faith that is given to me when I am saved." It literally reads, "I live by the faith *of* the Son of God."

Jesus's faith, as I have said many times, is faith that can walk on water. This is the saving faith which is given to you as a gift when the Holy Spirit regenerates you (Eph. 2:8, et.al.). When Jesus comes to live within you, by the indwelling Holy Spirit, you and He reside one alongside the other, within your inner man. In similar fashion, Jesus's faith resides within you side-by-side with your human belief. In fact...

Your human belief sprang forth from Jesus, and the faith of Christ within you, because He is the author of your faith.

These modern English versions of the Bible have lost this important truth (just as the Jews lost truth when the Pharisees changed the words of Isaiah 53 in the targums prior to the first advent of Christ). But the KJV, true to the underlying Greek, speaks of the faith *of* Jesus justifying us (and if you believe in verbal, plenary inspiration, every little word is important)....

We receive this gift of Jesus's faith in the following manner.

Colossians 2:12
12 Buried with him in baptism [i.e., Spirit Baptism, you being placed into Christ by the Holy Spirit upon regeneration], wherein also ye are risen with him through the faith of the operation of God, who hath raised him from the dead.

Lewis Sperry Chafer said at the very moment of our regeneration, the Holy Spirit does thirty-three things to us in a nanosecond, as I mentioned above.[32] I believe He does even more. This is what the "operation of God" is—what He does *TO* us on that operating table, during our "heart-transplant"!

Few would disagree that the Holy Spirit gives us the very same *agape* LOVE Christ has (because God *IS* love); is it so hard to believe that He also gives us the very FAITH OF Christ? (Some have not seen this in the Bible, but it is clearly so.) These two gifts are given to us the moment we are born again and are indispensable for us to be able to respond with our own belief, repentance, love and good works. This is because He saved us while we were "yet sinners." We were in our sin, without faith, without hope, without *agape*, and without God.

> **Ephesians 2:12**
> **12** That at that time ye were without Christ, being aliens
> from the commonwealth of Israel, and strangers from
> the covenants of promise, having no hope, and without
> God in the world:

Another gift He gives us at the time of our regeneration is that ***He seals Himself within us until the day of redemption.***

Think about this: if Christ comes to live *IN* you by the Holy Spirit's indwelling, then wouldn't it be true that His LOVE is also in you, and His FAITH is also in you? Isn't it also true that if someone gives you something, and you receive it, then it is now yours? i.e.,

---

[32] Lewis Sperry Chafer, op. cit.

your love, and your faith? But it remains true that the creator of this faith, and the **source** of it is God, not your flesh, not your mind; hence, it is God's love and Jesus's faith placed within you, and thus, God gets the glory for your very salvation.

Your human belief, then, becomes the *effect* of your regeneration, not the *cause* of it—the *cause* is the death of Christ on the cross, and His blood (as all the reformers agreed), and His vital work within you through the Holy Spirit's indwelling! If you focus on your human belief as the efficient cause of your salvation, then you must believe in salvation by works, salvation by self, which is, in effect, idolatry, for belief is a work of the mind, which requires human energy as any other work (John 6:28,29). So, the Holy Spirit gives you the gift of Christ's faith, faith that can walk on water, saving faith, when He regenerates you. Again, God gets the glory.

Another gift at the moment of salvation is that He makes you **positionally righteous** by giving you **the righteousness of Christ**. The doctrines of salvation are as broad as the heavens and as deep as the sea. These great doctrinal truths—such as justification, redemption, reconciliation, and forgiveness—are all gifts given to you at the moment of your regeneration by the Holy Spirit. Look at these next verses. They show that the Holy Spirit **gives** you the righteousness of Christ AND the **faith OF Christ**!

Hebrews 12:2
2 Looking unto Jesus the **author** and **finisher** of **our faith**; who for the joy that was set before him endured the cross, despising the shame, and is set down at the right hand of the throne of God.

Romans 3:20–23

20 Therefore by the deeds [i.e., works] of the law there shall no flesh be justified in his sight: for by the law *is* the knowledge of sin.

21 But now the righteousness of God without the law is manifested, being witnessed by the law and the prophets;

22 Even the ***righteousness of God*** *which is* by ***faith of Jesus*** Christ unto all and upon all them that believe: for there is no difference.

Verse 22 in the Greek/English Interlinear Bible reads like this:

"A righteousness of God through faith *of* Jesus Christ to all and upon all the (ones) believing...."[33]

The righteousness of God comes to us without us ***doing*** anything (i.e., without the works of the law). The only ones truly believing, are the ones that have been given the faith *of* Jesus Christ.

We first *receive* something, and then we *believe something* (v. 22).

We receive the faith *of* Christ, and then our human belief comes along beside His faith inside us and resonates with His faith. It actually all happens in the same moment of time. Why is this

---

[33] Jay P. Green, Sr. ed. and translator, *The Interlinear Hebrew–Greek–English Bible*, (Lafayett, In.: Authors For Christ, Inc., 2009), p. 480.

necessary? Because "all have sinned and come short of the glory of God," so we had to "be justified freely by His grace" (which means undeserved favour—we did not do anything to deserve it; we had to be justified [passive] by someone stronger and more powerful than us, the Saviour Jesus Christ).

Why is this true?

There are two reasons:

First, the Bible teaches that *not all men have faith.* However, those who do have faith have been established and kept by the faith, or faithfulness, of the Lord, and by the Lord's working in their lives, and his directing their hearts into the love for God and patient waiting for the coming of Christ! Our faith is a result of Christ faithfully working within us.

2 Thessalonians 3:2–5
2 And that we may be delivered from unreasonable and wicked men: *for all men have not faith.*
3 But the Lord is **faithful,** who shall stablish you, and keep *you* from evil.

faithful
pistŏs, trustworthy; *trustful*:—believe (-ing).

4 And we have confidence in the Lord touching you, that ye both do and will do the things which we command you.
5 And the Lord direct your hearts into the love of God, and into the patient waiting for Christ.

Second, because we were lost, not seeking God, and in our sin.

Romans 3:11

There is none that understandeth, there is none that seeketh after God.

Romans 3:23

For all have sinned, and come short of the glory of God.

He had to do something **_TO_** us to awaken us, and that is accomplished by the effectual calling and regenerating work of the Holy Spirit. He gave us the **_gifts of faith and love_**, and then we, as the bride, responded to the groom by believing in Him and loving Him. Verse 26 proves this is the correct rendering of these verses.

> **Romans 3:22** Even the **_righteousness of God_** _which is_ by **_faith of Jesus_** Christ unto all and upon all them that believe....
>
> **26** To declare, _I say_, at this time **_his_** righteousness: that he might be just, and the justifier of him which believeth in Jesus.

The Greek/English interlinear Bible provides this literal translation of verse 26:

> "In the forbearance of God; for the demonstration of the righteousness of Him in the present time, for the being of Him just and justifying the one of [having the] **_faith of Jesus_**."[34]

---

[34] Ibid.

Those who are able to believe are those who have been given the faith of Christ, and His righteousness. Jesus has justified (i.e., made righteous) the "one having the faith of Jesus."

So, the Greek would look like this: "It is righteous for Jesus to justify the one having **Jesus-faith**." Or, better in English, "It is righteous for Jesus to justify…the one who has the **faith of Jesus**." The important thing to remember, as stated above, is that in the Greek, the word "in" (Gk "**en**") is not found here in verse 26. God is just, and the justifier of the person who has in his heart, Christ's faith alongside and upholding his human belief. It is right for God to justify the true believer.

> **Rom. 3:27, 28**
> **27** Where *is* boasting then? It is excluded. By what law? of works? Nay: but by the law of faith.
> **28** Therefore we conclude that a man is justified by faith without the deeds of the law.

Your brain requires energy to think so to "believe" something requires physical work. But we are not saved by works. We are saved by grace through faith, and THAT faith is a gift from God (Eph. 2:8–9). Now this fits many other passages in Paul's epistles, which we will see later.

The idea of being justified by the faith _of_ Christ may be very new to you because its *effect*—personal belief in Jesus—is what most churches emphasize, and that is fine. But the *source* of faith is what is in view here. So, you might be surprised to learn that this is not a novel idea at all, and it certainly upholds the idea of Jesus being THE author of faith.

Many important scholars discuss the "subjective genitive" (faith *of* Christ), including:

- **G. Kittle**, (*πίστις Ἰησοῦ Χριστοῦ bei Paulus [Paul's faith of Jesus Christ]*, 1906);
- **J. HauBleiter** (*Genitivus auctoris [Faith Effected by Christ]*);
- **Deissmann** (*Paul: A Study in Social and Religious History, genitivus mysticus [Faith Experienced in Mystical Communion with Christ]*, 1926);
- **O. Schmitz** (*Characterizing Genitive [Christ-faith]*, 1924);
- **T. F. Torrance** (*One Aspect of the Biblical Conception of Faith*, 1956);
- **R. N. Longenecker** (*Paul, Apostle of Liberty,* 1964, Note: Whose works I read while studying N.T. at Baylor);
- **G. M. Taylor** (*The Function of ΠΙΣΤΙΣ ΧΡΙΣΤΟΥ [faith in Christ] in Galatians*, 1966);
- **G. Howard** (*The Faith of Christ*, 1967);
- **D.W.B. Robinson** (*Faith of Jesus Christ—A New Testament Debate*, 1970);
- **M. D. Hooker** (*πίστης χριστού [faith in Christ])*, the Presidential Address delivered in Cambridge], 1989); and
- **G. Wallis**, *The Faith of Jesus Christ in Early Christian Traditions*, 1995).

All these works were cited by **Richard B. Hays,**[35] in his book, *The Faith of Jesus Christ: The Narrative Substructure of Galatians 3:1–4:11*.

Hays explains why he believes that we are saved by the "faith OF Christ" which results in our belief "in" Christ:

> While Paul does not hold up the figure of Jesus Christ as an example to be imitated directly, there is in fact a pattern of correspondence between him and those who are "in" him.
>
> The Jesus Christ of the gospel story took the initiative to love and to give himself up (2:20), to bear vicariously the curse of the Law (3:13); thus, when Paul exhorts the Galatians to "bear one another's burdens and so fulfill the law of Christ" (6:2), we may see here a reflected image of the pattern enacted by Christ. When Paul says ἐν πίστει ζῶ τῇ τοῦ υἱοῦ τοῦ θεοῦ (I live by the faith OF the Son of God) (2:20), he does not mean that he strives to emulate Jesus's faith but that his ***own new life in faith*** is "the shadow cast on the plane of experience by the transformation wrought through Jesus Christ's faith...."[36]

Hays is not easy to read. He is very scholarly, and mostly seminary students read him; however, in plain English, he is saying that our faith is an ***effect*** of the faith OF Christ which the Holy Spirit placed within us (as a free gift) when He regenerated us. Our belief

---

[35] Richard B. Hays, *The Faith of Jesus Christ: The Narrative Substructure of Galatians 3:1-4:11*, (Cambridge, U.K.: William B. Eerdmans Publishing Company, 1983), p. 249.
[36] Ibid.

is the "transformation wrought through *Jesus Christ's faith* within us." Hays continues:

> In Galatians...Paul traces the story backward no farther than Abraham and forward no farther than the immediately controverted future of the Galatian churches. This limitation of scope is imposed in part, no doubt, by the particular problem that Paul is addressing here: the role of the Jewish Law in a Gentile Christian community.[37]

Hays is referencing the fact that Paul goes back to the Abrahamic Covenant in the letter to the Galatians to show that they are not saved, and they do not grow, by a combination of faith plus works, *but by faith alone, and the origin of this faith is the faith of Christ*.

I believe the Abrahamic Covenant may be used as proof of this, as follows.

We know, and I have always taught, that the Abrahamic Covenant was a covenant between the Father and Abraham, with the Eternal Son of God (Jesus) advocating and interceding on Abraham's behalf, while Abraham was asleep. Thus...

The source or origination of Abraham's faith was Jesus's faith, for Abraham was asleep when the covenant took place (Gen. 15:12-21).

---

[37] Ibid. p. 226.

This following verse in the N.T. refers to the unconditional "Promise" of God to Abraham:

Galatians 3:22
22 But the scripture hath concluded all under sin, that the ***promise*** by ***faith _of_ Jesus Christ*** might be given to them that believe.

This verse completely ties together the concept of us receiving the *faith of Christ* as a gift, and the Abrahamic Covenant! In fact, the Holy Spirit reveals through Paul, here, that the reason for this unconditional Abrahamic Covenant is the total depravity of man ("But the scripture hath concluded all under sin...."), and the promise of the covenant was brought into force only to "them that believe" by "faith of Jesus Christ." Unfortunately, few have seen this in our day, again, due to the mistranslations of all modern English versions of the Bible (other than the KJV, and the less popular Geneva Bible which came across the Atlantic on the Mayflower).

Most do not ever recognize that our salvation, according to Paul in the epistle of Galatians, is based upon the Abrahamic Covenant, which is an unconditional covenant between God the Father and Abraham. However, when the covenant was made, in Genesis Ch. 15, since Abraham was asleep (picturing resting in Christ) it was the Eternal Son in the form of a "burning lamp," Who exhibited faith in joining the Father (in the form of a "smoking furnace") in covenant on behalf of Abraham!

Even though Jesus did this in the place of Abraham, who was asleep, Abraham benefited because he responded to Christ's faith (and faithful act) with his own trust in this covenant, and it was counted to him as righteousness (Gal. 3:6).

We all know it is the righteousness of Christ that saved Abraham, but as Richard Hays has pointed out, it was also the faith of Christ, in making and later keeping the covenant with the Father, that saved Abraham (and all of us). The Son of God, according to Hebrew covenant tradition, said something like, "May I be as these dead animals if Abraham breaks the covenant with the Father." Abraham (and all of us) have broken the covenant, so Jesus died on the cross, as He promised.

He died for us (i.e., because of us and in the place of us) that we might be saved. At the deepest level, it was Jesus's faith and faithfulness in making and keeping this covenant with the Father, that saved us—therefore, we are justified by the "faith of Christ," not by anything we have done. We were just as asleep as Abraham on the day the Holy Spirit awakened us, at our calling and regeneration.

Galatians 2:16

16 Knowing that a man is not justified by the works of the law, but by the faith **of** Jesus Christ, even we have believed in Jesus Christ....

James D. G. Dunn takes the opposing view, i.e., that we are saved by our own belief in Christ, rather than by Christ's faith and faithfulness, and Hays had the fortitude to print it in an appendix at the back of his book. However, even Dunn says nice things about Hays's views.

I should make it clear that the *theology* of the subjective genitive reading is powerful, important and attractive. For anyone who wishes to take the humanness of Jesus with full seriousness "the faith of Jesus" strikes a strong and resonant chord.

Moreover, as a theological motif, it seems to me wholly compatible with Paul's theology; that is, not a component of Paul's theology but consistent with other emphases. As Hooker has noted, it follows naturally when we bring together the thought of God in Christ and the thought of God's faithfulness.[38]

So, many scholars have promoted the idea—an idea that I have long believed and taught—that we are saved by the faith OF Jesus, as the Holy Spirit indwells us at our regeneration, and gives us more than 33 things as a free gift, including the "faith of Christ." The effect of this gift is that our human belief, like one tuning fork next to another, rings at the same frequency as Christ's faith in us (Gal. 3:20).

I respect Dunn, who passed away in 2020, at the age of 80, as a genuine scholar, but I don't agree with his approach on this issue, because he argued on the most basic level that the phrase "faith in Christ" is used more often, so "faith of Christ" must mean the same thing. In truth, he was in agreement with most reformers. However, I believe this is a non sequitur, and therefore leads to a false conclusion. Nevertheless, here is how Dunn states this:

> The traditional "faith in Christ" makes consistently good sense of the line of thought…with repetition serving to reinforce the claim being made [that "faith of Christ" really means "faith in Christ"].[39]

My contention is that if the Holy Spirit, the author of the Bible, wanted "faith of Christ" to mean the same thing as "faith in Christ"

---

[38] Ibid. p. 269.
[39] Ibid. p. 254.

then He would have said so! He could have used the Greek word *en* throughout. Now, I believe that common sense alone would prove Dunn's logic is bad. For example, take this verse, and then change all the "of"s to "in"s, and look at the ridiculous redundance.

Galatians 2:16

16 Knowing that a man is not justified by the works of the law, but by the faith *in* Jesus Christ, even we have believed *in* Jesus Christ, that we might be justified by the faith *in* Christ, and not by the works of the law....

If this were the meaning, then the Holy Spirit could have just written:

Galatians 2:16

16 Knowing that a man is not justified by the works of the law, but by faith *in* Jesus Christ.

And, knowing how concise the Bible is, why repeat the same thing three times? I don't believe He would have. Apparently "faith of Christ" is something different than "faith in Christ," which means we should put thought into it. Little words like "of" and "in" are also "God-breathed" (*thĕŏpnĕustŏs)* and are therefore important.

However, Dunn then argues against the "faith of Christ" motif by simply saying Paul didn't write Ephesians, Colossians, 2 Thessalonians, 1 Timothy, 2 Timothy, and Titus! (This is what "deuteron-Pauline" means.) This is not an argument that would sway any conservative Bible thinker.

Higher critics of the Bible (liberal theologians) don't believe Moses wrote the first five books of the Bible, or that Paul wrote all his epistles, and they have many other theories which I now believe to be mostly based in pride. (They think they are "smart enough" to judge the Word of God, rather than being judged by it.) I studied under several of these types in Baylor University theology classes, and I rejected these professors as most likely lost (I'm not saying that about Dunn, but sadly, some people never get over seminary).

You'll see this liberal theology in Dunn's arguments. The N.T. books Paul penned, which would prove the "faith of Christ" motif to be true, Dunn says most likely were not written by Paul, so they prove nothing about Paul's writing style. (Of course, if, like most of us, you **_DO_** believe Moses wrote the Pentateuch and Paul wrote his letters, then Dunn's arguments fall apart). He follows this line below:

> The deutero-Paulines seem to have developed the formula, "faith in Christ Jesus (πίστις [anarthrous, i.e., nouns used with an article, in this case 'the'] ἡ ἐν Χριστῷ Ἰησοῦ) [i.e., you believe in Christ Jesus]" (1 Tim 3:13; 2 Tim 1:13; 3:15). An earlier version of it is Eph 1:15— "your faith in the Lord Jesus (τὴν καθ᾽ ὑμᾶς πίστιν ἐν τῷ κυρίῳ Ἰησοῦ)"—the definite article in this case required, of course, to indicate the particular faith (καθ᾽ ὑμᾶς) in view.

> This could be significant [in other words prove the "faith of Christ" motif], since it might indicate that a different phrase was current to denote "faith in Christ," and thus suggest that by "faith of Christ" Paul must have meant something else (Christ's faith).

> The difficulty of course is precisely that all the instances of the "in" phrase belong to the **_deutero-Pauline corpus_** and thus **_provide no evidence of Paul's own usage or of usage current at the time of Paul_**. The deutero-Pauline

usage therefore gives us *no assistance* in resolving the force of the genitive constructions in Paul.[40]

The word "corpus" means "a particular collection of writings" and is referring to those books that Dunn says Paul did not actually write.

Therefore, Dunn just cops out on the whole argument with: "Instances of the 'in' phrase belong to the *deuteron-Pauline corpus* and thus *provide no evidence of Paul's own usage or of usage current at the time of Paul*."

In reality, the writings of Paul show EVERY evidence of Paul's usage of the idea of faith OF Christ as something different, though related to, faith IN Christ.

This reveals a sad truth. Although the current theological world would say Dunn is a "conservative theologian," the yardage markers have moved so much since I was a young man, that what they call "conservative" now is *no doubt a liberal* to those of us older guys who think we are truly conservative.

I once heard it said that one of the most dangerous places for a Christian is a Christian bookstore. If something is on a bookshelf, it automatically gives a sense of authority. Therefore, we can find ourselves repeating theories for so long that they quickly become the "scholarly consensus."

Even good men, like Dunn, repeat these theories as if they are Scripture. We must always remember two things, in our search for truth:

---

[40] Ibid. p. 255.

(1) Scripture is, and must always be, *the* standard upon which we base everything else. For example, there is beautiful consistency between all 13 of Paul's letters. The Apostle Peter himself stated that Paul's inspired letters *are* Scripture (2 Pet. 3:15-16).

(2) We must *never* consider historical texts through the lens of *modern* ideas and understandings (to do so is something referred to as "anachronism").

Scholars often fall into this, and then create other dangerous theories to fulfill their anachronistic feelings about a passage. When they do this, they rob the historical figures (such as Paul, and all of the 1st and 2nd century Christians that accepted his 13 letters as Scripture) of their place in history, which is bad historiography by all standards. Sadly, Dunn (and many others in the last 150 years) have committed this error.

Also, I think Dunn doesn't see the forest for the trees in his vigorous analysis, and he definitely bought into the liberal theology he learned as a young man in seminary, which I tasted but rejected while at Baylor. The verse we used above is a great example.

Galatians 2:16

16 Knowing that a man is not justified by the works of the law, but by the *faith **of** Jesus* Christ, even we have *believed **in** Jesus Christ*, that we might be justified *by the faith **of** Christ,* and not by the works of the law: for by the works of the law shall no flesh be justified.

A literal translation in the Greek would be:

"Knowing that a man is not justified *by* (*ek* from the origin of) works...but ***through*** (*dia*) Christ-faith (subjective genitive, i.e., the faith comes from Christ), even we have believed into (*eis*) Jesus Christ (in this portion of the verse, the preposition "into" thus indicates our human belief *in* Christ), that we might be justified *from out of* (*ek*, denoting origin) Christ-faith (subjective genitive)."

The grammar is **_not_** unclear, as Dunn would want us to think. This is especially true if we allow the text to just say what it actually says! And, and we previously suggested, the verse makes no sense if each "faith of Christ" were translated "faith in Christ," because the redundancy would be ridiculous if we said the two "ofs" were "ins." However, they are not and the Greek word *en* is not in the text in the first and third phrases!

Paul is, no doubt, saying we are *justified by Jesus's faith* that the Holy Spirit placed within us when He called us (He gave us the faith *of* Christ as a free gift, Eph 2:8, 9), and then the *effect* was that we were able to believe *IN* Christ, because we were quickened—made alive—hearing and seeing Jesus for Who He really is for the first time.

Then the *cause* of the justification is emphasized by the purposeful redundance of the last phrase, "we have *believed in Jesus Christ*, that we might be justified *by the faith of Christ,* and not by the works of the law." The verse begins by us being justified by Christ's faith within us, and it ends the same way. The effect of this gift of faith from the Lord, is our human belief *in* Christ, found in the middle of the verse.

In the future, everyone found to be in heaven will have been given this heavenly gift of Christ's faith, and will have exhibited human belief in Christ, as personal Lord and Saviour, as a result. Both occur in the very moment of regeneration.

I will say again, when the *faith of Christ* is given to us, the kind of faith that can walk on water and move mountains, then our belief is like a tuning fork alongside HIS tuning fork.

Christ's faith and our human belief are like ONE TUNING FORK NEXT TO ANOTHER. When one is struck, the other vibrates at the same frequency.

Our belief moves along with Christ's faith within us.

So, we can now add the Apostle Paul's name to the list of renowned theologians above—all people who believe we are saved by the "faith OF Christ." He, together with Luke, James, and John taught this principle 2,000 years ago!

Romans 3:22
22 Even the righteousness of God *which is* by faith *of* Jesus Christ unto all and upon all them that believe: for there is no difference.

Romans 1:17
17 For therein is the righteousness of God revealed *from faith to faith*: as it is written, The just shall live by faith.

Philippians 3:9

9 And be found in him, not having mine own righteousness, which is of the law, but that which is through the faith **_of_** Christ, the righteousness which is of God by faith.

Galatians 2:20

20 I am crucified with Christ: nevertheless I live; yet not I, but Christ liveth in me: and the life which I now live in the flesh I live by the faith **_of_** the Son of God, who loved me, and gave himself for me.

Galatians 3:22

22 But the scripture hath concluded all under sin, that the promise by faith **_of_** Jesus Christ might be given to them that believe.

Ephesians 3:11–12

11 According to the eternal purpose which he purposed in Christ Jesus our Lord:
12 In whom we have boldness and access with confidence by the faith **_of_** him.

Luke, who wrote Acts, also agrees that the faith that saves us is "by Him," i.e., by Jesus:

Acts 3:16

16 And his name through faith in his name hath made this man strong, whom ye see and know: yea, the faith *which is __by__ him* hath given him this perfect soundness in the presence of you all.

James agrees as well:

James 2:1

1 My brethren, have not the faith *__of__* our Lord Jesus Christ, *the Lord* of glory, with respect of persons.

John, as well:

Revelation 2:13

13 I know thy works, and where thou dwellest, *even* where Satan's seat *is*: and thou holdest fast my name, and hast not denied *__my__* faith....

Revelation 14:12

12 Here is the patience of the saints: here *are* they that keep the commandments of God, and the faith *__of__* Jesus.

These phrases are not talking about faith *IN* Christ (while many other verses DO say "faith in Christ"); but here the Holy Spirit chose to say, "the faith *OF* Christ"—*Christ's very faith*, which is given to us as a gift.

Our human belief can quickly turn into doubt; it is up one day and down the next. However, once we are regenerated, *our human belief can then fall in line with Christ's forever faith.*

When our belief turns to doubt, as it does so often, His faith within us walks on the water, extends His hand, and lifts us back up onto the water with Him.

Charles Spurgeon, the "Prince of Preachers," put it this way in a sermon on Philippians 3:9:

> "'And be found in him, not having my own righteousness, which is from the law, but what is through the faith **of** Christ, the righteousness which is from God by faith.' It must be more glorious to be justified by God than by ourselves. It must be more safe to wear the righteousness of Christ than to wear our own. Nothing can so dignify our manhood as to have Christ himself to be 'the Lord our Righteousness.' This Paul chose in preference to everything else."[41]

We see that the faith of Christ is a gift given to us by the Holy Spirit when He regenerates us, and His righteousness is imputed to us with this faith. This faith is not a "self" faith, but a gifted faith.

Ephesians 2:8–9
8 For by grace are ye saved through faith; and that not of yourselves: *it is the gift* of God:
9 Not of works, lest any man should boast.

---

[41] Charles Spurgeon, *The Enemies of the Cross of Christ*, on August 28, 2018, No. 2553-44:37. A Sermon Delivered On Lord's Day Evening, October 26, 1884, By C. H. Spurgeon, At The Metropolitan Tabernacle, Newington, Answers in Genesis, https://answersingenesis.org/education/spurgeon-sermons/2553-enemies-cross-christ/.

All this must be in proper order, or our Christianity becomes nothing more than humanism.

This is God's order, and Paul exhorts us to be careful not to be beguiled by humanism (or liberal theologians)—giving us the idea that we can save ourselves.

Colossians 2:4, 8–13

4 And this I say, lest any man should beguile you with enticing words.

8 Beware lest any man spoil you through philosophy and vain deceit, after the tradition of men, after the rudiments of the world, and not after Christ.

9 For in him dwelleth all the fulness of the Godhead bodily.

10 And *ye are complete in him*, which is the head of all principality and power:

11 In whom also ye are circumcised with the *circumcision made without hands*, in putting off the body of the sins of the flesh by the circumcision of Christ:

12 Buried with him in baptism, wherein also ye are risen with *him* through the *faith of the operation of God*, who hath raised him from the dead.

13 And *you, being dead* in your sins and the uncircumcision of your flesh, *hath he quickened together with him*, having forgiven you all trespasses.

We were in Christ when He died; when He was buried, and when He came out of that grave, we were also in Him. Now that we have received Him, He is in us. This means His faith, His love, and His righteousness are in us! His faith has become our faith, His love our love, and His righteousness our righteousness. This is called, in v. 12, *"the operation of God."* Both the words "faith" and the phrase "operation of God" are subjective genitive! The operation stems from *God*. The faith stems from the *operation* of God. Again, if you saw this in the Greek it would look like this: "Through the faith from the God-operation." It means that Jesus's faith comes to US because of the operation God performs upon us.

Unfortunately, this beautiful truth of being saved by the faith *of* Christ is lost to many in the English-speaking world. I love the King James because it is, in my opinion, the most accurate English translation.[42]

The truth found in Hebrews 12:2, that Jesus is the only author of our faith, is in perfect harmony with the concept of being justified by Christ's faith within us. Jesus is the only author of our faith, and He is also the "finisher" of our faith!

Not only is Jesus the Author of our faith, but He is the FINISHER of our faith.

The whole book of Galatians in the New Testament is about the fact that we are saved by grace through faith, and we ***STAY saved*** the same way—by grace through faith. Also, any holiness we may

---

[42] The author spent two years studying manuscript evidence, but this is beyond the scope of this book. See Appendix 1 for information on Bibles and study helps.

attain comes by grace, through faith, not by works of the flesh. (The book of Galatians SHOUTS this truth.)

The Bible teaches that when we do good works, it is **because** we are saved; in other words, it is an EFFECT of salvation, **not** the CAUSE of it.

The great Charles Spurgeon, the Prince of Preachers, once said, "An effect can never be the cause of the cause." This is a true logical statement. Many are confused about cause and effect when it comes to salvation.

Once, I asked a close Roman Catholic friend of mine, "What do you think the cause of regeneration is?"

He thought for a moment and said, "Well, I believe in the idea of being born again." (Many Roman Catholics do not know about this, but my friend did.)

I asked, "So, what is the cause of it?" He could not answer. I said, "Let me give you a hint: there are a couple of verses that give us the answer." And I quoted to him these scriptures:

Colossians 2:13
13 And you, being dead in your sins and the uncircumcision of your flesh, hath he quickened together with him, having forgiven you all trespasses;

Ephesians 2:5
5 Even when we were dead in sins, hath quickened us together with Christ, (by grace ye are saved;)

I said, "While we were yet sinners, hath HE (here I pointed to the sky) quickened us (brought us from death to life). Who regenerated us?"

My dear friend said, "God?"

I exclaimed, "YES! ...and everything else that happened after that were EFFECTS; God was the cause."

I continued, "You have told me in the past it bothered you that we cannot all worship together in one church. Do you know why we cannot? All denominations, including the Catholics, look at DIFFERENT EFFECTS of salvation and claim they are the CAUSE.

"If they all understood that the ONLY CAUSE is that the Holy Spirit called us and opened our eyes to Christ, which made us desire Him, and that HE, the Holy Spirit, brought us to life, and that everything else we did later, such as believe, repent, be baptized, do good works, tithe, go to church, live better, etc. are EFFECTS, not the cause, then we could all go to church together. In fact, had the Catholics followed Augustine, we might have all been Roman Catholics and happy about that!"

So, Jesus is the Author (saves us) and the Finisher (keeps us saved) of our faith until we meet Him in person someday, perhaps soon.

Contemplate the following verses, and perhaps in a future book, we will go deeper into these amazing truths.

Romans 6:4–7

4 Therefore we are buried with him by baptism into death: that like as Christ was raised up from the dead by the glory of the Father, even so we also should walk in newness of life.

5 For if we have been planted together in the likeness of his death, we shall be also *in the likeness* of *his* resurrection:

6 Knowing this, that our old man is crucified with *him*, that the body of sin might be destroyed, that henceforth we should not serve sin.

7 For he that is dead is freed from sin.

Galatians 2:20–3:3

20 I am crucified with Christ: nevertheless I live; yet not I, but Christ liveth in me: and the life which I now live in the flesh I live by the faith of the Son of God, who loved me, and gave himself for me.

21 I do not frustrate the grace of God: for if righteousness *come* by the law, then Christ is dead in vain.

3:1 O foolish Galatians, who hath bewitched you, that ye should not obey the truth, before whose eyes Jesus Christ hath been evidently set forth, crucified among you?

2 This only would I learn of you, Received ye the Spirit by the works of the law, or by the hearing of faith?

3 Are ye so foolish? having begun in the Spirit, are ye now made perfect by the flesh?

2 Corinthians 5:17–18

17 Therefore if any man *be* in Christ, *he is* a **_new creature_**: old things are passed away; behold, all things are become new.

18 And **_all things are of God_**, who hath reconciled us to himself by Jesus Christ, and hath given to us the ministry of reconciliation.

Our salvation and our new life both come from God—by grace through faith, we are resurrected to new life in this lifetime and the next, and we live that new life for Him because we now love Him. LOVE is our motive for good works.

2 Corinthians 5:14–15

14 For the *love of Christ* constraineth us; because we thus judge, that if one died for all, then were all dead:

15 And *that* he died for all, that they which live should not henceforth live unto themselves, but unto him which died for them, and rose again.

29. Jesus is our Intercessor, our Advocate with the Father, and our High Priest.

All the Old Testament sacrifices pictured specific things that Jesus would eventually accomplish on the cross. They were the patterns; Jesus was the REAL, perfect Lamb of God that the patterns depicted.

He is both the offering and the offeror. He offered Himself to save us, and He KEEPS us saved by the integrity of His offering.

Many verses indicate HOW Christ keeps us saved, even though we live in a body of flesh, which sometimes seems to fight against what God and even we ourselves wish to do.

Remember this: when you do sin, and you are down on yourself, this life of a new man living in the old body of flesh is ON PURPOSE. It is God's will that we live with this constant struggle because it brings glory to Him. When we DO get it right, HE gets the glory! So, don't stay down on yourself—go directly to 1 John 1:9, and believe it! (See point number 35 below.) Then get right back up and *stand straight in this crooked world*.

This shows that God made you to be a "new creation," a "new man or woman" when He saved you, but you still live with the "old man," which pulls against what God desires, and even that which your NEW SELF desires.

But this state we live in, old man and new man, is God's will.

I've studied the Bible for 45 years and only realized this truth (in v. 7 below) in the last couple of years. However, it is a profound truth to help us keep going! You need to always remember that, once you're born again, *the real you is the new man*. However, the old man is always present until you go to meet the Lord.

2 Corinthians 4:6–7
6 For God, who commanded the light to shine out of darkness, hath shined in our hearts, to *give* the light of the knowledge of the glory of God in the face of Jesus Christ.
7 But we have ***this treasure*** in ***earthen vessels***, that the excellency of the power may be of God, and not of us.

"This treasure" is your new man walking hand in hand with Jesus. The "earthen vessel" is your fleshly body with all its urges. This life you live, fighting the good fight, brings glory to God and to God's power.

The reason you can win many of these battles, and ultimately the war, is because Jesus is your Advocate with the Father and your Intercessor before the throne of God. He is your attorney who stands up and says, "My child is innocent because I have paid their sin debt in full," every time Satan accuses you before the Father, every time you sin.

1 John 2:1
1 My little children, these things write I unto you, that ye sin not. And if any man sin, we have an ***advocate with the Father***, Jesus Christ the righteous:

Hebrews 7:25–27
25 Wherefore he is able also to **save them to the uttermost** that come unto God by him, seeing he ever liveth ***to make intercession for them***.
26 For such an high priest became us, *who is* holy, harmless, undefiled, separate from sinners, and made higher than the heavens;
27 Who needeth not daily, as those high priests, to offer up sacrifice, first for his own sins, and then for the people's: ***for this he did once***, when he offered up himself.

The patterns of the O.T. sacrifices were not sufficient. However, when Jesus came in the fullness of time and died for the sins of His people, He only offered Himself **ONCE. *He saved us <u>once and for all.</u>***

These verses in Hebrews are a little difficult to understand without much prayer, study, and meditation, and a good understanding of the book of Leviticus in the O.T., but they are all about Jesus, our High Priest, being the perfect sacrifice Who paid for our sins and ransomed us from the power of Satan and death.

Hebrews 6:18–20

18 That by two immutable things, in which *it was* impossible for God to lie, we might have a strong consolation, who have fled for refuge to lay hold upon the hope set before us:

19 Which *hope* we have as an anchor of the soul, both sure and stedfast, and which entereth into that within the veil;

20 Whither the forerunner is for us entered, *even* Jesus, made an high priest for ever after the order of Melchisedec.

Hebrews 7:22–25

22 By so much was Jesus made a surety of a better testament [the N.T.].

23 And they [in the O.T.] truly were many priests, because they were not suffered to continue by reason of death:

24 But this *man*, because he continueth ever, hath an unchangeable priesthood.

25 Wherefore he is able also to **save them to the uttermost** that come unto God by him, seeing he ever liveth to make intercession for them.

The fact that *Jesus's finished work*—the blood that He gave to *pay the sin-debt* of all His people—has been accomplished, AND the fact that He is *now seated at the right hand of God* in heaven and is our *Advocate before the Father,* is WHY a person, once truly saved, can never lose his salvation.

All of John Chapter 17 is an intercessory prayer of Jesus Christ for His sheep. In that chapter, He says:

John 17:2–4, 6, 8-9; 15–18
2 As thou hast given him power over all flesh, that he should give eternal life to as many as thou hast given him.
3 And this is life eternal, that they might know thee the only true God, and Jesus Christ, whom thou hast sent.
4 I have glorified thee on the earth: I have finished the work which thou gavest me to do. [FINISHED WORK OF CHRIST!]
6 I have manifested thy name unto the men which thou gavest me out of the world: thine they were, and thou gavest them me; and they have kept thy word.
8 For I have given unto them the words which thou gavest me; and they have received *them*, and have known surely that I came out from thee, and they have believed that thou didst send me.
9 I pray for them: I pray not for the world, but for them which thou hast given me; for they are thine.

15 I pray not that thou shouldest take them out of the world, but that thou shouldest keep them from the evil.
16 They are not of the world, even as I am not of the world.
17 Sanctify them through thy truth: thy word is truth.
18 As thou hast sent me into the world, even so have I also sent them into the world.

Once saved, you are <u>saved to the uttermost</u> (and you cannot get more saved than that)!

We are saved to bring glory to Christ, to be separate from the world system, to be sanctified and made more like Christ in this world, to receive and keep His Word, and to witness to everyone the Holy Spirit leads us to.

30. The Apostle Peter preached a sermon in the book of Acts and said that Jesus Christ was the <u>ONLY name</u> given under heaven among men, whereby we must be saved.

It is NOT true that all religions of the world are headed to heaven but down different roads. There is ***only ONE way, and that way is Jesus Christ.***

Acts 4:10–12
10 Be it known unto you all, and to all the people of Israel, that by the name of Jesus Christ of Nazareth,

whom ye crucified, whom God raised from the dead, *even* by him doth this man stand here before you whole.

11 This is the stone which was set at nought of you builders, which is become the head of the corner.

12 Neither is there salvation in any other: for there is *none other name under heaven given among men, whereby we must be saved*.

31. The Great Apostle Paul says that Jesus is declared to be the Son of God with power by His resurrection and that over 500 people who were still alive in Paul's day saw the resurrected Saviour.

Romans 1:3–4

3 Concerning his Son Jesus Christ our Lord, which was made of the seed of David according to the flesh;

4 And declared *to be* the Son of God with power, according to the spirit of holiness, by the resurrection from the dead.

1 Corinthians 15:3–8

3 For I delivered unto you first of all that which I also received, how that Christ died for our sins according to the scriptures;

4 And that he was buried, and that he rose again the third day according to the scriptures:

5 And that he was seen of Cephas, then of the twelve:

6 After that, *he was seen of above five hundred brethren* at once; of whom the greater part remain unto this present, but some are fallen asleep.

7 After that, he was seen of James; then of all the apostles.

8 And last of all he was seen of me also, as of one born out of due time.

Jesus was proven to be *THE* very Son of God by His resurrection.

The Apostle Paul recorded that Jesus was seen *after* His resurrection not only by Cephas and the rest of the twelve apostles but also by over five hundred brethren at one time. After that, Jesus

appeared to James and the other apostles and then, last of all, to Paul himself. Paul said that most of them were still alive when he wrote this letter—no one, not even the Jews, refuted this testimony in the days of Paul. There were just too many eyewitnesses to overlook.

Also, the personality of the apostles had been changed from cowardice to BOLDNESS in three days! What did they see that changed them? All of them but John were later killed, holding to the testimony that they had seen the risen Saviour—none recanted. In fact, they turned the world upside down in the days following the resurrection. The only thing that can explain this remarkable psychological change is—well, an actual resurrection.

The resurrection proved that Jesus was exactly who HE claimed to be—the Son of Man, the Son of God, the "I AM." (This is the name God told Moses to use for the Lord when speaking to the Israelites in Exodus 3:14.)

When Jesus died on the cross, perhaps Satan felt he had won. But three days later, Satan surely trembled when Jesus came out of that grave, walked among His people for forty days, and then ascended into heaven and presented His blood as a ransom for all God's children!

> **32. Paul also made it clear that salvation is by the FAITH OF Christ on the cross and not by works of righteousness which we could try to do. Righteousness comes to us only as we have the faith of Christ.**

Romans 3:22–24, 27–28

22 Even the righteousness of God *which is* **by faith _of_ Jesus Christ** unto all and upon all them that believe: for there is no difference:

23 For all have sinned, and come short of the glory of God;

24 Being justified freely by his grace through the redemption that is in Christ Jesus:

27 Where *is* boasting then? It is excluded. By what law? of works? Nay: but by the law of faith.

28 Therefore we conclude that a man is justified by faith without the deeds of the law.

Please take time here to quietly meditate upon the following passages and allow God, through HIS Word, to bless your heart with a full knowledge of the Gospel—the message of good news that men cannot save themselves but must BE saved by someone stronger, someone sinless, someone who desires to do the saving, and that is the Lord Jesus Christ!

It is a disgrace to Jesus Christ to suggest that His blood is not sufficient to ransom God's people from the slave market of sin and Satan.

Nothing But the Blood of Jesus...

Titus 3:5–7

5 Not by works of righteousness which we have done, but according to his mercy he saved us, by the washing of regeneration, and renewing of the Holy Ghost;
6 Which he shed on us abundantly through Jesus Christ our Saviour;
7 That being justified by his grace, we should be made heirs according to the hope of eternal life.

Romans 5:8–10

8 But God commendeth his love toward us, in that, while we were yet sinners, Christ died for us.
9 Much more then, being now justified by his blood, we shall be saved from wrath through him.
10 For if, when we were enemies, we were reconciled to God by the death of his Son, much more, being reconciled, we shall be saved by his life.

Ephesians 1:4–7

4 According as he hath chosen us in him before the foundation of the world, that we should be holy and without blame before him in love:

5 Having predestinated us unto the adoption of children by Jesus Christ to himself, according to the good pleasure of his will,

6 To the praise of the glory of his grace, wherein he hath made us accepted in the beloved.

7 In whom we have redemption through his blood, the forgiveness of sins, according to the riches of his grace.

Colossians 1:19–22

19 For it pleased *the Father* that in him should all fulness dwell;

20 And, having made peace through the blood of his cross, by him to reconcile all things unto himself; by him, *I say*, whether *they be* things in earth, or things in heaven.

21 And you, that were sometime alienated and enemies in *your* mind by wicked works, yet now hath he reconciled

22 In the body of his flesh through death, to present you holy and unblameable and unreproveable in his sight.

1 Peter 1:2–6

2 Elect according to the foreknowledge of God the Father, through sanctification of the Spirit, unto obedience and sprinkling of the blood of Jesus Christ: Grace unto you, and peace, be multiplied.

3 Blessed *be* the God and Father of our Lord Jesus Christ, which according to his abundant mercy hath begotten us again unto a lively hope by the resurrection of Jesus Christ from the dead,

4 To an inheritance incorruptible, and undefiled, and that fadeth not away, reserved in heaven for you,

5 Who are kept by the power of God through faith unto salvation ready to be revealed in the last time.

6 Wherein ye greatly rejoice, though now for a season, if need be, ye are in heaviness through manifold temptations.

Ephesians 2:1–10

1 And you *hath he quickened*, who were dead in trespasses and sins;

2 Wherein in time past ye walked according to the course of this world, according to the prince of the power of the air, the spirit that now worketh in the children of disobedience:

3 Among whom also we all had our conversation in times past in the lusts of our flesh, fulfilling the desires of the flesh and of the mind; and were by nature the children of wrath, even as others.

4 But God, who is rich in mercy, for his great love wherewith he loved us,

5 Even when we were dead in sins, hath quickened us together with Christ, (by grace ye are saved;)

6 And hath raised *us* up together, and made *us* sit together in heavenly *places* in Christ Jesus:

7 That in the ages to come he might shew the exceeding riches of his grace in *his* kindness toward us through Christ Jesus.

8 For by grace are ye saved through faith; and that not of yourselves: *it is* the gift of God:

9 Not of works, lest any man should boast.

10 For we are his workmanship, created in Christ Jesus unto good works, which God hath before ordained that we should walk in them.

Romans 3:23–28

23 For all have sinned, and come short of the glory of God;

24 Being justified freely by his grace through the redemption that is in Christ Jesus:

25 Whom God hath set forth to be a propitiation through faith in his blood, to declare his righteousness for the remission of sins that are past, through the forbearance of God;

26 To declare, I say, at this time his righteousness: that he might be just, and the justifier of him which believeth in Jesus.

27 Where *is* boasting then? It is excluded. By what law? of works? Nay: but by the law of faith.

28 Therefore we conclude that a man is justified by faith without the deeds of the law.

Romans 6:23

23 For the wages of sin is death; but the gift of God is eternal life through Jesus Christ our Lord.

Romans 10:9–10, 13

9 That if thou shalt confess with thy mouth the Lord Jesus, and shalt believe in thine heart that God hath raised him from the dead, thou shalt be saved.

10 For with the heart man believeth unto righteousness; and with the mouth confession is made unto salvation.

13 For whosoever shall call upon the name of the Lord shall be saved.

The N.T. makes it abundantly clear that we are "saved by grace (unmerited favor) through faith, and NOT of our own works, lest we should boast." The gospel is only good news because it teaches everywhere that salvation is a free gift, not earned by us, and therefore we cannot UN-earn it. We are BORN again; we cannot be UN-born. We can disobey, but we cannot be kicked out of our Father's family, we are held in the hand of Jesus AND in the Father's hand. Jesus said:

John 10:28–30

28 And I give unto them eternal life; and they shall never perish, neither shall any man pluck them out of my hand.

29 My Father, which gave them me, is greater than all; and no man is able to pluck them out of my Father's hand.

30 I and my Father are one. [Once again, the God-man.]

33. Paul teaches that Christ died for us before we even knew we wanted Him! He died in our place. This is known as the substitutionary death of Christ.

He paid our sin debt in full. The last thing He said before He died was, "It is finished." In Greek, this statement was written on bills that were paid off—it meant "paid in full." Our sin debt is completely paid by Jesus Christ so that we do not have to pay it. We are ransomed and justified by His blood (the finished work of Christ) and saved by His life (the continuing intercessory work on our behalf by the living Saviour). He did this for us while we were still sinners.

Romans 5:8–11

8 But God commendeth his love toward us, in that, while we were yet sinners, Christ died for us.

9 Much more then, being now justified by his blood, we shall be saved from wrath through him.

10 For if, when we were enemies, we were reconciled to God by the death of his Son, much more, being reconciled, we shall be saved by his life.

11 And not only *so*, but we also joy in God through our Lord Jesus Christ, by whom we have now received the atonement.

34. Paul says our salvation in Christ is a FREE GIFT. As such, we cannot lose it because we did not earn it and because Jesus's love for His sheep is eternal.

Romans 6:23

23 For the wages of sin *is* death; but the ***gift of God is*** eternal life through Jesus Christ our Lord.

Romans 8:1, 38–39

1 *There is* therefore now no condemnation to them which are in Christ Jesus, who walk not after the flesh, but after the Spirit.

38 For I am persuaded, that neither death, nor life, nor angels, nor principalities, nor powers, nor things present, nor things to come,

39 Nor height, nor depth, nor any other creature, shall be able to separate us from the love of God, which is in Christ Jesus our Lord.

Did God leave anything in the universe out?

The Apostle John agrees with Paul, of course, that NOTHING can separate us from God's love, as we have already seen.

John 10:27–30

27 My sheep hear my voice, and I know them, and they follow me:

28 And I give unto them eternal life; and they shall never perish, neither shall any *man* [Gk. anything] pluck them out of my hand.

35. The Scriptures teach that Jesus's death was the RANSOM paid to set us free.

Isaiah 35:10

10 And the ransomed of the Lord shall return, And come to Zion with songs And everlasting joy upon their heads: They shall obtain joy and gladness, And sorrow and sighing shall flee away.

Hosea 13:14
14 I will ransom them from the power of the grave; I will redeem them from death: O death, I will be thy plagues; O grave, I will be thy destruction....

Matthew 20:28
28 Even as the Son of man came not to be ministered unto, but to minister, and to give his life a ransom for many.

Mark 10:45
45 For even the Son of man came not to be ministered unto, but to minister, and to give his life a ransom for many.

1 Timothy 2:5–6
5 For *there is* one God, and one mediator between God and men, the man Christ Jesus;
6 Who gave himself a ransom for all, [i.e., GK pas = "all kinds of" men, Jew and Gentile, every race] to be testified in due time.

Think about what "ransom" means. If your child and another person's child were kidnapped, and they said the ransom is $1 million for your child to be set free and live; and let's say you paid the ransom, but the other person did not, whose child would be set free? The child whose parent paid the ransom would be set free; the other child for whom no ransom was paid would NOT.

If Jesus paid the ransom price for YOU (i.e., He gave His blood for your life), then YOU will be set free.

The Bible's teaching of Christ our ransom is a powerful picture of how Jesus actually paid the price to set God's sheep free from death and hell.

36. The Scriptures teach that Jesus's death propitiated Holy God's justice and hatred of sin.

Romans 3:23–26

23 For all have sinned, and come short of the glory of God;

24 Being justified freely by his grace through the redemption that is in Christ Jesus:

25 Whom God hath *set forth to be a propitiation through faith in his blood*, to declare his righteousness for the remission of sins that are past, through the forbearance of God;

26 To declare, *I say*, at this time his righteousness: that he might be just, and the justifier of him which believeth in Jesus.

We think of all the things Christ did for *us* when He died on the cross in our place. However, propitiation is something that Jesus accomplished *for God the Father* when He died. This is also part of His finished work.

To **propitiate** means *"to satisfy."* Look at this amazing Old Testament passage. (A fantastic place to use in witnessing to your Jewish friends.)

Isaiah 53:5–6

5 But he *was* wounded for our transgressions, *He was* bruised for our iniquities: The chastisement of our peace *was* upon him; And with his stripes we are healed.

6 All we like sheep have gone astray; We have turned every one to his own way; And the Lord hath **laid on him the iniquity of us**....

This is the **substitutionary death of Christ** on the cross. He died for us and because of us, to save us. He died in our place.

Isaiah 53:8, 10–11

8 ... For he was cut off out of the land of the living: For the transgression of my people was he stricken.

10 Yet it pleased the Lord to bruise him; he hath put *him* to grief: When thou shalt **make his soul an offering for sin....**

11 He shall **see of the travail of his soul**, *and* shall **<u>be satisfied</u>**: By his knowledge shall my righteous servant justify many; For he shall bear their iniquities.

When God the Father saw Jesus die on the cross, He was SATISFIED that His holiness and justice had been met, and He could now justly forgive His children's sins because, in the light of

His law, "the wages of sin is death," but the sin debt is now paid in full!

> **Psalm 85:9–10, 13**
> **9** Surely his salvation *is* nigh them that fear him; That glory may dwell in our land.
> **10** Mercy and truth are met together; ***Righteousness and peace have kissed each other.***
> **13** Righteousness shall go before him; And shall set *us* in the way of his steps.

When Jesus died on the cross, it allowed God's righteousness (i.e., His justice) and His peace (His mercy and desire to save His people by grace) to kiss each other.

God is now just (i.e., righteous) to justify His people (make them as if they have never sinned, make them righteous by placing the righteousness of His perfect Son upon His people).

This is why 1 John 1:9 is true!

> **1 John 1:9**
> **9** If we confess our sins, he is faithful and just to forgive us our sins, and to cleanse us from all unrighteousness.

Notice, once saved, it says God is ***faithful to forgive*** you (which means He does it every time), but it also says He is ***JUST to forgive you*** (which means it's right for Him to forgive you). Why? Because ***Jesus satisfied God's law on behalf of YOU when He died in your place***. He paid the wages of sin for you. ***God is satisfied, and*** *accepted that sacrifice; therefore, you may be saved.* You can also be cleansed from all unrighteousness every time you sin, utilizing 1 John 1:9, because as a saved person, Jesus propitiated God the Father's justice on your behalf.

37. Jesus says all true Christians bear fruit; also, He ascended to heaven and gave gifts to men.

Jesus taught about fruit-bearing through the beautiful parable below. Here, Jesus speaks of four types of people and how they respond to the Word of God. He uses the allegory of a farmer planting seeds and how the different types of soil respond to the seeds.

The farmer sowing the seeds represents the Christian witnessing together with the power of the Holy Spirit. The seed is the Word of God. The different types of soil typify the different kinds of people who hear the Word and how they respond to it. Those who remain lost, bear no fruit. Those who are truly saved ALL bear fruit.

Matthew 13:18–19
18 Hear ye therefore the parable of the sower.
19 When any one heareth the word of the kingdom, and understandeth *it* not, then cometh the wicked *one*, and catcheth away that which was sown in his heart. This is he which received seed by the way side.

The first type of soil is the ***hard path*** where the harvesters walk. The seed hits it but does not find its way into the depth of the soil (representing the heart and mind). This typifies a person who hears the Word preached, but pays no attention, and the truth does not sink down into his heart. Satan comes and snatches the idea out of his mind and he goes on his way toward oblivion.

> **20** But he that received the seed into stony places, the same is he that heareth the word, and anon with joy receiveth it;
> **21** Yet hath he not root in himself, but dureth for a while: for when tribulation or persecution ariseth because of the word, by and by he is offended.

This seed falls on *stony ground*, and it sprouts up quickly because there is a little soil on top of the rock, but then when the sun comes out (representing trials and tribulations of life), it withers and dies because it has no root. The root pictures Jesus Christ, so this person is not really saved; he just had a little "religion," was excited for a season, then disappeared from church, and he bears no fruit. The person is not really born again, but was outwardly religious for a short time.

> **22** He also that received seed among the thorns is he that heareth the word; and the care of this world, and the deceitfulness of riches, choke the word, and he becometh unfruitful.

This is a sad case. This soil, where the seeds fall on quite good soil, but where thorns are already growing, produces a Christian who no one really knows if he is saved or not. In my opinion, he is saved, because he bore fruit at first, but became unfruitful over time.

This is a carnal Christian. He started out well, received Jesus as his Lord and Saviour, and then the cares of the world (life hitting him hard), and/or the deceitfulness of riches (thinking money takes care of all troubles rather than relying upon the Lord for all things, or treating money as if it is God), or the lust of other worldly distractions come in (Mark 4:19). These distractions "choke the word" from the believer's life (he stops reading and studying the Bible).

Or worse, as the Mark passage says, these things "choke the word, and IT becomes unfruitful." This latter case is terrible because the believer is so worldly that as he or she reads the Bible, it does not fill the heart with joy and the life with growth—Bible reading has become a dry, rote work of the flesh. Jesus is no longer this believer's first love. For a season there is no more fruit, and the next phase will most likely be the chastening of the Lord.

Hebrews 12:5–6
5 And ye have forgotten the exhortation which speaketh unto you as unto children, My son, despise not thou the chastening of the Lord, nor faint when thou art rebuked of him:
6 For whom the Lord loveth he chasteneth, and scourgeth every son whom he receiveth.

And the last type of soil is called ***good ground.*** This person hears the Word with understanding (from the Holy Spirit) and bears fruit. Not everyone bears the same kind or amount of fruit, but every true believer is fruitful. The fruit become the outward proof of the inward regeneration that has taken place.

23 But he that received seed into the good ground is he that heareth the word, and understandeth *it*; which also beareth fruit, and bringeth forth, some an hundredfold, some sixty, some thirty.

Perhaps the greatest teaching on fruit-bearing was done by the Apostle Paul. In about A.D. 51, he wrote the letter to the Galatians. In this letter, he named the works of the flesh and said that they that do such things "shall not inherit the kingdom of heaven"!

Galatians 5:19–21
19 Now the works of the flesh are manifest, which are *these*; Adultery, fornication, uncleanness, lasciviousness,
20 Idolatry, witchcraft, hatred, variance, emulations, wrath, strife, seditions, heresies,
21 Envyings, murders, drunkenness, revellings, and such like: of the which I tell you before, as I have also told *you* in time past, that they which do such things shall not inherit the kingdom of God.

Then immediately after this, in contrast to the works of the flesh, ***Paul lists the fruit of the Spirit.*** It is clear that Paul is contrasting the outward life of a non-believer with the inward life of a believer, and the fruit that the world can see. (The Bible lists other fruits of the Spirit in other passages.) These types of fruit are actually "symptoms of salvation" that every believer in every age on this side of the cross will have. The ***fruit of the spirit never ceases to be available to the born-again person***. Here is Paul's list in Galatians:

Galatians 5:22–25

22 But the *fruit of the Spirit* is love, joy, peace, longsuffering, gentleness, goodness, faith,

23 Meekness, temperance: against such there is no law.

24 And they that are Christ's have crucified the flesh with the affections and lusts.

25 If we live in the Spirit, let us also walk in the Spirit.

My son, Ben, is the Associate Pastor at our church. He was teaching a Bible class recently and pointed out that Paul calls these, not fruits, but FRUIT (singular). Ben said, "This is because they all come in one package to the believer." I never thought about that, but it is true. All Christians display these types of fruits and they always have access to all of them, because they are produced by the root, Jesus Christ, Who lives in their hearts!

While not a complete list, this is a good representation of the types of fruit of the Spirit which God has made available to the Christian. These may be called "character fruit."

They may be divided into three groups:

1. Inward Fruit: love, joy, peace.

2. Outward Fruit: patience, gentleness, and goodness.

3. Upward Fruit: faith, meekness, and self-control.

Inward fruit makes us who we really are. Outward fruit extends toward other people and are how they perceive us. Upward fruit reaches toward God and make us more like Him.

We could group fruit another way. We could talk about *bearing fruit* and *gathering fruit*.

Bearing Fruit:

The fruit we listed above is *fruit we bear*. Jesus says we are the branches which bear the fruit. He is the root and the vine which creates and nourishes the fruit.

> **John 15:5, 7–8**
> **5** I am the vine, ye are the branches: He that abideth in me, and I in him, the same bringeth forth much fruit: for without me ye can do nothing.
> **7** If ye abide in me, and my words abide in you, ye shall ask what ye will, and it shall be done unto you.
> **8** Herein is my Father glorified, that ye bear much fruit; so shall ye be my disciples.

Here is a passage from Paul's letter to the Ephesians speaking of fruit that comes from the positional righteousness we have in Christ (His righteousness, given to us by imputation, see below).

Ephesians 5:6–11

6 Let no man deceive you with vain words: for because of these things cometh the wrath of God upon the children of disobedience.

7 Be not ye therefore partakers with them.

8 For ye were sometimes darkness, but now *are ye* light in the Lord: walk as children of light:

9 (For the *fruit of the Spirit* is in all goodness and righteousness and truth;)

10 Proving what is acceptable unto the Lord.

11 And have no fellowship with the unfruitful works of darkness, but rather reprove *them*.

He mentions the fruits of righteousness again in Philippians.

Philippians 1:11

11 Being filled with the *fruits of righteousness*, which are by Jesus Christ, unto the glory and praise of God.

Here, again, Paul contrasts the works of the flesh, which are "unfruitful," with the fruit of the Spirit. He exhorts us to avoid the workers of darkness. He then broadens the list of fruits of the Spirit to include *every good, righteous, and true thing* that comes out of a born-again person. *All of it comes from Jesus, the Root of Jesse, the vine that nourishes us and gives us life, that we may bear fruit!*

People who claim to be Christians, but lack fruit, are not spiritually well. It is possible that they are saved but are not studying the Bible regularly (perhaps believing that Bible study from years past is enough—the *thorny soil*). After all, the Bible is a large part of what sanctifies the believer. Just as the O.T. saints in the wilderness could not save manna and eat it the next day (they had to gather fresh manna every morning), we need new spiritual food from the Bible; we cannot rely upon yesterday's manna.

Or, sad to say, an unfruitful person could be still lost, never having been born again. Fruits are the effect (not the cause) of salvation. However, one must ask, if there are no effects, was there ever really a cause? One does not exhibit the fruit of the Spirit by trying in the flesh to be good, or to stop being bad. For a truly saved person, the fruit comes automatically when they are walking with the Lord and are in His Word.

If you are saved, but unfruitful, then you just need revival regarding personal Bible study, prayer, and church attendance at a Bible-believing, Bible-teaching church. Also, consider who you're spending time with. Spiritual people help you grow (Pr. 13:20; 27:17; Heb. 10:24–25). Carnal people stunt your growth (1 Cor. 15:33; 2 Ti. 2:21).

If you make the above corrections in your course and begin to willfully communicate with the Lord throughout the day (hold His hand), you will begin to walk down the right path with the Saviour. Your renewed relationship and fellowship with Jesus will produce the fruit. It will just hang off of you, and people will see it. You do not **produce** it; you **present** it, and the world sees it.

The best way to stop producing the works of the flesh, which hurt yourself and others, is to be busy presenting the fruits of the Spirit.

In addition to Paul's list of the fruit of the Spirit in Galatians, the Bible speaks of other types of fruit.

Philippians 4:17 and Romans 15:28 speak of the *"fruit of giving"* to support your local church and missions, or the poor, etc.

Romans 6:22 speaks of the *fruit of "holiness."*

Romans 7:4–6 speaks of *walking in newness of spirit* and not in the oldness of the letter of the Law. We are crucified with Christ, but now we are risen with Him and "married to Him" (rather than to the Law), and so we may now "bring forth *fruit unto God, serving in newness of spirit."*

Hebrews 13:15 speaks of us now having the ability to "offer the *sacrifice of praise* to God continually, that is, *the fruit of our lips giving thanks to His name.*" We also have the ability to do good.

James 3:18 says, "the *fruit of righteousness* is sown in peace of them that make peace." This is a reference to *experiential righteousness* (us having the ability to *decide* to live right).

Hebrews 12:11 informs us that when we sin, the Lord sometimes chastens us, and this *chastening brings forth "the peaceable fruit of righteousness"* (experiential righteousness).

Gathering fruit:

Gathering fruit is the fruit we gain when we win a soul to Christ. Paul writes in the letter to the Roman church:

Romans 1:11
11 For I long to see you, that I may *impart unto you some spiritual gift,* to the end you may be established.

We must remember that this passage is still in the early stages of the Apostolic Age, and sign gifts were still in play. Verse eleven is most likely speaking of Paul, in his apostolic office, imparting some types of **sign gifts** to the church at Rome to authenticate their message to the world around them so that they might grow and "be established." Later these gifts would cease until the last half of the tribulation period, when they are re-established by God (see Chapters 14 and 15, and Chapters 16–21 in Vol. 2).

However, in verse thirteen, he is no longer speaking of spiritual gifts but of *fruit of the Spirit,* which the Holy Spirit makes available to all Christians in all ages. I believe Paul is also referencing **gathering souls for Christ**, as he had done in other Gentile churches, and he wishes to gather some in Rome.

Romans 1:13, 16–17

13 Now I would not have you ignorant, brethren, that oftentimes I purposed to come unto you, (but was let hitherto,) that *I might have some fruit among you* also, even as among other Gentiles.

16 For I am not ashamed of the gospel of Christ: for it is the power of God unto salvation to every one that believeth; to the Jew first, and also to the Greek.

17 For therein is the righteousness of God revealed from faith to faith: as it is written, The just shall live by faith.

Spiritual Gifts:

Not only do we have the fruit of the Spirit given to us as a gift from the Holy Spirit, but we also have ***spiritual gifts: special talents or abilities for serving God.***

The book of Ephesians speaks of gifts which Christ disburses to His sheep according to God's sovereign will. Notice that these are called "gifts" (plural). This is because, unlike the fruit of the Spirit, no one of us possesses all of the gifts; some Christians may only possess one or two. These are disbursed according to God's will for each believer, and according to God's plan for their lives.

Ephesians 4:4–8
4 *There is* one body, and one Spirit, even as ye are called in one hope of your calling;
5 One Lord, one faith, one baptism,
6 One God and Father of all, who *is* above all, and through all, and in you all.
7 But ***unto every one of us is given grace according to the measure of the gift of Christ***.
8 Wherefore he saith, When he ascended up on high, he led captivity captive, and ***gave gifts unto men.***

The first portion of this passage speaks of ***gifts*** that Christ was able to give to men after His death, burial, resurrection, and ascension into heaven. When we are called by the Holy Spirit and regenerated, after that we are given the portion of grace that we need to fulfill our mission on this earth, and we are equipped with the gifts and talents we need for this service.

These gifts of the Spirit (and spiritual fruit in the section above) are operative throughout the church age, while the *sign gifts* have ceased temporarily until the last half of the tribulation period, as we have said.

The next portion of Ephesians Chapter 4 speaks of gifts the Lord Jesus *gives to the church*—gifted ministers to lead us until we meet the Lord and then have "unity of faith."

Ephesians 4:11–14

11 And he gave some, apostles; and some, prophets; and some, evangelists; and some, pastors and teachers;
12 *For the perfecting of the saints*, for the work of the ministry, for the edifying of the body of Christ:
13 Till we all come in the *unity of the faith*, and of the knowledge of the Son of God, unto a perfect man, unto the measure of the stature of the fulness of Christ:
14 That we *henceforth* be no more children, tossed to and fro, and carried about with every wind of doctrine, by the sleight of men, *and* cunning craftiness, whereby they lie in wait to deceive.

Some of these gifts to the church are apostolic in nature and only lasted as long as the apostles and the associated prophets and disciples were alive in the first years of the early church. When the apostles died, and the church obtained the whole canon of the N.T., I will say again, the sign gifts ceased. *Apostles and prophets* had the job of being the *foundation* upon which everything else would be built, ***Jesus being the chief Cornerstone.*** The foundation was only built once, and it was completed by the end of the first century A.D.

Then after the ***Apostolic Age was completed,*** and the foundation they built together with Jesus was laid, there being no more apostles or N.T. prophets, the remainder of the church began to be built upon their foundation. The Apostolic Age was over, and the mature church age continued for the next 2,000+ years. During that time evangelists, pastors, and teachers carried on the mission to the present day. The offices of the apostle and the N.T. prophet were no longer necessary, and thus ceased to exist in the mature church. Paul said that when "that which is perfect is come," then the gift of prophecy would cease, and it did.

> **38. Jesus made us righteous by giving us HIS righteousness. This is called <u>positional</u> righteousness. This righteousness comes because of the great <u>Doctrine of Imputation</u>. We call it "positional" because nothing we can do can remove it. We stand straight in a position of righteousness. We didn't do anything to gain it. Jesus gained it for us through His finished work.**

1 Peter 2:24
24 Who his own self bare our sins in his own body on the tree, that we, being dead to sins, should live unto righteousness: by whose stripes ye were healed.

2 Corinthians 5:21
21 For he hath made him *to be* sin for us, who knew no sin; that we might be made the righteousness of God in him.

These two verses together describe the great **Doctrine of Imputation.** It is like **an accounting term.** If you're saved, it is because God took your sins back 2,000 years and placed them upon Jesus Christ when He was on the cross as if HE had done them. God the Father imputed your sins to Christ. He took your sins out of your account and placed them into Jesus's account.

Then God took the righteousness of Christ and reached forward 2,000 years and placed that upon YOU. God took Jesus's righteousness out of His account and placed it into YOURS!

So, now you have the righteousness of Christ once you have received Him as your personal Lord and Saviour.

You are saved on the basis of HIS righteousness, which YOU now own.

I heard of an old black preacher once who explained it like this to his people: "Now God sees us all dressed up in Jesus." This is why He saves us once and for all—God the Father sees us as positionally righteous all the time. He sees us as already glorified!

Romans 8:30
30 Moreover whom he did predestinate, them he also called: and whom he called, them he also justified: and whom he justified, *them he also glorified.*

Notice from the Father's viewpoint that if you're saved, you are already "glorified." This is past tense—it has already happened in God the Father's mind, and this is Christ's righteousness in you, which the Father always sees from outside of time where He dwells. The Father sees YOU as already perfect in Christ.

Now, "God with us" in time, through Jesus and/or the Holy Spirit, sees our sins and sometimes must chasten us for our good, but I'm convinced that if we asked the Father to forgive us, He would say "For what?" This is because He, and He alone, has the ability to FORGET sin. He dwells outside of space and time and is not in the presence of sin.

He sees your sins as having been placed on Christ the day He died, and He sees Christ's righteousness as having been placed on you forever. He sees YOU "all dressed up in Jesus" with His robes of righteousness upon you.

When the Apostle John was given the revelation of the end times, he said:

> "And one of the elders answered, saying unto me, What are these which are arrayed in **white robes**? And whence came they? And I said unto him, Sir, thou knowest. And he said to me, These are they which came out of great tribulation, and have washed their robes, and made them white in the blood of the Lamb."
>
> **—Revelation 7:13–14**

Chapter 10

The Doctrine of Christ—

THINGS GOD SAID ABOUT JESUS CHRIST; AND ADDITIONAL WORKS OF CHRIST

39. Perhaps the greatest testimony of all is God the Father's. He said exactly Who Jesus is.

Mark 1:9–11

9 And it came to pass in those days, that Jesus came from Nazareth of Galilee, and was baptized of John in Jordan.

10 And straightway coming up out of the water, he saw the heavens opened, and the Spirit like a dove descending upon him:

11 And there came a voice from heaven, *saying*, Thou art my beloved Son, in whom I am well pleased.

Hebrews 1:8

8 But unto the Son he [God] saith, Thy throne, O God, is for ever and ever: a sceptre of righteousness is the sceptre of thy kingdom.

Here, we see God the Father calling Jesus "God."

Jesus Christ loves us, for He is our Groom, and we are His Bride. He loves us because we are His brothers and sisters. He loves us because we are God's children.

The dimensions of Jesus's love for us are beyond anything we can understand in this three-dimensional world. Notice His love is four-dimensional.

Ephesians 3:17–21

17 That Christ may dwell in your hearts by faith; that ye, being rooted and grounded in love,

18 May be able to comprehend with all saints what *is* the ***breadth, and length, and depth, and height***;

19 And to <u>know the love of Christ,</u> which passeth knowledge, that ye might be filled with all the fulness of God.

20 Now unto him that is able to do exceeding abundantly above all that we ask or think, according to the power that worketh in us,

21 Unto him *be* glory in the church by Christ Jesus throughout all ages, world without end. Amen.

Did God leave anything out? We do not know how many dimensions God's love for us fills because neither death nor life, neither angels nor principalities, powers in the heavenlies, things now or in eternity future—in fact, *no creation of God can separate us from the love of God, WHICH IS IN CHRIST OUR LORD*.

40. Jesus's LOVE for us caused Him to become our SUBSTITUTE (He died in our place).

Romans 5:8–9
8 But *God commendeth his love toward us*, in that, while we were yet sinners, Christ died for us.
9 Much more then, being now justified by his blood, we shall be saved from wrath through him.

If you read this carefully, it is pretty different than what we hear in church nowadays. We are often told that WE do something to become saved. Actually, the Scriptures teach clearly here, and elsewhere, that we are still in a state of sin and rebellion when GOD saves us. God does the saving through Jesus dying in our place to pay our sin debt. It is Jesus's finished work on the cross that saves us, plus the Holy Spirit's calling and regenerative act.

While we are dead due to our sins, HE hath quickened us (brought us from death to life) together with Christ, and thus, we are saved through grace (undeserved favour from God). So, we are dead, and cannot save ourselves, and we are still in that state of spiritual death when God saves us, so obviously, we play no role in our own salvation. Dead men and woman can do nothing! The very word "saved" implies this!

You have to be saved by someone else. Someone stronger and more capable than yourself. You see all this in the following verse:

Ephesians 2:5
5 Even when we were dead in sins, hath quickened us together with Christ, (by grace ye are saved).

Even when we were dead in our sins, we were quickened by God. This is known as the effectual calling of the Holy Spirit, theologically. It is the Holy Spirit's work to awaken us and show Christ to us as He really is (i.e., open our spiritual eyes to Who He actually is). This opening of the eyes and ears and quickening of the heart is called regeneration. All of this occurs before we do anything, because prior to that, we cannot do anything, nor do we wish to do anything ("…there is none that seeketh after God," Romans 3:11 et.al.). This is the great CAUSE of regeneration; everything after that (which we do) is an effect, not the cause. The following verses speak of the substitutionary death of Jesus FOR us, so that the Holy Spirit may righteously quicken us.

Galatians 1:4
4 Who gave himself for our sins, that he might deliver us from this present evil world, according to the will of God and our Father:

Romans 4:25–5:1
25 Who was delivered for our offences, and was raised again for our justification.

5:1 Therefore being justified by faith, we have peace with God through our Lord Jesus Christ:

41. Jesus's DEATH Reconciled us to God.

Romans 5:10, 11

10 For if, when we were enemies, *we were reconciled* to God by the death of his Son, much more, being reconciled, we shall be saved by his life.

11 And not only *so*, but we also joy in God through our Lord Jesus Christ, by whom we have now received the atonement.

Reconciliation is a key doctrine in the Bible. Obviously, vs. 10 above indicates that we were enemies of God while in our natural state (though it may not feel like we were, this means we wished to be our own rulers rather than submitting to the Lordship of Jesus Christ). Only after the Holy Spirit quickens us as He calls us and opens our eyes to Who Jesus is (a better Lord of our lives than we ourselves are) can we see that we were running away from God. It is the very death of Christ on the cross, with His arms open wide showing His love for us sinners even as we would have nailed Him to the cross—it is THAT kind of love that drew us to Him and that reconciles, i.e., restores friendship, with our God.

42. Jesus's finished work Justified us.

Justified means "just as if I'd never sinned." He gave you the righteousness of Christ (imputation). The Father now sees you as without sin.

When we say "I've been saved," most likely we really mean "I've been justified." Jesus has taken my sins away and, at the same time, He has given me His righteousness.

This is something God does to YOU. He makes you right with Himself by giving His Son for you and to you, and because He lives in your heart, His faith is in you!

Galatians 2:16
16 Knowing that a man is not justified by the works of the law, but by the faith <u>of</u> Jesus Christ.

43. Jesus gave His blood to Redeem us.

Redeem means "to set free by paying a price." The price was Jesus's blood.

1 Peter 1:18–21
18 Forasmuch as ye know that ye were not redeemed with corruptible things, *as* silver and gold, from your vain conversation *received* by tradition from your fathers;
19 But *with the precious blood of Christ*, as of a lamb without blemish and without spot:

20 Who verily was foreordained before the foundation of the world, but was manifest in these last times for you,

21 Who *by him do believe in God*, that raised him up from the dead, and gave him glory; that your faith and hope might be in God.

Notice that "by him do we believe in God." This is the effectual calling, and the faith of Christ in us—the operation of God.

44. Because we experienced a co-resurrection with Christ, we are FORGIVEN all our trespasses—PAST, PRESENT, AND FUTURE.

Colossians 2:13

13 And you, being dead in your sins and the uncircumcision of your flesh, hath he quickened [brought to life] together with him, having forgiven you all trespasses;

Heb.7:25

25 Wherefore he is able also to save them to the uttermost that come unto God by him, seeing he ever liveth to make intercession for them.

We were "quickened together with Him." Therefore, God the Father, who is not bound by time, took our sins back in time and placed them upon Jesus while He was on the cross. At that time, ALL our sins were future sins. Now, because we were crucified with

Christ, they are all already paid for! And, when He arose, we arose with Him to new life, everlasting life. Thus, we are SAVED to the UTTERMOST.

In summary, Jesus is the Son of God; He is all the fullness of the Godhead in a body; He is the brightness of God's glory and the express image of His Person; if you have seen Him, you have seen the Father; He is the Prince of Peace, the mighty God, the everlasting Father; He is the I AM; He is the Creator and Sustainer of all things; all things were made BY Him and FOR Him and without Him was not anything made that was made; He is the Bread of Life; He is the Water of Life that if one drinks, he shall never again thirst; He is the only DOOR to the sheepfold (heaven); Jesus is the Good Shepherd which laid down His life for the sheep; He is the ONLY WAY to heaven; He is TRUTH; He is LIFE; He is LIGHT; He is our Intercessor and Advocate with the Father, KEEPING us saved for all eternity.

He is the only name whereby men may be saved; He is the only one Who has seen the Father; He is the Bread of Life and the Water of Life; the One Who is preparing a place for us in heaven; the One Who sent the Holy Spirit to live within us; the true Lamb of God which all the O.T. sacrifices pictured; the Son of God with Power who was resurrected, proving His perfect life; the ONE who FINISHED the work to save us, and the One in Whom we rest; the One Who LOVED US and died for us even before we wanted Him; the One Who paid the wages of death so that we may have salvation as a FREE GIFT; the One Who freed us by paying the ransom price—His blood; the One Who gave us His righteousness and took our sins away; the One Who satisfied God and freed up His mercy to not contradict His justice and who accomplished this by being the "Beloved Son of God in Whom I am well pleased." He is "the Alpha and the Omega, the beginning and the end, the first and the last" (Revelation 22:13).

To close these 10 chapters on the Doctrine of Christ, there is perhaps no more beautiful passage than the one found in 1 Peter Chapter One.

It speaks of the new birth made possible by the death, burial, and resurrection of Jesus Christ for the sins of His people. It speaks of our eternal security and our incorruptible inheritance that cannot fade away, RESERVED in heaven for us, who are KEPT by the power of God through faith unto salvation. It speaks of trials we must go through but never alone, for Jesus is our Shepherd and is always with us, leading us and protecting us. It speaks of a life of obedience which we can live only in the power of "Christ in us, the hope of glory." It speaks of the fact that we are not redeemed by tradition or church or works but by the precious blood of Jesus.

When we walk hand in hand with Jesus, we can walk on water, and we can *stand straight in a crooked world!*

1 Peter 1:3–25

3 Blessed *be* the God and Father of our Lord Jesus Christ, which according to his abundant mercy hath begotten us again unto a lively hope by the resurrection of Jesus Christ from the dead,

4 To an inheritance incorruptible, and undefiled, and that fadeth not away, reserved in heaven for you,

5 Who are kept by the power of God through faith unto salvation ready to be revealed in the last time.

6 Wherein ye greatly rejoice, though now for a season, if need be, ye are in heaviness through manifold temptations:

7 That the trial of your faith, being much more precious than of gold that perisheth, though it be tried with fire, might be found unto praise and honour and glory at the appearing of Jesus Christ:

8 Whom having not seen, ye love; in whom, though now ye see *him* not, yet believing, ye rejoice with joy unspeakable and full of glory:

9 Receiving the end of your faith, *even* the salvation of *your* souls.

10 Of which salvation the prophets have inquired and searched diligently, who prophesied of the grace *that should come* unto you:

11 Searching what, or what manner of time the Spirit of Christ which was in them did signify, when it testified beforehand the sufferings of Christ, and the glory that should follow.

12 Unto whom it was revealed, that not unto themselves, but unto us they did minister the things, which are now reported unto you by them that have preached the gospel unto you with the Holy Ghost sent down from heaven; which things the angels desire to look into.

13 Wherefore gird up the loins of your mind, be sober, and hope to the end for the grace that is to be brought unto you at the revelation of Jesus Christ;

14 As obedient children, not fashioning yourselves according to the former lusts in your ignorance:

15 But as he which hath called you is holy, so be ye holy in all manner of conversation;

16 Because it is written, Be ye holy; for I am holy.

18 Forasmuch as ye know that ye were not redeemed with corruptible things, *as* silver and gold, from your vain conversation *received* by tradition from your fathers;

19 But with the precious blood of Christ, as of a lamb without blemish and without spot:

20 Who verily was foreordained before the foundation of the world, but was manifest in these last times for you,

21 Who by him do believe in God, that raised him up from the dead, and gave him glory; that your faith and hope might be in God.

22 Seeing ye have purified your souls in obeying the truth through the Spirit unto unfeigned love of the brethren, *see that ye* love one another with a pure heart fervently:

23 Being born again, not of corruptible seed, but of incorruptible, by the word of God, which liveth and abideth for ever.

24 For all flesh *is* as grass, and all the glory of man as the flower of grass. The grass withereth, and the flower thereof falleth away:

25 But the word of the Lord endureth for ever. And this is the word which by the gospel is preached unto you.

This needs no explanation. Isn't it beautiful? Isn't JESUS beautiful when you see WHO He actually is?

Do you think about where you might end up if you died? Do you have a sense that God is watching you, even though perhaps you have not yet received Jesus as your Lord and Saviour—you know

He sees you when you sin, and you feel uncomfortable about that? Well, then that is a very good sign, because goats don't consider these things, nor do they care about them. But sheep do, even lost sheep.

My prayer for you right now is that the Holy Spirit would gently lift your chin, so that your eyes are focused upon the face of Jesus in a different way than ever before. I pray that your eyes are opened and you see that He is the Shepherd and YOU are His sheep. I pray that you will realize you are hungry and only He has the food. Now, just receive Him as your personal Lord and Saviour—you'll never be the same!

Are you already a Christian, but you feel God is far away, or you are far away from Him? You would be surprised what a renewed hunger for the Word of God would do for you. Get back into the Bible. A small taste will create a larger hunger for it. Read the Psalms. Read the N.T. books of John and Romans. These are excellent places to start if you need to be encouraged, strengthened, and refreshed.

Your growth, your sanctification, is directly proportional to the amount of time you are spending pondering the Word of God while asking the Holy Spirit to be your teacher and keeping the rules of proper Bible interpretation (to be discussed often in the remaining chapters of this book).

Chapter 11

The Foundation of
Repentance From Dead Works

*"Therefore leaving the principles of the doctrine of Christ,
let us go on unto perfection; not laying again
<u>the foundation of repentance from dead works</u>...."*
—Hebrews 6:1

The first ten chapters were about our first Core Doctrine—the Doctrine of Christ. This is our second Core Doctrine, "repentance from dead works": We must repent from believing that our dead works will earn us entrance into heaven or produce a happy, fulfilling life on earth. Obviously, we have two important questions to answer—what is repentance? ... and what are dead works?

What is repentance?

First, let's talk about what the Bible meaning of repentance is **not.** I played in several rock bands in high school and through my young adult years. My favorite lead guitar part to play was "Stairway to Heaven" by Led Zeppelin. (Isn't it everyone's?) Remember that idyllic blues/rock song? Rolling Stone Magazine called it "the greatest song in rock and roll history." This is the era in which I grew up—I was a sophomore in high school when Zeppelin's first album came out. I was just beginning to play guitar with my friends, Billy P. and Billy S. Later, I played in college with a group of four other guys, Mark, Jay, Kevin, and Dave. And we *all* knew this song.

I must give the band's young guitarist Jimmy Page, who wrote the music, and front man and lead singer Robert Plant, who wrote the lyrics, great credit. They wrote exactly what the majority of humans have believed, in every culture, in every corner of the world, and throughout all the ages—***that man can rise up and reach God and heaven on his own terms.*** This is a song about humanism, ***man building his own stairway to Heaven.***

I recently heard Dan Rather interview Robert Plant about his famous song, *Stairway to Heaven*. Rather said, "I've heard that in your later years, it was not your favorite song to sing?" Plant gave this reply:

> It was a song written about fate, and something very British and abstract, but it was coming out of the mind of a 23-year-old guy. I think as time goes on you may find another period of your life that's got a little bit more substance or that's more relative, later on down the line,

you know. So, as much as I like it, I'm not wedded to that whole deal now."[43]

As Robert Plant aged and gained wisdom, he apparently no longer held to the same philosophies as in his youth.

This year, in 2025, he is touring Europe with a heavy metal Christian group. I am wondering if Robert might be a Christian in his older age? I hope he is. He is a modern Shakespeare. I imagine he now knows that man cannot build his own stairway to heaven.

At the age of 23, he may not have been a Christian at the height of his rock stardom, yet there are some amazing allusions to important truths about life in the lyrics of his famous song. The song has several lines of thought, though mostly it is a song of mysterious fantasy. Underneath the fantasy is most likely a subconscious sense of reality in the young poet's mind, which brings out real, valuable *questions about life*. Let's explore some of those questions as we hear the lyrics of the song in our memories. (You can also look up the words to the song online if you're not familiar with them. The poetry is beautiful.)

If you remember, in the song there was a lady who believed the old saying, "All that glitters is gold." She thought she could buy her way into heaven. Heaven, to her, was gaining materialistic things, but the stores were closed so she felt she could get pleasure with her cleverness, her enticing words, and her own intuition. To me, this leads to the young songwriter's first question about life:

---

[43] ***Robert Plant on "Stairway to Heaven"***, https://youtu.be/IFwU2qlEttg.

- **Question 1: "What's more important: the value of Materialism** (i.e., trying to buy happiness) **or Intuition** (attempting to gain things through wily wisdom of the world, and outsmarting people)?"

The young girl in the song is seeking material possessions, believing that "things" will bring her "heaven on earth." She later learns that, as a beautiful young woman, she doesn't even need gold: she can get things with her words, her looks, and her ways, but she is still seeking "heaven on earth" through sensual pleasures and covetousness.

She then sees a sign on the wall and wonders if it is pointing her in the right direction. The next question of life comes when she sees this sign on the wall but wants to be careful because she understands that words can have more than one meaning.

- **Question 2: "Who can I believe when there are many voices telling me which way to go?" (People, like Satan, deceive by craftily changing the meaning of words.)**

"I'm still not sure which way I should go," she thinks. "Do I go with Materialism and try to buy 'heaven,' or Intuition, and outsmart, deceive, and seduce people into giving me 'heaven?'" People and religions are giving her answers, but she cannot tell who is telling the truth.

The song then takes a turn, which leads to a third question about life. It speaks of a tree by a river, and a bird singing from the tree, and the young girl muses, but realizes even her own thoughts might deceive her.

And, she wonders:

- ## Question 3: "Could my own thoughts be misleading me?"

As the songbird in the peaceful place of her meditations sings, she wonders, *Are these pretty thoughts true?* The song continues, and now—rather than the young girl speaking—it seems to be the songwriter himself pondering life. In fact, even the young girl was used to picture his own questions about life! He is getting a sad feeling as he looks toward the western horizon. This could typify looking toward the end of one's life. The poet sees, in his imagination, smoke rings through trees in the distance and hears voices of those watching him.

Now it is clear that the poet, Robert Plant himself, is the muse. He contemplates what it might be like when the brief moment of fame that most rock stars enjoy is over, and he looks to the west as he walks out of the daylight, sad because he has left the spotlight behind.

- ## Question 4: "What will it look like when I'm out of the spotlight and the climax of my life is over?"

The crowd, pictured as circles of smoke behind the trees, standing and watching, is now watching another star as a very different genre of music arises out of nowhere. (Plant may have feared this, but of course, his fame never really vanished; Zeppelin's fans followed him into each decade, up until this day. The poet is as popular now as he was then, and rightfully so!)

The next part of the song brings yet another life question, as the lyrics speak of the future for people who endure the long, hard days and years of time as they watch the world around them frolic in its gaiety. The question comes to mind:

- **Question 5: "Can joy come with simple endurance? Can I find joy if I simply don't give up and quit?"**

The next lines speak of the May Queen, which implies preparing for the pagan May festivals that Brits enjoy each year, so we ask:

- **Question 6: "Can the carnal joy which comes from pagan festivals in the Spring, and all that they imply (humanism and/or Satanism), bring true happiness?"**

Then comes a more important line of this amazing song, speaking of two paths you could go down, suggesting that there is still plenty of time to change the path you're on. This is perhaps the most dangerous worldly thought that enters the mind of the very young—do I have plenty of time to change my life direction?

- ## Question 7: "Do we KNOW that there is still time to change the road we're on?"

The song itself provides the answer.

Ultimately, the "piper is calling"—death is inevitable.

You never know if you will have time to change the road you're on. Don't procrastinate—get on the right road now! I think it is a beautiful thing that Plant's gifts for poetry and philosophy even at a young age, whether on purpose or subliminally, urged him to write again and again the thought that all this made him wonder about life.

He is warning you to WONDER if you really have time to change the road you're on!

In fact, in almost all the questions of life in the song, the poet "wonders."

And then, the poet exhorts the lady from the beginning of the song with the strongest line in the song. He asks the lady if she can hear the wind blow and exhorts her that her stairway lies on the wind!

I find this to be the climax of the song. It so closely follows the gospel, it is amazing. This may not have been intended by the young songwriter. Or, he may have known exactly what he was writing. Most likely in the hugely creative time of his youth, he did not even understand all that he was saying, but it does not matter. God in His sovereignty uses all things to benefit His own.

It is interesting that many of the O.T. prophets wrote Scripture and often they had no idea what it meant. Not that Plant is a "Rock Prophet," but still, it would not be so strange (especially understanding the sovereignty of God) that as a young man, he could have written things for us to contemplate, which he did not fully understand. Certainly this happened to the O.T. prophets.

Ephesians 3:5

5 Which in other ages was not made known unto the sons of men, as it is now revealed unto his holy apostles and prophets by the Spirit;

Now, I am not implying that Plant's inspiration is the same as the inspiration of Scripture—not even close. Plant used the gifts God gave him to bring pleasure and joy to the world, including Christians like myself. But, the meaning of biblical "inspiration" is "God-breathed," and that is for those who penned the Scriptures only—it is an infinitely higher level. Nevertheless, God is Sovereign, and He used Plant even in his younger years to bless the world with beautiful lyrics.

And the most important of all the questions that the song brings to mind is this: did the young lady hear the wind blow and realize that her stairway to heaven was in the wind?

- **Question 8: Can YOU hear the wind blow?**

The poet reminds me of someone who is witnessing! How many times did Jesus say, "If any man has ears to hear, let him hear?" The Holy Spirit and the Church proclaim the invitation. Can *you* hear it?

> ***"And the Spirit and the bride say, Come.*** And let him that heareth say, Come. And let him that is athirst come. And whosoever will, let him take the water of life freely."—*Revelation 22:17*

Jesus Christ Himself cries out to the carnal Laodicean church, filled with both lost sheep and saved sheep:

> "Behold, I stand at the door, and knock: if any man hear my voice, and open the door, I will come in to him, and will sup with him, and he with me."—*Revelation 3:20*

- **Question 9: Do you know YOUR <u>stairway lies on the still small voice of the wind</u>?"**

Our Lord Jesus Christ explained to the spiritually blind religious leader, Nicodemus:

> "Marvel not that I said unto thee, Ye must be born again.
> ***"<u>The wind bloweth where it listeth</u>,* and thou hearest the sound thereof,** but canst not tell whence it cometh, and whither it goeth: *<u>so is every one that is born of the Spirit.</u> "*

"Nicodemus answered and said unto him, *How can these things be?"*

[Jesus replied]:

"If I have told you earthly things, and ye believe not, how shall ye believe, if I tell you *of* heavenly things?"
—John 3:7–9, 12

The end of "Stairway to Heaven" is the sad picture of a person who never finds the truth and spends her life searching for happiness in "things." Her mortal shadow is taller than her immortal soul, in her own eyes. She ends her life following the false, glittering light of covetousness, and she is a false light to people who are influenced by her words. It will be too late for her when, as the song says, just as the Scriptures say, "all are one." For, this is at the end of time.

"And when all things shall be subdued unto him, then shall the Son also himself be subject unto him that put all things under him, *that God may be all in all.*"
—1 Corinthians 15:28

The song, interestingly enough, ends with what sounds like an evangelic invitation! As we watch the worldly young woman walk on down her road, we must learn from her mistakes. She saw her shadow (made by her body of flesh) as being taller than her soul. We should NOT allow our flesh, a mere shadow, influence us more than our soul (which is eternal), even though the flesh is at first stronger (i.e., taller). The poet want us to listen well and learn from this story that the TRUE ROCK (Jesus) is the answer, and we should become a little rock; be like Him, not rolling on through life in the flesh, as a rolling stone, still attempting to buy a stairway to Heaven.

But as the song would have it, she does not. Her time runs out. I can still hear the sad ending now, as she was still building her own stairway to heaven.

I would like for you to go out and take a look at the lyrics of this amazing song. All these themes winding in and out of the song present a very accurate worldview of how life is so often wrongly perceived from the natural human viewpoint. Without the light of the gospel, we would all be doomed to ignorance and eternal death.

Before you're saved:

- You think "all that glitters is gold."
- You rely upon materialism and intuition to build your own stairway to heaven (happiness and fulfillment, but they are counterfeit).
- You never know who's telling you the truth: words can have more than one meaning. (Nefarious people today, in both politics and religion, change the meaning of words to bring confusion and to support their lies.)
- Sometimes you cannot trust our own thoughts—self-deceit.
- You sense life is slipping away, but you procrastinate on spiritual things, opportunities to better yourself, and family. It's like looking towards the west, or the end of life, but then forgetting that, and putting off important things.

- You believe by just working hard and enduring, you'll be happy.
- You still believe there are two roads you could go down, and that later you'll have time to change your direction and live right.
- You put out of your mind that, ultimately, death is inevitable.
- But the most life-altering question of all, is do you hear THIS message? The answer is in the still quiet voice of the Holy Spirit, as pictured by the wind.

The most important idea is the ***warning not to procrastinate: listen when you hear the wind blowing*** (the Holy Spirit speaking the gospel message that Jesus died to pay your sin debt)!

The second most important warning is this: You never know who's telling you the truth. ***Liars change the meaning of words***, and this problem comes into play with ***the idea of Repentance.***

"Repent" is virtually a universally misunderstood Bible concept.

There are entire denominations built upon the idea that to be saved, you must "repent." And, by this they mean you must "build your own stairway to heaven" and be saved by your own efforts. They have changed the meaning of the word "repent" (as Plant says, words can have more than one meaning).

This is particularly dangerous, because this is man's humanistic idea of salvation; it is not God's way, and it cannot lead to heaven. It actually builds only a stairway to the basement!

"Repentance" is not building your own "stairway to heaven." Yet, the belief that a member of the fallen human race may redeem himself by somehow building a stairway to heaven is universal. Most feel that good works, religious acts, giving to charity, treating people right, attending church, reading the Bible, praying, practicing the Eucharist (Holy Communion), or "turning over a new leaf" will cause God to usher them into heaven with a hearty, "Well done, my good and faithful servant." However, here is what God says about this idea:

(My best interpretation of the verse below is: "IT DOESN'T WORK THAT WAY!")

> "Not by works of righteousness which we have done,
> but according to his mercy he saved us, by the washing
> of regeneration, and renewing of the Holy Ghost."
> **—Titus 3:5**

What is "repentance," then? Let's look at the context of this verse and see what it reveals.

Titus 3:5, 6
5 Not by works of righteousness which we have done, but according to his mercy he saved us, by the washing of regeneration, and renewing of the Holy Ghost;
6 Which he shed on us abundantly through Jesus Christ our Saviour.

Most of the Bible is written for everyday people to understand, when read plainly (following the rules of reading and understanding any type of literature). Context is most important. To understand context, you'll need to ask questions such as:

- "Who is this written to?"
- "What is this about?"
- "Does this pertain only to the person or persons it is written to, or to everyone?"
- "How do the ideas before and after this verse affect the plain meaning of the verse in question?"
- "What light does the rest of the Bible shed on this passage?"

(For a complete list of the rules of proper Bible interpretation, go to ChristianPosture.com.)

This passage is certainly straightforward.

> **5 *Not by works of righteousness which we have done*,**
> but according to his mercy he saved us....

It begins by saying what does ***not*** gain an entrance into heaven— "good works which we have done."

There goes our "stairway to heaven." It fell infinitely short of getting us there! Good works—giving to charity or treating people right—do not gain us an entrance into heaven. Religious acts— attending church, reading the Bible, praying, practicing the Eucharist (Holy Communion)—do not open the pearly gates for anyone.

"Turning over a new leaf" is insufficient.

Let's discuss this last one, "turning over a new leaf." Many people believe—perhaps because many pastors seem to preach this—that believing and repenting are the two things required for us to be ushered into heaven someday. To be fair, there are verses that sound like they teach this.

Luke 13:5
5 I tell you, Nay: but, except ye <u>repent</u>, ye shall all likewise perish.

Yet, if you study the context of this, you will see immediately following this, Jesus told a parable about a fig tree, which shows how repentance works—and it is probably not what you think. True repentance is caused by something the Lord Himself does TO you, as the context shows. Therefore, the cause of your regeneration cannot be YOU repenting. Repentance must be an *effect* of something God did to you (which we will continue to discuss).

So, repentance is **_not_** the *cause* or the "trigger" of regeneration.

As we said earlier, repentance is likely not what you think it is. Most think "repentance" means to quit smoking, quit drinking, quit cursing, quit womanizing, quit overeating, quit stealing, quit lying, and quit hanging out with those who do. Now, even if it did mean "quit everything bad," who is going to quit every urge with which their particular carnal body hampers them, and "never do that again" for the rest of their lives? If you did quit everything for a season, then broke one law, look at the result....

James 2:10
10 For whosoever shall keep the whole law, and yet offend in <u>one *point*</u>, he is guilty of all.

If you are not perfect in keeping the whole law, you are guilty!

So, if repentance is what saves us, and it means to quit everything bad, then **no one** will enter a perfect heaven where a Holy God (absent from the presence of sin) resides.

The Apostle Paul said:

> **Galatians 3:11–12**
> **11** But that **no man** is justified [made right with God] by the law in the sight of God, *it is* evident: for, The just shall live by faith.
> **12** And the law is not of faith: but, The man that doeth them shall live in them.

If you are going to try to live by the law to enter heaven, you must live perfectly IN the law. However, Paul says this is a curse because you cannot perfectly live in the law. Paul knows the solution:

> **Galatians 3:13**
> *Christ hath redeemed us* from the curse of the law, being made a curse for us: for it is written, Cursed *is* every one that hangeth on a tree.

And, the Apostle Peter says…

1 Peter 2:24–25

24 [Jesus] Who ***his own self bare our sins in his own body*** on the tree, that we, being dead to sins, should live unto righteousness: by whose stripes ye were healed.
25 For ye were as sheep going astray; but are now returned unto the Shepherd and Bishop of your souls.

Jesus lived a perfect life, fulfilled the law, and then died for your sins, giving His blood as the redemption price that sets you free from sin and Satan. He was made a curse for you. He had no sin of His own, but God placed YOUR sins (and mine) on Him while He was on the cross. He died in your place. God then gave every true believer Jesus's righteousness. (This is the Doctrine of Imputation.) This is the only solution to the curse of the law.

The word "gospel" means good news, and the good news is that repentance does not mean "to quit doing bad."

Here is what repent DOES mean in the Greek:

Luke 13:3
3 I tell you, Nay: but, except ye repent, ye shall all likewise perish.

repent
mĕtanŏĕō, to *think differently.*
FROM
meta—*against*
+
nŏiĕō—to *exercise* the *mind:*—*to think.*
"To exercise the mind against," or...

"Repent" in the Greek means "to change your mind."

The first thing you must change your mind about is "WHO is God?" God is … and He is **_not_** ME. It is not your stairway to heaven devised in your mind based upon human philosophy that saves you; it is God's way that saves you. Jesus is **_THE WAY,_** the truth, and the life, and He said, "No man comes to the Father but by me" (John 14:6). THIS is a big changing of the mind!

You could be thinking, after reading the prior chapters, "If I am depraved and not seeking God, how **_can_** I repent so that I do not perish?"

The answer is part of the genuine good news (the gospel) message of the New Testament. Look at the context of Jesus's words:

Luke 13:5–9

5 I tell you, Nay: but, except ye repent, ye shall all likewise perish.

6 He spake also this parable; A certain *man* had a fig tree planted in his vineyard; and he came and sought fruit thereon, and found none.

7 Then said he unto the dresser of his vineyard, Behold, these three years I come seeking fruit on this fig tree, and find none: cut it down; why cumbereth it the ground?

8 And he answering said unto him, Lord, let it alone this year also, till I shall dig about it, and dung *it*:

9 And if it bear fruit, *well*: and if not, *then* after that thou shalt cut it down.

It was the man who planted the fig tree in his vineyard who was **responsible** to cause it to be fruitful. He must dig around it and place fertilizer beneath it in order for it to bear fruit. This pictures the Sovereign God acting in a person's life *FIRST*. (The tree could not fertilize itself.)

Then v. 9 pictures the man responding to God's love and action upon his life.

Repentance, therefore, is your mind being changed by the active work of God in your heart and mind, opening your eyes to who Jesus really is and who you really are.

This "opening of the eyes" is the *effectual calling of the Holy Spirit,* and it is something we mention many times in this book because it is a lost phrase in many modern churches. HE opens your eyes to who Jesus is, who you are, and who you are not—you are not God and should not be Lord of your own life. Jesus is a better Lord, and He will set you free from every lesser lord.

The great Apostle Paul said it this way:

Romans 2:4
4 ...Knowing that the goodness of God leadeth thee to repentance.

Just as God leads us to believe, by giving us the gift of Jesus's faith through the calling of the Holy Spirit, He leads us to repent at the effectual calling. In other words, repentance is also a gift given. Simply by opening our blind eyes and deaf ears, quickening our dead spirit, and then showing Jesus to us, He leads us to *change our minds* about who we are and who Jesus is. *This is repentance.*

The Bible clearly teaches that repentance is a gift given to us by the Holy Spirit at the moment of our calling.

2 Timothy 2:25–26

25 In meekness instructing those that oppose themselves; if God peradventure will *give them repentance* to the acknowledging of the truth;

26 And that they may recover themselves out of the snare of the devil, who are taken captive by him at his will.

Acts 11:18

18 When they heard these things, they held their peace, and glorified God, saying, Then hath *God also to the Gentiles granted repentance* unto life.

As with any gift, once we receive the gift of repentance, it becomes ours. Once the Holy Spirit changes our mind, and our "want to" concerning Jesus, we then have the capacity to repent, and we act on it. However, this is an *effect* of our regeneration, not the cause. While we were yet sinners, the Holy Spirit "quickened us." He brought us from death to life. He gave spiritual birth to us. We did not cause it, He did.

A baby does not cause his birth; the mother does. Yet, after the birth, there are many effects which the babe and mom enjoy. Spiritual birth is like this. But, never underestimate the importance of the effects (see the book of James, which is predominately about the effects of salvation).

I was driving to work the day the Lord called me in the spring of 1972. The Holy Spirit led me to see I was a terrible "boss" of my own life, and that Jesus would be a perfect, benevolent, loving "Boss" who could actually run my life well. I asked Jesus to do just that, to be the boss of my life. I asked because the Holy Spirit had changed my mind, changed my "want to" (Phil. 2:13). I asked this because I genuinely, for the first time in my life, WANTED Jesus in my life for the rest of my life.

Ten minutes before this, I did NOT want Him. What changed? Did I "work up" belief in my own mind like a mental pep rally? What about my heart? Did I turn it from hard to malleable all at once of my own free will? From within my carnal, lost mind, did I just decide on my own all at once that I would change my mind 180 degrees?

Or did God, in His mercy, send His Holy Spirit into my car that day, into my heart and mind, and give me a heart transplant? Was it God or me who initiated my salvation? Was my repentance the cause of my salvation (regeneration), or an effect of it? Let's review.

Colossians 2:12–13
12 Buried with him in baptism, wherein also ye are risen with *him* through the *faith of the operation of God,* who hath raised him from the dead.

13 And you, being dead in your sins and the uncircumcision of your flesh, hath he quickened together with him, having forgiven you all trespasses.

These Scriptures show that the faith I suddenly had was a gift that sprang from the "operation of God." The Bible shows that while I was still in my sin, still in rebellion against God, GOD quickened me. He brought me from death to life. God Himself, from heaven, regenerated me. This was the great CAUSE of my salvation.

All the things I desired to do for God immediately after my regeneration by the Holy Spirit were EFFECTS of my salvation; they did not cause it. I believed and repented as an effect of Christ's faith which the Holy Spirit had already given me, and the repentance (change of mind) which He led me to in my car that day. I repented, changed my mind, because He led me to repentance—He changed my "want to."

So, I CHANGED MY MIND (because I wanted to for the first time ever) about who I was (I'm not God), and who Jesus was (God, and the Lord of my life who would free me from every lesser lord).

Now this is an interesting process that the modern church knows little of, but the Puritans were well versed in. There were some things I immediately quit—drinking and cursing were two—because my New Lord, Jesus, freed me from slavery to these sins. This may have led passersby to believe that I "quit" these things to get religion. The opposite is true. I received Christ as my personal Lord and Saviour because the Holy Spirit had shown Him to me in a way that allowed me to really see He was my Shepherd, and I was His sheep; I was hungry, and He had the food. Jesus was at that moment, for the first time in my life, *irresistible* to me.

When I received Him, He freed me from every lesser lord that had controlled my life. He instantly freed me from some "lords," like the two I named above, and some He is still working on, but nothing owns me now but Him.

I was saved while I was still a sinner, and the effect was that these things went away, and some are in the process of going away. I am made more like Christ every day by the power of the Holy Spirit and the truth of the Word of God which cleanses the body and renews the mind—by the "washing of the word."

If I was saved while I was still a sinner, then I must have been saved before I repented. Therefore, repentance is not a cause of our regeneration; it is an effect.

Romans 5:6, 8–11

6 For when we were yet without strength, in due time Christ died for the ungodly.

8 But God commendeth his love toward us, in that, while we were *yet sinners*, Christ died for us.

9 Much more then, being now justified by his blood, we shall be saved from wrath through him.

10 For if, when *we were enemies*, we were reconciled to God by the death of his Son, much more, being reconciled, we shall be saved by his life.

11 And not only *so*, but we also joy in God through our Lord Jesus Christ, by whom we have now received the atonement.

The atonement points back to the O.T. sacrifices that were a picture of the true Lamb of God, Jesus Christ. When they offered the sacrificial animals, this atoned for (covered) the sins of the O.T.

saints. Jesus is our sacrifice, once and for all, and because of HIS work our sins are not only covered, **but done away**.

But the thing to notice in the above passage is that you are regenerated (born again) while you are "without strength" and still a rebellious sinner. You are saved from wrath by HIS blood, not by anything you do or don't do (and not by anything you decide to "quit").

Man's way of thinking—that we must quit things to be saved or do good works to save ourselves—is totally useless and would actually be a curse (how much good would *ever* be enough to cover the sins we had already done?). But Christ set us free from the curse of the law by keeping every jot and tittle of the law, and then dying for us on the cross with our sins in His body! So, the true gospel (good news) message is that we cannot save ourselves and we do not have to. We cannot build our own stairway to heaven.

We trust the blood of Christ to atone for our sins. It is the only thing that can. God is not satisfied with anything else.

We respond when the Holy Spirit calls us to see Jesus for Who He is and see ourselves for who we aren't— we are not God. This change of mind is the repentance.

When I changed my mind (repented) about Christ and received Him as my Lord, yes, I quit some things, but that was the EFFECT of having a new Lord that I loved more than those old masters. The repentance was not the CAUSE of my salvation.

So…

Titus 3:5

5 Not by works of righteousness which we have done, but according to his mercy he saved us, by the washing of regeneration, and renewing of the Holy Ghost.

In the second half of verse 5, after showing what is NOT His way (good works, religion), God begins to describe what IS ***His*** way of salvation very clearly.

> **Titus 3:5b** …But according to his mercy he saved us, by the washing of regeneration, and renewing of the Holy Ghost;
>
> **6** Which he shed [Gk "poured forth"] on us abundantly through Jesus Christ our Saviour.

- **Salvation is a "washing!"**

washing
lŏutrŏn – a *bath*
FROM
lŏuō, a primary verb; to *bathe* the *whole* person.

regeneration
paliggĕnĕsia, (spiritual) *rebirth*
FROM
palin, anew
+
genesis, nativity; FROM *gĕnĕtē,* fem. of *gĕnĕa, birth.*

So, He saves you by the ***washing of the new birth***—you being "born anew" or "born again."

We could paraphrase:

"Jesus, according to His tender passion, saves you by regenerating you (birthing you anew), and the washing that comes from that, i.e., He bathed you with His righteousness, and the Holy Spirit placed you into Christ so that you are one with Him, you in Him and He in you." (This is called ***Spirit baptism*** which we will discuss in Chapter 13.)

- **Salvation is a "renewal!"**

The Holy Spirit accomplished all of this within you at His effectual calling, when—while you were still a sinner—He RENEWED you! He made you a whole new man or woman as a newborn babe.

Now, the world, even the religious world, does NOT understand this or like it at all. It takes all power away from the church, its traditions, its dogma; it takes all money away as well. This, really, is why Jesus was crucified, from the human viewpoint. He took all the power away from the Pharisees, the religious leaders of Israel. He mocked their tradition and directed the people to the Scriptures instead. They hated it and hated him, and the same is true today.

Notice Jesus's talk with the Pharisee, Nicodemus.

John 3:2–4
2 The same came to Jesus by night, and said unto him, Rabbi, we know that thou art a teacher come from God:

for no man can do these miracles that thou doest, except God be with him.

Nicodemus offered a complement, "We know that thou art a teacher come from God...."

> **3** Jesus answered and said unto him, Verily, verily, I say unto thee, Except a man be born again, he cannot see the kingdom of God.

Jesus completely ignored his compliment and said, "You must be born again, or you will never see the Kingdom of God."

> **4** Nicodemus saith unto him, How can a man be born when he is old? can he enter the second time into his mother's womb, and be born?

You see, God's way of salvation makes about as much sense to the masses of humanity as entering a second time into one's mother's womb. It makes no sense at all. So why would anyone just "decide" to repent? This is why repentance must be a gift from God, something God gives you upon regeneration. And it is clear that the Holy Spirit must open your eyes and ears to see and hear the truth.

After all, Nicodemus was a man who had spent his life studying the biblical law, thinking that keeping the law saves a person. DOING things for God must be the way to heaven, he thought. Jesus took this completely away from Nicodemus.

> **John 3:5** Jesus answered, Verily, verily, I say unto thee, Except a man be born of water and of the Spirit, he cannot enter into the kingdom of God.

Jesus teaches that it takes two things to be saved. You must, (1) be born of the water of the Word of God, and (2) be called by the Holy Spirit. Neither of these things have to do with human effort. Our part is simply to respond by receiving the gift we have been given. Once we receive the gift of salvation, it is ours—together with many other things the Holy Spirit gives us at regeneration.

We know the "water" here is the Word of God, including the gospel message itself (Jesus died, was buried, and rose again for the sins of His people), because Ephesians 5:26 tells us:

> **Ephesians 5:26**
> **26** That he might sanctify and cleanse it with the *washing of water by the word*.

It takes a combination of the Word of God and the work of the Holy Spirit for men to be saved.

For Nicodemus, this is bad, but it gets worse … at least with respect to his system of salvation which he had spent a lifetime studying and teaching.

> **John 3:6** That which is born of the flesh is flesh; and that which is born of the Spirit is spirit.
> **7** Marvel not that I said unto thee, Ye must be born again.

- **The Parable of Physical Birth**

Jesus likens spiritual birth to physical birth. This is a sort of parable, in a sense—a physical story to explain a spiritual phenomenon which we know little, if anything, about.

We understand physical birth, so perhaps this will help us understand what Nicodemus is having a hard time with—the fact that spiritual regeneration has nothing to do with HIS system of works. Good works that Nicodemus required men to do for God.

Regeneration is an operation which God performs upon man, not something man does for God. The way regeneration works, according to Jesus Christ, is backward from Nicodemus's idea of the process.

When speaking to a crowd, I often ask the room how many mothers there are. They raise their hands. I ask, "How much did the baby help you when you were giving birth?" They laugh, and sometimes one will shout out, "The baby did not help; it was the problem!" Of course, this is true. The baby did not help at all with its own birth. The mom did ALL the hard work.

Then I will ask, "How much of the planning and pre-birth work did the baby do?" The fact is, again, none of it. All the work and planning were done by the parents. The baby had nothing to do with it at all. The baby did not even desire his own birth—the parents had all the love and all the desire, did all the planning, and birthed the baby. Then the baby was born—he was not, but now is. He enjoys his mother's nourishment, and his dad's protection, and takes part in all that the family owns, and yet he deserves none of it due to anything he did—he owns it all simply because he is the child of the parents.

Spiritual birth is the same. We have nothing to do with planning it. We have nothing to do with desiring it or causing it to happen. We don't deserve it, and we are not born again because we did anything good or bad. Our Father in heaven did all the planning, all the loving, and Jesus did all the work to give us this new life, and then the Spirit of Christ birthed us. In one moment of time we are not here, and in the next, we are.

The Before-Time Aspect of Salvation:

Ephesians 1:4–5
4 According as he hath chosen us in him before the foundation of the world, that we should be holy and without blame before him in love:
5 Having predestinated us unto the adoption of children by Jesus Christ to himself, according to the good pleasure of his will.

Some expositors wish not to accept the fact that God knew His own children (with an intimate knowledge) before time began and wilfully chose this same group of people to be adopted into His family later in time and space. These teachers say that God only predestined that those who are saved would do good works.

It is true that verse 4 (above) says we are predestined to be holy, but usually these expositors leave out the very next verse. Verse 5 says we are also predestined to be adopted as the children of God by (or through) Jesus Christ, according to God's good pleasure (i.e., He chooses whom He wishes to choose, and God's will is the basis upon which they are chosen). All of this happened before time began—before Genesis 1:1.

The In-Time Aspect of Salvation:

2 Corinthians 5:17
17 Therefore if any man *be* in Christ, *he is* a new creature: old things are passed away; behold, all things are become new.

On each of our time lines, if we ever have a concern for our souls, if we ever fear God and His judgement, it is because He knew us before time, and has sent His Holy Spirit to call us to Jesus, to open our eyes to the Wonder of the Eternal Son of God, our Great Shepherd, and to regenerate us. To use another metaphor, He brings us to life, opens our eyes of understanding, gives us ears that hear, and a new heart which desires the Lord, and can love God, so that we have the ability to respond to the bridegroom, as He offers Himself to us. And, as we say "yes" to the most wonderful relationship of our lives, His bride we become. At that time we become a "new creation," old ungodly desires of our "old man" and many of our sin habits pass away, and all things become new. Our "new man (or woman)" is risen from the crypt of this body of death, and our old man now has the standing of having been crucified with Christ. This is the "in time" aspect of salvation.

Colossians 3:9–10
9 …Seeing that ye have put off the old man with his deeds;
10 And have put on the new *man*, which is renewed in knowledge after the image of him that created him.

The next teaching on salvation, by Jesus Christ Himself, shows us that just as the before-time part of salvation was all about God, and His will, in like manner the in-time aspect of salvation is caused by God, not us. The Holy Spirit, and the regenerative act He performs upon us, is the great CAUSE of salvation. Everything *we* do is an effect. An effect can never be the cause of the first cause. Therefore, what *we* do does NOT cause our salvation. However, we respond, as a bride to the Bridegroom, and receive salvation as a free gift of love, extended first by the Groom. "We love him, because he first loved us," 1 John 4:19.

Here we see Jesus continuing the "in-time" lesson on salvation for Nicodemus, a top theologian of the Jews:

John 3:8
8 The wind bloweth where it listeth, and thou hearest the sound thereof, but canst not tell whence it cometh, and whither it goeth: so is every one that is born of the Spirit.

This was a very hard lesson for Nicodemus, as it is for all human beings. Natural man hates this lesson most of all. This lesson drove the Jews to try to kill Jesus more than once before He was crucified, due to their hatred of this teaching!

Jesus taught this religious man that true salvation, being born again, is like the wind.

• **The Parable of the Wind**

The wind blows where it wants (listeth). You can hear the sound of it, but you cannot control where it came from or where it is going. This is a picture of how the Holy Spirit selects whom He will light upon and call to salvation. A person can only be saved IF the Holy Spirit calls him. No human can control this any more than he can control the wind. It is out of our hands entirely.

Since this is true, religion—the church, the denominations—cannot control *who* gets saved, *when* they get saved, or *if* they get saved. The job of the true church is simply to tell the gospel to the world—this is the Water of the Word. Then the Holy Spirit must come to the individual and awaken him, regenerate him, give birth to him, or there is no real salvation. To whom does He come? Ephesians 1:5 above answers this, along with many other verses in the Bible: "…according to the good pleasure of his [God the Father's] will." The Holy Spirit comes to whom the Father sends Him. The Father controls exactly when, where, and how His Spirit moves—no man can tell from where He comes or where He will go next.

Are we saying man has no control over who is saved from this fallen human race? We can only read what God has written. However, does this logic demand that man plays no role in his own salvation? Here again, we read what is written:

The Apostle John set up the story of Nicodemus in Ch. 3, with this idea in Chapter 1:

John 1:12–13

12 But as many as *received him*, to them gave he power to become the sons of God, *even* to them that believe on his name:
13 Which were born, not of blood, nor of the will of the flesh, nor of the will of man, but of God.

John made it clear that the *mode of salvation* is belief in Jesus's name, and therefore, receiving Him (see below). But John makes it equally clear that this born-again experience is not caused by "the blood [line]" i.e., the family we are born into (example: "My grandpa was a preacher so I'm okay," does not work); not caused by "the will of the flesh," our natural man does not *WANT* salvation, and *does not seek it* (Romans 3:11); and regeneration is not caused by "the will of man." Our own flesh does not desire salvation, and our own will does not cause salvation; nor does the will of our mother, father, preacher, or any man cause it.

The Holy Spirit calls whom He will to salvation, and *this call* is *"as the wind, which bloweth where it listeth [desires]."*

"The wind bloweth where it listeth, and thou hearest the sound thereof, but canst not tell whence it cometh, and whither it goeth: so is every one that is born of the Spirit."—**John 3:8**

The phrase "born again" is interesting. We know what "born" means, but look at the Greek word for "again."

again

anōthĕn, from above; by analogy from the first; by implication anew:—from above, again, from the beginning (very first).

Jesus told Nicodemus he must be *"born from above."* In other words, he must be *"born from the first"* (i.e., from before the foundation of the world, Ephesians Ch. 1; Romans Ch. 8, et.al.).

Now, see if the following verse makes more sense, in the light of John 3:3. We were chosen before the foundation of the world to be adopted as God's children—born from the first, from the beginning, from above.

Ephesians 1:4–8, 11–12

4 According as he hath chosen us in him *before the foundation of the world,* that we should be holy and without blame before him in love:

5 Having *predestinated us unto the adoption of children by Jesus Christ* to himself, according to the good pleasure of his will,

6 To the praise of the glory of his grace, wherein he hath made us accepted in the beloved.

7 In whom we have redemption through his blood, the forgiveness of sins, according to the riches of his grace;

8 Wherein he hath abounded toward us in all wisdom and prudence;

11 In whom also we have *obtained an inheritance, being predestinated according to the purpose of him*

who worketh all things after the counsel of his own will:

12 That we should be to the praise of his glory, who first trusted in Christ.

Here, the passage shows the mode of salvation and the result of salvation:

The Mode of Salvation (Our Part):

Ephesians 1:13

13 In whom ye also *trusted*, after that ye heard the word of truth, the gospel of your salvation: in whom also after that ye believed....

You trust Christ AFTER you HEAR the Word of truth (i.e., the Word of God—you are born of the water of the Word).

Now, we know that Jesus said many times, "He who has ears to hear, let him hear." Dead people do not have the ability to hear God. However, when the Holy Spirit calls us and quickens us (brings us to life) He opens our ears, and we then HEAR the Word of God with understanding for the first time. (This is being born of the Spirit, which allows us to hear the Word of God.) *We are born of the water [the Word of God] and the Spirit.*

The Result of our Salvation:

Ephesians 1:13b, 14.

13b…Ye were sealed with that holy Spirit of promise.

(a) The Holy Spirit indwells you and you become the temple of the living God.

> **14** Which is the earnest of our inheritance until the redemption of the purchased possession, unto the praise of his glory.

(b) This indwelling of the Spirit is the "earnest money" (as in real estate) that guarantees you will someday be IN the house, i.e., obtain your inheritance in heaven, because it has already been purchased for you by the death of Christ on the cross. God receives all the glory for this plan of salvation.

Back to our parable in John Chapter 3:

> **John 3:9** Nicodemus answered and said unto him, How can these things be?

Of course! This is what most church members in America say today. "How can THIS be the plan of God? We like a plan that includes doing good works and being religious for salvation! We want to be in control! We want to be seen doing good things." Nicodemus, the Pharisee, would agree with this sentiment!

John 3:10 Jesus answered and said unto him, Art thou a master [teacher] of Israel, and knowest not these things?

14 And as Moses lifted up the serpent in the wilderness, even so must the Son of man be lifted up:

15 That whosoever believeth in him should not perish, but have eternal life.

18 He that believeth on him is not condemned: but he that believeth not is condemned already, because he hath not believed in the name of the only begotten Son of God.

19 And this is the condemnation, that light is come into the world, and men loved darkness rather than light, because their deeds were evil.

(This speaks of the depravity of man and proves Jesus's point: Nicodemus cannot save himself by keeping the rules—he is depraved. He can only be saved by the water and the Spirit.)

Now we come full circle back to Titus Chapter 3:

Titus 3:5–6

5 Not by works of righteousness which we have done, but according to his mercy he saved us, by the washing of regeneration, and renewing of the Holy Ghost;

6 Which he shed on us abundantly through Jesus Christ our Saviour.

Three last points:

(1) We are made right with God (justified) by God's grace [unmerited favor];

(2) We will be made heirs according to the hope of eternal life. (Note: the phrase "should be" in English is not in the Greek—it is implied that we "*will* be made heirs.");

(3) AFTER the CAUSE of our salvation happens, i.e., we have received the gifts of faith and repentance, and now believe, then the EFFECT is that we become joint-heirs with Christ (we own everything He owns); and we should be careful to maintain good works, which are good and profitable to men.

> **Titus 3:7** That being justified by his grace, we should be made heirs according to the hope of eternal life.
> **8** *This is* a faithful saying, and these things I will that thou affirm constantly, that they which have believed in God might be careful to maintain good works. These things are good and profitable unto men.

Repentance is changing your mind. You stop believing that YOU are God and a good lord of your own life, and start believing that Jesus Christ would be a better Lord of your life. And repentance is a gift from God given to you, which the Holy Spirit gives you when He calls you, when *He changes your "want to"* so that for the first time you desire Christ to be your Saviour and Lord.

It is fascinating for many Christians to discover the fact that both the faith and the repentance that save us are actually given to us by the Holy Spirit as He regenerates us.

- **Proof that true saving faith is a gift GIVEN to you by the Holy Spirit upon your regeneration:**

Ephesians 2:8–9

8 For by grace are ye saved through faith; and that not of yourselves: *it is* the gift of God:

9 Not of works, lest any man should boast.

James 1:16–18

16 Do not err, my beloved brethren.

17 *Every good gift* and every perfect gift *is from above*, and cometh down from the Father of lights, with whom is no variableness, neither shadow of turning.

18 Of his own will begat he us with the word of truth, that we should be a kind of firstfruits of his creatures.

2 Peter 1:1–4

1 Simon Peter, a servant and an apostle of Jesus Christ, to them that *have obtained* like *precious faith* with us through the righteousness of God and our Saviour Jesus Christ:

2 Grace and peace be multiplied unto you through the knowledge of God, and of Jesus our Lord,

3 *According as his divine power hath given unto us* all things that *pertain* unto life and godliness, through the knowledge of him that hath called us to glory and virtue:

4 *Whereby are given unto us exceeding great and precious promises: that by these ye might be partakers of the divine nature,* having escaped the corruption that is in the world through lust.

Philippians 1:29

29 For unto you *__it is given__* in the behalf of Christ, not only to believe on him, but also to suffer for his sake.

Acts 3:16

16 And his name through faith in his name hath made this man strong, whom ye see and know: yea, **the faith which is *__by him__*** hath given him this perfect soundness in the presence of you all.

- **Proof that it is NOT your own belief (mental peprally belief) that saves you:**

James 2:19

19 Thou believest that there is one God; thou doest well: the devils also believe, and tremble.

Demons believe in God, and they believe in Christ; however, they are not saved. They have not been given saving faith.

- **Proof that true repentance is a gift GIVEN to you by the Holy Spirit upon your regeneration:**

Romans 2:4

4 …Knowing that the goodness of God leadeth thee to repentance.

2 Timothy 2:25

25 …If God peradventure will **give them repentance** to the acknowledging of the truth;

- **Proof that it is NOT your own fleshly repentance that saves you:**

Matthew 27:3–5

3 Then Judas, which had betrayed him, when he saw that he was condemned, *repented himself*, and brought again the thirty pieces of silver to the chief priests and elders,

4 Saying, I have sinned in that I have betrayed the innocent blood. And they said, What *is that* to us? see thou *to that*.

5 And he cast down the pieces of silver in the temple, and departed, and went and hanged himself.

Matthew 26:24–25

24 The Son of man goeth as it is written of him: *but woe unto that man by whom the Son of man is betrayed! it had been good for that man if he had not been born.*

25 Then Judas, which betrayed him, answered and said, Master, is it I? He said unto him, Thou hast said.

Judas betrayed Christ. Later, within his own mind, he worked up human repentance. He was NOT forgiven, and he died and went to hell. True repentance is a gift from God, imparted by the Holy Spirit at the time the elect saints are called. The desire to repent is something that is placed within us by the Holy Spirit upon our regeneration. It is not the cause of regeneration; rather, it is one of the many effects of it. True, born-again Christians repent, because their "want to" is changed by the Holy Spirit.

Now we must ask, "What is the opposite of true repentance?"

What are dead works?

It is interesting that the Bible teaches that faith without works is dead.

> **James 2:20–23**
> **20** But wilt thou know, O vain man, that faith without works is dead?

True faith, the kind that is given to us by the Holy Spirit on our spiritual birthday, always has the effect of producing good works in the life of the true believer. Here is how it works:

> **22** Seest thou how faith wrought with his works, and by works was faith made perfect?
> **23** And the scripture was fulfilled which saith, Abraham believed God, and it was imputed unto him for righteousness: and he was called the Friend of God.

The word **"wrought"** in v. 22 in Greek is:

sunĕrgĕō, to *be a fellow-worker; to work together with.*

Faith is a fellow-worker with the good works, and by works, faith is made whole.

So, if true, then think about this:

If faith is always a "fellow-worker" together with TRUE good works, then the definition of DEAD works must be works that do NOT have true faith accompanying them.

Not only is it true that faith without works is dead, it is also true that WORKS WITHOUT FAITH ARE DEAD.

So, dead works are *works done in the flesh*, through human effort alone, and *not driven by the faith of Christ* within us.

The following are Bible examples of people who had good works and/or religious works, but their works were dead works, and they were walking dead men (who thought they were saved). Jesus said:

Matthew 23:27–28

27 Woe unto you, scribes and Pharisees, hypocrites! for ye are like unto whited sepulchres, which indeed appear beautiful outward, but are within full of dead *men's* bones, and of all uncleanness.

28 Even so ye also outwardly appear righteous unto men, but within ye are full of hypocrisy and iniquity.

Jesus made it clear that these same Pharisees who were doing many "works," yet without faith, were actually on their way to hell. Their works were *dead* works.

John 8:21, 23–24

21 Then said Jesus again unto them, I go my way, and ye shall seek me, and shall die in your sins: whither I go, *__ye cannot come__*.
23 And he said unto them, *__Ye are from beneath__*; I am from above: ye are of this world; I am not of this world.
24 I said therefore unto you, that *__ye shall die in your sins: for if ye believe not that I am he, ye shall die in your sins.__*

Revelation 3:1–2

1 And unto the angel of the church in Sardis write; These things saith he that hath the seven Spirits of God, and the seven stars; *I know thy works, that thou hast a name that thou livest, and art dead.*
2 Be watchful, and strengthen the things which remain, that are ready to die: for I have not found thy works perfect before God.

In the next passage, Jesus first spoke to Jews who believed on Him, and then He spoke to the Pharisees and other Jews who rejected Him.

John 8:31–32

31 Then said Jesus to those Jews which believed on him, If ye continue in my word, *then* are ye my disciples indeed;

32 And ye shall know the truth, and the truth shall make you free.

Then he turned to the unbelieving Jews:

John 8:38-45

38 I speak that which I have seen with my Father: and ye do that which ye have seen with your father.

39 They answered and said unto him, Abraham is our father. Jesus saith unto them, If ye were Abraham's children, ye would do the works of Abraham.

40 But now ye seek to kill me, a man that hath told you the truth, which I have heard of God: this did not Abraham.

41 Ye do the deeds of your father. Then said they to him, We be not born of fornication; we have one Father, *even* God.

42 Jesus said unto them, If God were your Father, ye would love me: for I proceeded forth and came from God; neither came I of myself, but he sent me.

43 Why do ye not understand my speech? *even* because ye cannot hear my word.

44 Ye are of *your* father the devil, and the lusts of your father ye will do. He was a murderer from the beginning, and abode not in the truth, because there is no truth in him. When he speaketh a lie, he speaketh of his own: for he is a liar, and the father of it.

45 And because I tell *you* the truth, ye believe me not.

So, there are many people who do what they think are works for God, but they are dead works, not having true God-given faith accompanying them, and these people will not see the Kingdom of heaven.

Matthew 7:21–24

21 Not every one that saith unto me, Lord, Lord, shall enter into the kingdom of heaven; but he that doeth the will of my Father which is in heaven.

22 Many will say to me in that day, Lord, Lord, have we not prophesied in thy name? and in thy name have cast out devils? and in thy name done many wonderful works?

23 And then will I profess unto them, I never knew you: depart from me, ye that work iniquity.

24 Therefore whosoever heareth these sayings of mine, and doeth them, I will liken him unto a wise man, which built his house upon a rock:

True good works are built upon the Rock, and the Rock is Jesus Christ. **Dead works** are performed in the flesh; Good works are derived from and energized by the faith of Christ, which is given to the believer upon his regeneration.

Dead works are sometimes called "will-worship" in the Bible. They are said to be "a show" of wisdom; in other words, they feign wisdom and humility, and they satisfy the flesh.

Colossians 2:21

21 (Touch not; taste not; handle not;

22 Which all are to perish with the using;) after the commandments and doctrines of men?

23 Which things have indeed a shew of wisdom in will worship, and humility, and neglecting of the body; not in any honour to the satisfying of the flesh.

Only the blood of Christ, and faith in that blood can purge us from dead works.

Hebrews 9:14, 24, 26–28

14 How much more shall the blood of Christ, who through the eternal Spirit offered himself without spot to God, purge your conscience from ***dead works*** to serve the living God?

24 For Christ is not entered into the holy places made with hands, *which are* the figures of the true; but into heaven itself, now to appear in the presence of God for us:

26 …But now once in the end of the world hath he appeared to put away sin by the sacrifice of himself.

27 And as it is appointed unto men once to die, but after this the judgment:

28 So Christ was once offered to bear the sins of many; and unto them that look for him shall he appear the second time without sin unto salvation.

This is the profound enigma to mankind—it makes no sense that we are not saved by doing good things, or that people are not saved just because they seem to be nice people.

The only thing that our HOLY God is pleased with to remove the stain of sin is the sacrificial, substitutionary blood of the Son of God, the Lamb of God. God only accepts THAT sacrifice as the ransom for His people.

It makes sense if you just think about it. How much good must an unclean sinner do to erase the bad he has already done? No amount of "dead works" done by a dead person who is part of a fallen race which is unpleasing to God, can erase even one of the bad things already done! Only Jesus's blood can satisfy God's law, because the wages of sin is death, and HE paid the price FOR you!

Hebrews 10:10, 12, 14, 16–17
10 By the which will we are sanctified through the offering of the body of Jesus Christ once *for all.*
12 But this man, after he had offered one sacrifice for sins for ever, sat down on the right hand of God;
14 For by one offering he hath perfected for ever them that are sanctified.

You cannot get more perfected than *"perfected forever."* This is why you cannot lose your salvation once Christ gives it to you.

16 This *is* the covenant that I will make with them after those days, saith the Lord, I will put my laws into their hearts, and in their minds will I write them;

You no longer need a list of good works. You simply walk each moment of each day holding Jesus's hand, and He will never lead you toward sin.

> **17** And their sins and iniquities will I remember no more.

Once you are saved, all the sins of your whole life—past, present, and future—have been placed upon the body of Jesus while He was on the cross. They are removed from you, and God the Father forgets them.

Now, not only can you do good works which spring from the faith within you, but you can also get your prayers answered!

> **Hebrews 10:19–24**
> **19** Having therefore, brethren, boldness to enter into the holiest by the blood of Jesus,
> **20** By a new and living way, which he hath consecrated for us, through the veil, that is to say, his flesh;
> **21** And *having* an high priest over the house of God;
> **22** Let us draw near with a true heart in full assurance of faith, having our hearts sprinkled from an evil conscience, and our bodies washed with pure water.
> **23** Let us hold fast the profession of *our* faith without wavering; (for he *is* faithful that promised;)

And finally, you are exhorted to use that prayer life, to pray for others that they may also be provoked to love and true good works.

24 And let us consider one another to provoke unto love and to good works.

In the end, everyone will be judged according to whether they had dead works or living works, which can only spring from the faith of Christ within their hearts.

Revelation 20:13–15

13 And the sea gave up the dead which were in it; and death and hell delivered up the dead which were in them: and they were judged every man according to their works.

14 And death and hell were cast into the lake of fire. This is the second death.

15 And whosoever was not found written in the book of life was cast into the lake of fire.

Galatians 2:16

16 Knowing that a man is not justified by the works of the law, but by the faith _of_ Jesus Christ, even we have believed in Jesus Christ, that we might be justified by the faith _of_ Christ, and not by the works of the law: for by the works of the law shall no flesh be justified.

John 6:28–29

28 Then said they unto him, What shall we do, that we might work the works of God?

29 Jesus answered and said unto them, This is the work of God, that ye believe on him whom he hath sent.

Jesus made it clear that true work that is of God, work that pleases God, can only come through belief in the Messiah.

Faith works together with the good works—otherwise the works are dead.

The world's definition of "repent" is incorrect—it is not "quitting this and that," but rather it is changing one's mind about who God is (not me, not you). Its idea that one must "quit this and that bad thing" to be saved is topsy-turvy, upside-down, and backward from the actual truth. In fact, the quitting of these things for salvation would be considered "dead works" by God, and summarily dismissed as "wood, hay, and stubble." Any works that are done in the flesh, and not activated by faith in Christ, are dead works.

True repentance is in fact a gift from God, which He gives you as a part of the "operation of God."

When the Holy Spirit calls you and changes your "want to," when all of a sudden Jesus Christ is irresistible to you, whereas yesterday you easily resisted Him and remained lord of your own life, then He also gives you many things, including the "faith OF Christ" and the "desire to change the mind."

All of this happens in one big package called regeneration. But remember, contrary to what the world believes, regeneration is "the operation of God," not the work of yourself. You don't DO anything to be saved. You receive something, as a free gift. That's actually the good news.

Doing dead works can never save a single human soul. Once you ARE saved, then real good works come forth from the "New

Man"—from the inside out. God receives these as gold and silver, because they are a result of the united, quickened spirit and the Holy Spirit, as they become one spirit—the New Man (which is the real "you").

Chapter 12

The Foundation of
Faith Toward God

**"Therefore leaving the principles of the doctrine of Christ,
let us go on unto perfection; not laying again <u>the foundation
of repentance from dead works, and <u>of faith toward God</u>."</u>
—Hebrews 6:1**

Our third Core Doctrine is "Faith *toward* God." But, what is this? Is it the same as "faith in God" or "the faith of Christ" or "faith in Christ"? Actually, it is related to these concepts, but a little different. And the difference is important because "faith toward God" relates more to our practical day-to-day living after we are born again.

Hebrews 6:1
1 …Laying again <u>the foundation of faith toward God</u>.

There are several Greek words for "toward" in the N.T. In this verse, the word is:

epi, which means to superimpose.

Webster's Dictionary defines **superimpose** as: "To place or lay over or above something."

To get a better idea of what this means, to have faith **toward** God, let's allow the **Bible** to teach us the Bible. (By the way, this is a very important rule of proper Bible interpretation—every true principle or doctrine in the Bible must harmoniously fit all the other teachings of the whole Bible.) First, let's look at another passage with the same word, "*epi*."

Ephesians 2:4–7

4 But God, who is rich in mercy, for his great love wherewith he loved us,

5 Even when we were dead in sins, hath quickened us together with Christ, (by grace ye are saved;)

6 And hath raised *us* up together, and made *us* sit together in heavenly *places* in Christ Jesus:

7 That in the ages to come he might shew the exceeding riches of his grace in *his* kindness **_toward_** us through Christ Jesus.

The idea here is that we have God's kindness **placed upon** us through Christ. If we parallel this meaning with our verse on having "faith toward God," then this is what we see.

**Faith "toward" God is
you placing your faith upon God.**

We could say it this way: "It is your faith moving in the direction of God."

Or, perhaps even better: "It is the eye of your faith gazing UPON God, not other things."

This gets us closer to the meaning. Perhaps it is best described by contrast. We could have faith that moves in the direction of the world system, or in the direction of money, or our position in the community or church, or toward a spouse or boyfriend or girlfriend. We could have faith toward our government, or our president, our college professor, or our preacher. But our faith should be toward God FIRST, rather than any of these.

This whole idea can be described perfectly by our Lord Jesus Himself.

Matthew 6:24–34

24 No man can serve two masters: for either he will hate the one, and love the other; or else he will hold to the one, and despise the other. Ye cannot serve God and mammon.

25 Therefore I say unto you, Take no thought for your life, what ye shall eat, or what ye shall drink; nor yet for your body, what ye shall put on. Is not the life more than meat, and the body than raiment?

26 Behold the fowls of the air: for they sow not, neither do they reap, nor gather into barns; yet your heavenly Father feedeth them. Are ye not much better than they?

27 Which of you by taking thought can add one cubit unto his stature?

28 And why take ye thought for raiment? Consider the lilies of the field, how they grow; they toil not, neither do they spin:

29 And yet I say unto you, That even Solomon in all his glory was not arrayed like one of these.

30 Wherefore, if God so clothe the grass of the field, which to day is, and to morrow is cast into the oven, *shall he* not much more *clothe* you, O ye of little faith?

31 Therefore take no thought, saying, What shall we eat? or, What shall we drink? or, Wherewithal shall we be clothed?

32 (For after all these things do the Gentiles seek:) for your heavenly Father knoweth that ye have need of all these things.

33 But ***seek ye first the kingdom of God, and his righteousness;*** and all these things shall be added unto you.

34 Take therefore no thought for the morrow: for the morrow shall take thought for the things of itself. Sufficient unto the day *is* the evil thereof.

If our faith looks towards the kingdom of God first, and God's imputed righteousness, then all the things we need will be given to us by the Lord. If our faith is *not* toward God, then it will be toward money, according to Jesus. ("Mammon" in Matthew 6:24 means money.)

However, the wonderful thing to know (that many do NOT know) is that if your faith IS TOWARD God and NOT toward the money, ***then money will not hurt you***.

Proverbs 10:22

22 The blessing of the Lord, it maketh rich, And he *addeth no sorrow with it.*

On the contrary, money becomes a blessing to the family. There is nothing wrong with God's people being rich. It is all about what you DO with the money and how you THINK of the money. I teach our church family and TRADEway clients that money is just a TOOL God uses to work through us to help our families and others. You must not love the money. If you think of it as a tool, not to be hoarded, then the money will not hurt your family; it will be a blessing to them and to others in need.

To a believer, riches come from God's blessing, never from ill-begotten gain. Verses which people often take out of context to try to demonstrate that Jesus was against wealth are only teaching that He hated ill-begotten gain. Jesus rebuked the Pharisees who got rich off of widows, much like "faith-healers" today! However, the Spirit of Christ who wrote the Proverbs certainly did not teach that it was evil for God's people to obtain wealth.

If this weren't true, then the Bible would contradict itself. Consider these "friends of God" who were the wealthiest men of their time: Abraham, Job, Solomon, King David, and even the Apostle Paul who was a tent maker by trade and "knew how to abound" financially (Philippians 4:12). In fact, Solomon was the wealthiest man who ever lived (in today's money, he would have over two trillion dollars)! If money is evil, then these men could not have been the friends of God. In general, if wealth is evil, then the Bible would be in error when it says:

Psalm 128:1–2

1 Blessed *is* every one that feareth the Lord; That walketh in his ways.

2 For thou shalt eat the labour of thine hands: Happy *shalt* thou *be*, and *it shall be* well with thee.

If we look at the above verse through the eyes of the Israelite, we learn something valuable. If the Jew of the O.T. said, "I am more blessed by God than you," he meant he had more cattle, more sheep, more camels than his neighbor—God had "blessed" him. The livestock was his money! He knew the blessing came from God. Think about that for a moment.

To be more explicit, the Bible actually SAYS riches are a *blessing* from God to the person whose faith is TOWARD GOD.

Proverbs 8:10–11, 18–19

10 Receive my instruction, and not silver; And knowledge rather than choice gold.

11 For wisdom *is* better than rubies; And all the things that may be desired are not to be compared to it.

18 Riches and honour *are* with me; *Yea, **durable riches*** and righteousness.

19 My fruit *is* better than gold, yea, than fine gold; And my revenue than choice silver.

Proverbs 24:3–5

3 Through wisdom is an house builded; And by understanding it is established:
4 And by knowledge ***shall [thy] chambers be filled With all precious and pleasant riches.***
5 A wise man *is strong.*

The Bible teaches us that through knowledge, understanding, and wisdom from God, God's people gain riches. The riches come directly from the wisdom God gives His child through His Word. So, riches are not bad in and of themselves.

If one has faith TOWARD God, then the money will not hurt his family but becomes like a "moat around his castle" (and his castle is his home). That is what the last verse means, "A wise man [whose chambers are filled with all precious and pleasant riches] is STRONG," i.e., safe.

The N.T. is even more explicit. In TRADEway meetings around the country, I will always find a pastor or two in the crowd who is learning to trade in the stock market. I'll ask one of them, "Pastor, can you show me a verse in the Bible that says if you skip next week's revival meeting, you are worse than an infidel?"

He says, "No sir, that's not in the Bible."

So, I ask another pastor, "Sir, can you show me a verse in the Bible that says if you don't tithe, you are worse than an infidel?"

"No, that's not in there."

Then I say, "But there IS a verse that says if you do not take care of your family financially, you are worse than an infidel and have denied the faith." And the phrase "the faith" is a word formula in the N.T. that simply means the whole of the Christian faith.

"Wow!" the crowd is thinking, "We've never seen that one."
And here it is:

1 Timothy 5:8

8 But if any provide not for his own, and specially for
those of his own house, he hath denied the faith, and is
worse than an infidel.

Then I will define wealth for the people in the room: "Wealth is
money left over after all your expenses are paid each month—it's
the extra saved month after month." I'll add, "Can you tell me how
you could obey the next two imperatives (N.T. commandments from
God) without creating some amount of wealth?"

2 Corinthians 12:14–15

14 ...for the children ought not to lay up for the parents,
but the parents for the children.

Then, the Bible takes it further in Proverbs and includes the
grandchildren!

Proverbs 13:22

22 A good *man* leaveth an inheritance to his children's
children: And the wealth of the sinner *is* laid up for the
just.

These three passages taken together show that God gives us imperatives to create wealth so that we can lay aside for our children and grandchildren, and take care of our family financially.

There is no contradiction in the Bible. Mammon is only bad if we "serve" it—if we love it and trust it more than God. If we consider it a gift from God and use IT to SERVE our FAMILY and others, then this is a holy work.

If our faith is toward the money, it kills our family. If our faith is toward God, the money is a safety net, a moat of protection around our castle.

With faith toward God, as Jesus exhorts us in the above passage from Matthew Chapter 6, we may, "Take no thought for your life, what ye shall eat, or what ye shall drink," etc. We don't have to worry.

God takes care of the birds of the air and feeds them; will He not also feed us?

> "Wherefore, if God so clothes the grass of the field, which to day is, and to morrow is cast into the oven, *shall he* not much more *clothe* you, O ye of little faith?"—**Matt. 6:30**

Not just "little faith," but little faith **toward** God! Our faith may sometimes be aimed at things, or money, but it *should* always be aimed **toward God.** Then we need not worry, and entrepreneurial fear shrinks! (This is one reason the "Protestant Ethic" built the great economies of Western society!)

"For after all these things do the Gentiles seek: for your heavenly Father knoweth that ye have need of all these things."—**Matt. 6:32**

Faith toward God can be summed up with Jesus's last teaching in this passage:

"But seek ye first the kingdom of God, and his righteousness; and all these things shall be added unto you."—Matthew 6:33

This is the perfect definition of *The Foundation of Faith Toward God.*

Chapter 13

The Doctrine of Baptisms

"Therefore leaving the principles of the doctrine of Christ, let us go on unto perfection; not laying again the foundation of repentance from dead works, and of faith toward God.
Of <u>the doctrine of baptisms</u>...."
—Hebrews 6:1–2

Our fourth Core Doctrine is the "doctrine of baptisms." Most people only think of one type of baptism—water baptism. Also, there is disagreement on the mode of baptism. Some churches sprinkle, some pour, and some immerse, but most believe water baptism is all there is.

Regrettably, some people believe (and even more sadly, some teach) that baptism in water—whether sprinkled, poured upon, or immersed—saves you, or is required for salvation. The topic of baptism can be confusing. We intend to help you decipher all of this, and more, within this chapter on the doctrine of baptisms.

Notice that I said baptism(s), plural. This is because Hebrew 6:2 speaks of "the doctrine of baptisms," which proves the Bible teaches more than one kind of baptism.

In fact, the Bible teaches seven different baptisms! This is a surprise to many Christians and to almost all outside the church.

Before we begin to teach the different types of baptism, we should assess one verse in particular, because it seems to teach that there is only one baptism. A wise old preacher once said, "It does not matter what the Bible says.... What matters is what the Bible MEANS." True. Usually when we miss the true meaning, we have not examined the context of the verse well enough. Here is the verse in question:

Ephesians 4:4, 5
4 There is one body, and one Spirit, even as ye are called in one hope of your calling.
5 One Lord, one faith, one baptism.

This verse does seem to teach there is only one baptism, upon first glance; however, if we examine the context, we find it is expressing that you only need to be baptized one time. You only have one Lord, there is only one true faith, and you only need to be baptized one time. (This is a good study of why context is important and how to use it when interpreting different verses or passages.) Let's look at the context. I'll make a few comments along the way.

Ephesians 4:1

> **1** I therefore, the prisoner of the Lord, beseech you that ye walk worthy of the vocation wherewith ye are called.

First, we need to know who "you" is in verse one. The context tells us **WHO** Paul wrote this letter to if we look back. In Ephesians 3:1, we find one hint. The letter is written predominately *to Gentiles*.

Ephesians 2:1 provides another clue. It is written *to "quickened" Gentiles (i.e., saved Gentiles).*

Chapter 1 tells us precisely who Paul wrote this to, in more detail:

Ephesians 1:1–7

> **1** Paul, an apostle of Jesus Christ by the will of God, *to the saints which are at Ephesus*, and to *the faithful in Christ Jesus.*

The Apostle Paul wrote the letter to "saints" in the church at Ephesus. He also wrote it to all the faithful in Christ. (We must interject here the Catholics make a "saint" to be a very special Christian, usually from the past, whereas the Bible usage of the word "saint" means simply, "any saved person.") So, Paul wrote this letter to "saved people" at Ephesus, and everywhere, who were predominately Gentiles, and who walked abiding IN Christ, and were therefore faithful to Him. And what did he say?

> **2** Grace *be* to you, and peace, from God our Father, and *from* the Lord Jesus Christ.

3 Blessed *be* the God and Father of our Lord Jesus Christ, who hath blessed us with all spiritual blessings in heavenly *places* in Christ.

These believers were blessed with ***all spiritual blessings*** in heavenly places, when they were called and regenerated by the Holy Spirit and placed into Christ (we will touch on what it means to be "in Christ" later).

Eph. 1:4 According as he hath chosen us in him before the foundation of the world, that we should be holy and without blame before him in love:
5 Having predestinated us unto the adoption of children by Jesus Christ to himself, according to the good pleasure of his will,
6 To the praise of the glory of his grace, wherein he hath made us accepted in the beloved.
7 In whom we have redemption through his blood, the forgiveness of sins, according to the riches of his grace.

Paul's letter is written to believers, chosen (elected) to be in Christ by the Father before the foundation of the world, and predestinated to be adopted into God's family (by Christ, unto the Father) according to the good pleasure of God's own will. So, the letter to the Ephesians is written to believers, the ones chosen by God to be saved out of a fallen race. It is not written to the lost world. The ***WHO*** in the passage, then, refers to believers.

Ephesians 4:1 tells us ***WHAT*** the chapter is talking about.

"I beseech you that ye walk worthy of the vocation wherewith ye are called."

The word "vocation" is *klēsis*, an invitation (figuratively)—a calling.

Paul, in Ephesians Chapter 4, is exhorting the predominately Gentile believers in Ephesus to walk WITHIN their calling—to utilize the gifts they were given to serve the Lord.

When the Holy Spirit calls you, He gives you the gifts that Jesus told Him to give you, so that you would be equipped for the exact purpose God called you to have on this earth.

The passage in Ch. 4 continues:

> **Ephesians 4:3** Endeavouring to keep the unity of the Spirit in the bond of peace.
> **4** *There is* one body, and one Spirit, even as ye are called in one hope of your calling;
> **5** One Lord, one faith, *one baptism*,
> **6** One God and Father of all, who *is* above all, and through all, and *in you all*.
> **7** But unto every one of us is *given grace according to the measure of the gift of Christ*.

The immediate context here speaks of Christians endeavoring to keep unity by walking in the Spirit. Then in vv. 4 and 5, it reveals the fact that all believers are united into one body, by the one true Holy Spirit, at the ONE time He called you with the effectual calling (on your spiritual birthday).

Now we know the context is speaking of what happens at the very first moment of your calling.

At this moment of awakening, you recognize only one Lord, Jesus Christ. You have only one faith, HIS faith, i.e., the faith OF Christ. And you are baptized into Christ (Spirit Baptism) only one time—you cannot be saved twice. (This is a very important theme fleshed out later in Chapter 6 of Hebrews, and discussed in Chapter 17.)

We see, in context, the passage is NOT teaching that there is only one KIND of baptism, but rather, you only experience Spirit Baptism ONCE.

Spirit Baptism is the most important of all seven types of baptism taught in the Bible, and we will discuss it fully, below.

The concept of the "one (Spirit) baptism" in Ephesians 4:3–7 is one of the most important ideas in the N.T. because Paul calls it a *mystery* that God sent him to teach the church. Spirit Baptism is what causes Christ to dwell in us by His Spirit, and this is all about "Christ in us, the hope of glory," the great mystery which the O.T. prophets looked into but could not understand for thousands of years. No one on earth understood it until Paul explained it through the inspiration of the Holy Spirit.

Verse 6 teaches us that God the Father, Who dwells outside of time and space, projects Himself into us, and literally indwells our bodies through the work and presence of the Holy Spirit, Who is *omnipresent*. This is made possible by the sacrificial death and resurrection of His Son, Jesus.

Verse 7 teaches us that at the same time we are regenerated and indwelt by the Holy Spirit, He does over 33 things to us and for us (we know this from various other Scriptures throughout the N.T.). This includes giving us grace and spiritual gifts according to the measure that Christ wanted us to have *for our journey through this life.* The next few verses speak of the giving of gifts.

> **Ephesians 4:8** Wherefore he saith, When he ascended up on high, he led captivity captive, and gave gifts unto men.

Verse 11 names some of just a few of the types of gifts given, and their purpose.

> **Ephesians 4:11** And he gave some, apostles; and some, prophets; and some, evangelists; and some, pastors, and teachers;
> **12** For the perfecting of the saints, for the work of the ministry, for the edifying of the body of Christ:
> **13** Till we all come in the unity of the faith, and of the knowledge of the Son of God, unto a perfect man, unto the measure of the stature of the fulness of Christ:

Verses 15–16 speak of the whole group of believers in all human history, as one body, of which Christ is the Head. Verse 16 speaks of the *different parts of the body exercising their appointed gifts*, so that the whole body is strengthened.

15 But speaking the truth in love, may grow up into him in all things, which is the head, *even* Christ:

16 From whom the whole body fitly joined together and compacted by that which every joint supplieth, according to the effectual working in the measure of every part, maketh increase of the body unto the edifying of itself in love.

Verses 22–24 reveal that a regenerated person is now two men. An *old man* (the corrupt fallen body we live in) and a *new man* (the real you, the man or woman which was born on your spiritual birthday, who is one with the Holy Spirit).

Ephesians 4:22 That ye put off concerning the former conversation the old man, which is corrupt according to the deceitful lusts;

23 And be **renewed in the spirit of your mind**;

24 And that ye **put on the new man**, which after God is created in righteousness and true holiness.

Verse 30 reveals the awesome truth that when we are regenerated, the *Holy Spirit seals Himself within our bodies*, and our bodies become the temple of the Living God! This is a seal that *cannot be broken* by any created thing, and the Holy Spirit remains in us until we meet Jesus, face to face some day.

30 And grieve not the holy Spirit of God, whereby *ye are sealed unto the day of redemption.*

The next three verses speak of some of the results of this NEW BIRTH, and the new man, *indwelt* by the Holy Spirit and *full of spiritual gifts.* For the first time we can be Christ-like. In fact, as long as we walk in the new man, we WILL be Christ-like because we will be holding His hand; our spirit will be one with the Holy Spirit within us.

> **32** And be ye kind one to another, tenderhearted, forgiving one another, even as God for Christ's sake hath forgiven you.
>
> **Ephesians 5:1** Be ye therefore followers of God, as dear children;
> **2** And walk in love, as Christ also hath loved us, and hath given himself for us an offering and a sacrifice to God for a sweetsmelling savour.

Two broad things are happening at the moment of regeneration, *(1) the baptism of the Holy Spirit* (i.e., the one-time indwelling, and *(2) the giving of spiritual gifts* and equipment the believer will utilize his whole life. Our topic now is the first thing: the baptism of the Holy Spirit. (We have already discussed the giving of spiritual gifts in Chapter 9.)

What is this *one baptism* that is of utmost importance? When the Scripture says "one baptism," it is not speaking in terms of *types* of baptisms, for there are several baptisms; but it is speaking in terms of the power and permanence of the *one-time indwelling and sealing, or baptism of the Holy Spirit* at the moment of salvation.

This is the first and most important baptism that is taught in the Scriptures, and we call it *"Spirit Baptism,"* theologically.

The Bible says in this context there is only *ONE baptism*, because this only happens *ONE time* in the life of the believer. It is a once-and-done event at the inception of every believer's regeneration.

Before we move on, let me explain the use of the phrase *"indwelling of the Spirit."* The phrase is a theological concept, or doctrine. The word "indwelling" is not actually found in the Bible (much like "trinity" or "rapture" are not, but which are also useful theological constructs), but the PRINCIPLE is taught throughout the N.T. (and even the O.T. where the indwelling was prophesied).

Here are just a few of the verses from which the principle is derived, and the word *"indwelling"* of the Holy Spirit is a very good word to use for the study of this concept. Each speaks of the Holy Spirit *"dwelling within"* (thus, indwelling) the believer from the time of the baptism of the Holy Spirit at his or her regeneration, or spiritual birthday.

I point this out because the "baptism" of the Holy Spirit is almost synonymous with the "indwelling" of the Holy Spirit because they happen at the same moment. The former is the CAUSE of the latter. Therefore, it is not out of place, nor confusing, to use these two terms interchangeably in most cases.

As you may remember, we have already discussed the "filling of the Holy Spirit" back in Chapter 8. It is very different, in that being "filled" is an imperative, i.e., a command from the Lord, and is active, whereas the indwelling is passive; in other words, it is something God does to us.

Indwelling of the Holy Spirit

Romans 8:9–11

9 But ye are not in the flesh, but in the Spirit, if so be that *the Spirit of God dwell in you.* Now if any man have not the Spirit of Christ, he is none of his.

10 And if Christ *be in you,* the body *is* dead because of sin; but the Spirit *is* life because of righteousness.

11 But if the Spirit of him that raised up Jesus from the dead *dwell in you*, he that raised up Christ from the dead shall also quicken your mortal bodies by *his Spirit that dwelleth in you*.

Think about this verse: "Now if any man have not the Spirit of Christ, he is none of his."—**Romans 8:9b**

This verse makes it clear that the indwelling is permanent, and happens at the moment of spiritual birth, i.e., when baptized by the Holy Spirit, because if you are NOT indwelt, you are NOT saved!

John 14:20

20 At that day ye shall know that I *am* in my Father, and *ye in me, and I in you.*

The Spirit Baptism immerses us into Christ, seals the Spirit of Christ within us, and connects us to the Father, to Jesus, and to every Christian throughout history.

John 14:23

23 Jesus answered and said unto him, If a man love me, he will keep my words: and my Father will love him, and *we will come unto him, and <u>make our abode with him</u>.*

Romans 8:1

1 *There is* therefore now no condemnation to *them which are in Christ Jesus,* who walk not after the flesh, but after the Spirit.

John 14:17

17 *Even* the Spirit of truth...ye know him; for he dwelleth with you, and *shall be in you.*

Acts 9:17

17 And Ananias went his way, and entered into the house; and putting his hands on him said, Brother Saul, the Lord, *even* Jesus, that appeared unto thee in the way as thou camest, hath sent me, that thou mightest receive thy sight, and be filled with the Holy Ghost.

There are several examples (such as Acts 9:17, above, and Acts 2:4, below) in the early stages of the Apostolic Age where the phrase "filled with the Holy Ghost" means that your body was "filled up" with Him when you were born again, at which time you received the *baptism of the Spirit.* This can be confusing, because in cases like these it does not refer to the theological idea of "being Spirit filled," but rather the doctrine of the "indwelling of the Spirit."

Adding to the confusion, in the very beginning of the Apostolic Age—which was almost totally Jewish—a few times the baptism of the Spirit was imparted to Jewish believers shortly after salvation by the laying on of hands by an apostle (such as with Ananias and Saul above). This practice stopped as the church became mostly Gentile and began to grow explosively (the apostles could not possibly get around to all the converts to lay hands on them by this time), and the sign gifts had by-and-large authenticated the Gospel message and messengers. After that, the born-again experience included the ***immediate baptism of the Holy Spirit*** (the indwelling) for each believer as in Acts 10, without the laying on of hands, and it has continued this way until the present time.

Below is another example where the phrase "filled with the Holy Ghost" actually means "indwelt" by the Holy Ghost. This is the initial "filling up" of the Holy Spirit when He comes to live in the body of the Christian. Jesus had prophesied this would happen after He ascended into heaven and sent the Comforter, Who had been with them, but Who now would be ***IN THEM***.

After the people who were already saved from the O.T. economy (like many of the disciples of John the Baptist and Jesus Christ) were indwelt after Pentecost, then later The Holy spirit began to fall upon people immediately ***AS they heard*** and believed and were saved. But in Acts 9:17 above, "filled" means ***indwelt*** for the first time, and forever.

Later these same people who had been indwelt once and for all could be "spirit filled" in the theological sense; in other words, they would not only have the Holy Spirit living within their bodies (the indwelling), but could also CHOOSE to be connected as one spirit with Him for power to evangelize the world (by becoming Spirit-filled). Being Spirit-filled was a moment-by-moment, willful decision of the believer, as it is now—this is what being "filled" is all about.

Therefore, theologically, we use the term *indwelling* to speak of the initial baptism of the Spirit at salvation. The indwelling includes the first time a person was "filled up" with the Holy Spirit permanently (as in the Acts chapter 2 passage below), the Holy Spirit being sealed within the believer, and the Holy Spirit connecting the believer to Jesus, to the Father, and to all other believers.

We use the phrase *"spirit filled"* in the sense of Eph. 5:18, "…Be filled with the Spirit," to describe the moment-by-moment choice a believer can make each day. The indwelling is permanent, is performed by God, and happens only once at Spirit Baptism. During the early transitional stages of the Book of Acts, the terminology can be confusing, but may be discerned by the context. Leter in the N.T., it is easier to distinguish between the indwelling and the filling of the Spirit. Just remember, the filling is a choice being made many times each day by the believer, and is something the believer desires and willfully chooses to do. The indwelling is "once and done." The following passage describes the first time believers were indwelt by the Holy Spirit, as Jesus had promised the apostles would happen.

Acts 2:1–4, 7-8

1 And when the day of Pentecost was fully come, they were all with one accord in one place.

2 And suddenly there came a sound from heaven as of a rushing mighty wind, and it filled all the house where they were sitting.

3 And there appeared unto them cloven tongues like as of fire, and it sat upon each of them.

4 And *they were all filled* with [indwelt by] the Holy Ghost, and began to speak with other tongues, as the Spirit gave them utterance....

7 And they were all amazed and marvelled, saying one to another, Behold, are not all these which speak Galilaeans?

8 And how hear we every man in our own tongue, wherein we were born?

"Filled" here is, in the Greek, *plēthō*, and "to fill up" is a perfect English translation.

However, in the following verse, a different word for "filled" is used of Jesus.

Luke 4:1

1 And Jesus being *full of the Holy Ghost* returned from Jordan, and was led by the Spirit into the wilderness.

plērēs, Gk. replete, or covered over; by analogy complete:—full.

This word is not used of the believer being filled with the Spirit, but only of Jesus being FULL of the Spirit. We have the Spirit *by measure;* He has the Spirit *without measure* (Ephesians 4:7; John 3:34, 35).

The following passages describe the *indwelling* of the Holy Spirit.

1 Corinthians 6:19

19 What? know ye not that your body is the temple of *the Holy Ghost which is in you*, which ye have of God, and ye are not your own?

2 Corinthians 4:16

16 For which cause we faint not; but though our outward man perish, yet the inward *man* is renewed day by day.

Colossians 2:10

10 And ye are *complete in him*, which is the head of all principality and power:

Since you are complete in him, you do not need a so-called "second blessing."

1 Corinthians 15:22

22 For as in Adam all die, even so *in Christ* shall all be made alive.

As the following verse in Romans chapter 8 teaches, a person cannot even BE saved *if not indwelt* by the Holy Spirit, so all true Christians are indwelt at the moment of salvation.

Romans 8:9

9 But ye are not in the flesh, but in the Spirit, if so be that the Spirit of God dwell in you. Now if any man have not the Spirit of Christ, *he is none of his*.

Colossians 3:10

10 And have put on the *new man*, which is renewed in knowledge after the image of him that created him.

The new man is your human spirit connected as *ONE with the Holy Spirit* Who dwells within you. He always lives in you (the indwelling), but you must make the choice to be *"filled"* with the Spirit, and thus connected as one with Him. In this mode, again, you cannot sin (1 John 5:18).

Now, here are verses that fall under the category, theologically, of being "Spirit filled." This first passage actually references both the *indwelling* and the *spirit filled experience*.

Ephesians 3:16–21

16 That he would grant you, according to the riches of his glory, to be *strengthened with might by his Spirit in the inner man;*
17 That Christ may *dwell in your hearts by faith*; that ye, being rooted and grounded in love,
18 May be able to comprehend with all saints what *is* the breadth, and length, and depth, and height;

Verses 16–18 reference the *indwelling Spirit*, which is something God did TO you once and for all at salvation (He entered your body).

Verses 19–21 reference the ***spirit filled*** experience, which is a choice of the believer to walk in this mode at any given moment in time, hand in hand with Christ (or not to).

> **19** And to know the love of Christ, which passeth knowledge, that ye might **<u>be filled</u> with all the fulness of God.**
> ***Eph. 3:20*** Now unto him that is able to do exceeding abundantly above all that we ask or think, according to ***the power that worketh in us,***
> **21** Unto him *be* glory in the church by Christ Jesus throughout all ages, world without end. Amen.

As you walk in the new man, filled with the Spirit, God gets the glory for good works which you may do (because you are not doing them in the flesh by yourself but in the Spirit together WITH Him).

Ephesians 4:24
24 And that ye ***put on the new man***, which after God is created in righteousness and true holiness.

It is a choice at any given moment to decide to be filled with the Spirit by becoming one with Christ; this is "putting on the new man." This is only possible because you have already been baptized by the Spirit into the body of Christ at the moment of your new birth (the indwelling).

Luke 1:67
67 And his father Zacharias was filled with the Holy Ghost, and prophesied, saying.

The above verse was before Pentecost; therefore, Zacharias was NOT indwelt, but he could be filled as all O.T. saints could be from time to time—very different than the benefit we have now through being permanently indwelt by the Spirit. The verse below, also before Pentecost, is a reference to John the Baptist being Spirit filled (but not indwelt).

Luke 1:15

15 For he shall be great in the sight of the Lord, and shall drink neither wine nor strong drink; and he ***shall be filled*** with the Holy Ghost, even from his mother's womb.

Acts 13:9–10

9 Then Saul (who also *is called* Paul), ***filled with the Holy Ghost***, set his eyes on him,

10 And said, O full of all subtilty and all mischief, *thou* child of the devil, *thou* enemy of all righteousness, wilt thou not cease to pervert the right ways of the Lord?

Paul was indwelt already, and permanently, but at this moment he was *choosing* to be *"**Spirit filled" for power*** to deal with Elymas the sorcerer. The important thing to notice is that in the early stages of the Apostolic era, when people were born again and baptized with the Spirit (indwelt), they sometimes spoke with tongues. When they are later "filled with the Spirit" for power, they do not speak with tongues. (This contradicts the false Pentecostal and charismatic teaching of the "second blessing.")

The example below shows this. The filling caused them not to speak with tongues, but *to be filled with the power of the Holy Spirit to speak the Word of God with boldness* (I need this often, especially as I step behind the pulpit to preach on Sunday mornings).

Acts 4:7–10, 31
7 And when they had set them in the midst, they asked, By what power, or by what name, have ye done this?
8 Then Peter, filled with the Holy Ghost, said unto them, Ye rulers of the people, and elders of Israel,
9 If we this day be examined of the good deed done to the impotent man, by what means he is made whole;
10 Be it known unto you all, and to all the people of Israel, that *by the name of Jesus Christ* of Nazareth, whom ye crucified, whom God raised from the dead, *even* by him doth this man stand here before you whole.
31 And when they had prayed, the place was shaken where they were assembled together; and they were all *filled with the Holy Ghost, and they spake the word of God with boldness.*

Ephesians 5:18
18 And be not drunk with wine, wherein is excess; but *be filled* with the Spirit;

"Be filled" is *present tense*, *imperative,* which is a command, and so you have the choice of your will to either be filled or choose to walk in the flesh. You make this decision every moment of every day, whereas the indwelling is a once-and-for-all sealing.

Acts 4:31–33

31 And when they had prayed, the place was shaken where they were assembled together; and they were all filled with the Holy Ghost, and they spake the word of God with boldness.

32 And the multitude of them that believed were of one heart and of one soul: neither said any *of them* that ought of the things which he possessed was his own; but they had all things common.

33 And with *great power gave the apostles witness* of the resurrection of the Lord Jesus: and great grace was upon them all.

They were "filled with the Spirit," no one spoke with tongues, and the power was for witnessing.

Acts 13:48–52

48 And when the Gentiles heard this, they were glad, and glorified the word of the Lord: and *as many as were ordained* to eternal life *believed*.

49 And the word of the Lord was published throughout all the region.

50 But the Jews stirred up the devout and honourable women, and the chief men of the city, and *raised persecution against Paul and Barnabas,* and expelled them out of their coasts.

51 But they shook off the dust of their feet against them, and came unto Iconium.

52 And the disciples were *filled with joy, and with the Holy Ghost.*

Again, this *filling was for witnessing in power*, and many were saved because of it. There was no speaking in tongues because this was not the baptism of the Spirit but the "filling of the Spirit" for power.

Now we will discuss the seven types of baptism taught in the Bible, beginning with the most important.

1. Spirit Baptism

The phrase "Spirit Baptism" is not in the Bible, but rather is a theological term for a doctrine found in both the Old and New Testaments.

The first mention of the concept of Spirit Baptism is found in the book of Joel, written more than 800 years before Jesus Christ was born in Bethlehem. In Chapter 2, the prophet begins to talk about the future coming of Israel's Messiah. The chapter refers primarily to the second coming of Christ at the end of the church age. However, there is a secondary application of the prophecy which has to do with the first advent, and we know this because the N.T. writers quoted Joel and interpreted the near prophecy as having to do with certain occurrences surrounding the first advent of Christ. But it is clear that the first couple of verses speak of the second coming (the "Day of the Lord") and Armageddon.

Joel 2:1–2

1 Blow ye the trumpet in Zion, and sound an alarm in my holy mountain: Let all the inhabitants of the land tremble: For the day of the Lord cometh, for *it is* nigh at hand;

2 A day of darkness and of gloominess, A day of clouds and of thick darkness, As the morning spread upon the mountains: A great people and a strong; There hath not been ever the like, Neither shall be any more after it, *Even* to the years of many generations.

Later in the passage we find:

Joel 2:27–28

27 And ye shall know that I *am* in the midst of Israel, And *that* I *am* the Lord your God, and none else: And my people shall never be ashamed.

28 And it shall come to pass afterward, *That* **I will pour out my spirit upon all flesh**; And your sons and your daughters shall prophesy, Your old men shall dream dreams, Your young men shall see visions.

This has an early fulfillment at Christ's first coming, and a latter fulfillment at His second coming in our future.

The early fulfilment is found in this passage quoted by Jesus Christ in the N.T.

John 14:16–21

16 And I will pray the Father, and he shall give you another Comforter [the Holy Spirit], that he may abide with you for ever;

17 *Even* the Spirit of truth; whom the world cannot receive, because it seeth him not, neither knoweth him: but ye know him; for he dwelleth with you, and ***shall be in you***.

This is Jesus's early teaching about the indwelling of the Holy Spirit. He spoke of a time when all who are saved will have the Holy Spirit sealed within them at the first moment of their salvation, and He will remain within them until the day of redemption (the Second Coming).

In the O.T., the Spirit would come upon people, but then He would later withdraw, then come upon them again for power. As Jesus said, "for He dwelleth WITH you…." King David said, "Take not thy Spirit from me," thus illustrating that the Holy Spirit did not permanently indwell O.T. saints.

However, Jesus said, "and He shall be IN you." This is one of the key things that marks the N.T. as different and superior to the O.T. economy—the indwelling of the saints.

Jesus goes on, speaking of the fact that He will soon be crucified, but after His ascension into heaven, He would send the Holy Spirit to be the Comforter for all believers.

John 14:18 I will not leave you comfortless: I will come to you.

19 Yet a little while, and the world seeth me no more; but ye see me: because I live, ye shall live also.

20 At that day ye shall know that I *am* in my Father, and ye in me, and I in you.

Jesus speaks more specifically about this in Chapter 16 of John.

John 16:5–7, 16, 28-33

5 But now I go my way to him that sent me; and none of you asketh me, Whither goest thou?

6 But because I have said these things unto you, sorrow hath filled your heart.

7 Nevertheless I tell you the truth; It is expedient for you that I go away: for if I go not away, ***the Comforter*** will not come unto you; ***but if I depart, I will send him unto you.***

16 A little while, and ye shall not see me: and again, a little while, and ye shall see me, because I go to the Father.

28 I came forth from the Father, and am come into the world: again, I leave the world, and go to the Father.

29 His disciples said unto him, Lo, now speakest thou plainly, and speakest no proverb.

30 Now are we sure that thou knowest all things, and needest not that any man should ask thee: by this we believe that thou camest forth from God.

31 Jesus answered them, Do ye now believe?

32 Behold, the hour cometh, yea, is now come, that ye shall be scattered, every man to his own, and shall leave me alone: and yet I am not alone, because the Father is with me.

33 These things I have spoken unto you, that in me ye might have peace. In the world ye shall have tribulation: but be of good cheer; I have overcome the world.

After Jesus died, was buried, and rose again the third day, He walked among His disciples for forty days, then He ascended into heaven. The clouds received Him out of their sight. During this event, Jesus spoke of a day—ten days in the future, at the Feast of Pentecost (50 days after His crucifixion)—when the Holy Spirit would come and permanently indwell believers for the first time. This would then become the first day of the church age, and to be indwelt by the Holy Spirit upon salvation would become the norm for N.T. believers from then until now.

Luke 24:46–53

46 And said unto them, Thus it is written, and thus it behoved Christ to suffer, and to rise from the dead the third day:

47 And that repentance and remission of sins should be preached in his name among all nations, beginning at Jerusalem.

48 And ye are witnesses of these things.

49 And, behold, *I send the promise of my Father upon you* [this is the promised indwelling of the Holy Spirit in the heart of believers]: but tarry ye in the city of Jerusalem, until ye *be endued with power from on high.*

50 And he led them out as far as to Bethany, and he lifted up his hands, and blessed them.

51 And it came to pass, while he blessed them, he was parted from them, and carried up into heaven.

52 And they worshipped him, and returned to Jerusalem with great joy:

53 And were continually in the temple, praising and blessing God. Amen.

This enduement of power from on high is recorded in the book of Acts, as we have seen already.

Acts 2:4

4 And they were all filled with the Holy Ghost, and began to speak with other tongues, as the Spirit gave them utterance.

There were Jews from all over the world visiting Jerusalem for Pentecost, and when Peter preached, every man heard the gospel in his own language. This was the apostolic gift of languages (i.e., tongues). These tongues were not gibberish but actual world languages, and people miraculously heard the gospel in their own language and were saved.

Acts 2:7–8

7 And they were all amazed and marvelled, saying one to another, Behold, are not all these which speak Galilaeans?

8 And how *hear we every man in our own tongue*, wherein we were born?

There has been a problem with the fact that in Greek the only word for "language" is "tongue," (*glossa*, in Greek). This Greek word is translated literally into "tongues" in the English Bible, and I personally feel a less literal and more natural translation would have been more helpful here, because in our English mind, we do not often call a language a "tongue."

In verse 8 above, it should say, "And how hear we every man in our own *language*, wherein we were born?"

Here is an example of the problem:

Acts 19:6

6 And when Paul had laid *his* hands upon them, the Holy Ghost came on them; and they spake with *tongues*, and prophesied.

The word for "tongue," in Greek, *glōssa*, means the actual *tongue*; but also, by implication, a *language* (specifically, one naturally unacquired). There is no other word than this for "language" in Greek.

We know it means languages in the context because the text names the various world languages of the day. Therefore, a more natural translation of Acts 19:6 would be:

"And when Paul had laid *his* hands upon them, the Holy Ghost came on them; and they spake with *known languages of the world*, and prophesied."

Instead, it was translated "tongues," and this has led some (through ignorance) to believe "tongues" in the Bible is gibberish. In reality, it should have been translated more plainly into the word "languages." They spoke in existing languages (not gibberish).

The next few verses named all the known world languages that were miraculously spoken by the disciples after the Holy Spirit indwelt them. The reason it was a miracle is because they had never studied these languages.

Acts 2:9
"Parthians, and Medes, and Elamites, and the dwellers in Mesopotamia, and in Judaea, and Cappadocia, in Pontus, and Asia...." etc. and many more.

The ability for these unlearned men to speak foreign languages that they had never studied, was a miracle. These were ***sign gifts*** given for a short time to authenticate their new message of the N.T. gospel, and the Kingdom of Christ, which would be replacing the O.T. economy of the Law of Moses. Of course, the Jews would never have believed their message without the signs and miracles to authenticate Jesus and His disciples.

When the people heard the men preaching with such joy, some believed they were drunk. Peter speaks up and corrects them, and this is where he quoted the O.T. prophet Joel.

Acts 2:13–19
13 Others mocking said, These men are full of new wine.

14 But Peter, standing up with the eleven, lifted up his voice, and said unto them, Ye men of Judaea, and all *ye* that dwell at Jerusalem, be this known unto you, and hearken to my words:

15 For these are not drunken, as ye suppose, seeing it is *but* the third hour of the day.

16 But this is *that which was spoken by the prophet Joel;*

17 And it shall come to pass in the last days, saith God, *I will pour out of my Spirit upon all flesh:* and your sons and your daughters shall prophesy, and your young men shall see visions, and your old men shall dream dreams:

18 And on my servants and on my handmaidens I will pour out in those days of my Spirit; and they shall prophesy:

19 And I will shew wonders in heaven above, and signs in the earth beneath; blood, and fire, and vapour of smoke.

Peter continued to preach quite a long message to these people.

Acts 2:22–24, 36–42

22 Ye men of Israel, hear these words; Jesus of Nazareth, a man *approved of God among you by miracles and wonders and signs*, which God did by him in the midst of you, as ye yourselves also know:

23 Him, being delivered by the determinate counsel and foreknowledge of God, ye have taken, and by wicked hands have crucified and slain:

24 Whom God hath raised up, having loosed the pains of death: because it was not possible that he should be holden of it.

36 Therefore let all the house of Israel know assuredly, that God hath made that same Jesus, whom ye have crucified, both Lord and Christ.

37 Now when they heard *this*, they were pricked in their heart, and said unto Peter and to the rest of the apostles, Men *and* brethren, what shall we do?

38 Then Peter said unto them, Repent, and be baptized every one of you in the name of Jesus Christ for the remission of sins, and ye shall receive the gift of the Holy Ghost.

39 For the promise is unto you, and to your children, and to all that are afar off, *even* as many as the Lord our God shall call.

40 And with many other words did he testify and exhort, saying, Save yourselves from this untoward generation.

41 Then they that gladly received his word were baptized: and the same day there were added *unto them* about three thousand souls.

42 And they continued stedfastly in the apostles' doctrine and fellowship, and in breaking of bread, and in prayers.

This was the beginning of the church age, on the day of Pentecost when the Holy Spirit first indwelt believers permanently.

The key components of church life today should be the same as those found in v. 42, "And they continued stedfastly in the apostles' doctrine and fellowship, and in breaking of bread, and in prayers." They also witnessed, giving the gospel to as many as the Lord led them to. The church programs included Bible study and preaching, fellowship, meals together, prayers, and telling people everywhere the good news of Christ dying for the sins of God's people.

In Acts Chapter 8, the apostles laid hands on Jewish people who had believed, and they were indwelt by the Holy Spirit. The laying on of hands was a Jewish tradition from O.T. times. As Peter continued to preach over the next weeks, Gentiles began to be saved in the same fashion, except there was no laying on of hands with them, since they were not Jews (we will discuss this in a later chapter). They were just indwelt the moment they heard the gospel and believed, and that is how it still works today.

The book of Acts is a transitional book, moving from a mostly Jewish group of believers with Jewish traditions, toward a mixed church with more Gentiles. Thus, we see the laying on of hands when Jews were saved, and then by Chapter 10, when Gentiles were saved, they were indwelt by the Holy Spirit as they heard the Word, with no laying on of hands. Here is an example of the Gentile, Cornelius, and his friends being saved.

Acts 10:21–22

21 Then Peter went down to the men which were sent unto him from Cornelius; and said, Behold, I am he whom ye seek: what *is* the cause wherefore ye are come?

22 And they said, Cornelius the centurion, a just man, and one that feareth God, and of good report among all the nation of the Jews, was warned from God by an holy angel to send for thee into his house, and to hear words of thee.

Peter came to Cornelius' house and preached Jesus to the Gentiles:

> **Acts 10:42** And he commanded us to preach unto the people, and to testify that it is he which was ordained of God *to be* the Judge of quick and dead.
>
> **43** To him give all the prophets witness, that through his name whosoever believeth in him shall receive remission of sins.
>
> **44** *While Peter yet spake these words, the Holy Ghost fell on all them which heard the word.*
>
> **45** And they of the circumcision which believed were astonished, as many as came with Peter, because that on the Gentiles also was poured out the gift of the Holy Ghost.
>
> **46** For they **heard them speak with tongues**, and magnify God. Then answered Peter,
>
> **47** Can any man forbid water, that these should not be baptized, which have received the Holy Ghost as well as we?
>
> **48** And he commanded them to be baptized in the name of the Lord. Then prayed they him to tarry certain days.

These were Gentile believers, and there was no laying on of hands—they heard the word, and the Holy Spirit came upon them and indwelt their bodies upon regeneration. Thus, again, Acts is a transitional book from O.T. to N.T., from law to grace, from the

Apostolic age to the church age, and from an early Jewish church to later, more predominately Gentile churches. Being a transitional book, it is NOT the best book for local churches to base their doctrinal stance upon. The pastoral epistles of 1 and 2 Timothy, Titus, etc. are better for the church age.

Later, when Paul went to Jerusalem, he recounted the story to the Jewish believers in the mother church:

Acts 11:11–18

11 And, behold, immediately there were three men already come unto the house where I was, sent from Caesarea unto me.

12 And the spirit bade me go with them, nothing doubting. Moreover these six brethren accompanied me, and we entered into the man's house:

13 And he shewed us how he had seen an angel in his house, which stood and said unto him, Send men to Joppa, and call for Simon, whose surname is Peter;

14 Who shall tell thee words, whereby thou and all thy house shall be saved.

15 *And as I began to speak, the Holy Ghost fell on them, as on us at the beginning.*

16 Then remembered I the word of the Lord, how that he said, *John indeed baptized with water; but ye shall be baptized with the Holy Ghost.*

17 Forasmuch then as *God gave them the like gift as he did unto us, who believed on the Lord Jesus Christ;* what was I, that I could withstand God?

18 When they heard these things, they held their peace, and glorified God, saying, ***Then hath God also to the Gentiles granted repentance unto life.***

These passages record some of the first believers, both Jew and Gentile, hearing that Jesus had died, was buried, and rose again to take their sins away, believing this, and instantly being indwelt by the Holy Spirit.

"Spirit Baptism" initiates and causes the "indwelling," therefore, they are, for all practical purposes, the same event.

The Holy Spirit places us "into Christ" and places Christ into us. After this, they were then baptized in water, picturing the Spirit Baptism that had already taken place.

Here is a good time to discuss why there is some confusion between Spirit Baptism and water baptism. We discussed in Chapter 9, above, that the word "baptism" in English is NOT a translation of the Greek word used—it is a transliteration. This means rather than translating the word, when the English Bible was first translated and printed, they simply made up a new English word that sounded like the Greek word.

The Greek word for "baptize" is:

Bap-ti´-zo; it means to *make whelmed.*

Websters defines *"whelmed" as*—to turn (something, such as a vessel) upside down, usually to cover something: cover or engulf completely.

This is first a nautical term. This is what happens when a ship sinks, it is "whelmed." It is completely surrounded in all directions with water. Or one could say when a space craft re-enters earth's atmosphere, it is "whelmed" with air. So, it really has nothing to do with water—***baptizo*** just means to be surrounded or engulfed by, or placed into something, or connected vitally to something or someone.

Since the translators didn't use the real meaning but they transliterated *"**baptizo**"* into "baptized," generations of English-speaking Christians have been confused. Many believed it just meant "dunked in water." Not so.

Spirit Baptism is when the Holy Spirit immerses us into Christ. It has nothing to do with water.

God is all around us, but after salvation, He is also IN us, so we are completely engulfed by Him—He in us and us in Him. This is what ***baptize*** means.

John the Baptist, the forerunner of Christ, spoke about the difference between water baptism (which he performed) and Spirit Baptism, which only Christ could accomplish (because it is spiritual).

Mark 1:6–8

6 And John was clothed with camel's hair, and with a girdle of a skin about his loins; and he did eat locusts and wild honey;

7 And preached, saying, There cometh one mightier than I after me, the latchet of whose shoes I am not worthy to stoop down and unloose.

8 I indeed have baptized you with water: but *he shall baptize you with the Holy Ghost.*

This is Spirit Baptism. What does it mean again?

Spirit Baptism: It means that upon hearing and believing the gospel, the believer would be *baptized*, by the Holy Spirit, into the body of Christ. This means He places you into Christ, He engulfs you, He whelms you, He enters your body and is sealed there forever. He connects you to God the Father, to Jesus, and to every Christian who ever lived, spiritually. The omnipresent Holy Spirit not only surrounds the believer but now also is SEALED WITHIN the believer.

Christ lives in our hearts by the Holy Spirit indwelling us (and so does the Father). For the Holy Spirit is the Spirit of the Father, and the Spirit of the Son. This is one of the most defining differences between how the O.T. saint lived and how we live now, permanently indwelt by the Holy Spirit. The baptism of the Holy Spirit gives us a towering advantage!

An important passage on *Spirit Baptism* is found in Romans Chapter 6.

Romans 6:3–6

3 Know ye not, that so many of us as were baptized into Jesus Christ were baptized into his death?

4 Therefore we are buried with him by baptism into death: that like as Christ was raised up from the dead by the glory of the Father, even so we also should walk in newness of life.

5 For if we have been planted together in the likeness of his death, we shall be also *in the likeness* of *his* resurrection:

6 Knowing this, that our old man is crucified with *him*, that the body of sin might be destroyed, that henceforth we should not serve sin.

There is no water here, therefore this passage is not discussing water baptism. This is all about a spiritual event—Spirit Baptism. We are placed into Christ by the Holy Spirit when He saved us. Now, we must understand that God is not bound by time. Once we are connected to Christ by Spirit Baptism, God can transcend time and take us back 2000 years to the time Jesus was on the cross and place us into Him spiritually.

When you are saved, you are thereby "baptized into (immersed into, or connected to) Jesus's death." When He died, your OLD MAN died with him. When He was buried, your OLD MAN was "buried with him by baptism into death." And, when Christ rose from the dead, you were in Him, and "like as Christ was raised up from the dead by the glory of the Father, even so YOU also are raised" a new man or woman. All of this happened to you at the moment of your salvation, and also transcended time back to the death, burial, and resurrection of Christ, because you were spiritually baptized into (immersed into, or connected to) Christ upon your regeneration. Yes, this is mystical, but it is also actually true, both from our in-time viewpoint, and God the Father's outside-of-time viewpoint.

You can now walk in newness of life due to Spirit Baptism. Verse 6 says that since your OLD MAN is (already) crucified with Christ, the body of sin (OLD MAN) has been destroyed, and so now you should not serve sin with your body.

None of this has anything to do with water; this is a spiritual event. It is part of "the operation of God." The Holy Spirit does the work of placing you into Christ, and He into you. When the Holy Spirit enters your body upon salvation, all of this is accomplished in the blink of an eye. In this sense, and this sense only, are you saved by baptism (Spirit Baptism).

You can see how some whole denominations are fooled by false preachers into believing that they are saved by *water baptism*, when really it is *Spirit Baptism* which saves us—the water baptism is a physical picture of this life-changing spiritual event, and you will understand this better when you get to point no. 4, below.

Paul's letter to the Galatians sheds further light on this truth.

Galatians 3:26–29
26 For ye are all the children of God by faith in Christ Jesus.
27 For *as many of you as have been baptized into Christ have put on Christ.*

28 There is neither Jew nor Greek, there is neither bond nor free, there is neither male nor female: for ye are all one in Christ Jesus.

29 And if ye *be* Christ's, then are ye Abraham's seed, and heirs according to the promise.

Because the Holy Spirit, dwelling within each of us, connects us to each other, to God, to Christ, because He is omnipresent, then we are all one in Christ.

The connection we have should cause complete unity within the body of Christ (however, our enemy Satan is always working to cause division).

1 Corinthians 12:11–13

11 But all these worketh that one and the selfsame Spirit....

12 For as the body is one, and hath many members, and all the members of that one body, being many, are one body: so also *is* Christ.

13 For ***by one Spirit are we all baptized into [immersed into; connected to] one body***, whether *we be* Jews or Gentiles, whether *we be* bond or free; and have been all made to drink into one Spirit.

And the Apostle Paul goes even deeper into this subject:

Colossians 2:12–15

12 Buried with him in baptism, wherein also ye are risen with *him* through the faith of the *operation of God*, who hath *raised him from the dead.*
13 And you, being dead in your sins and the uncircumcision of your flesh, hath he quickened [made alive] together with him, having forgiven you all trespasses;
14 Blotting out the handwriting of ordinances that was against us, which was contrary to us, and took it out of the way, nailing it to his cross;
15 *And* having spoiled principalities and powers, he made a shew of them openly, triumphing over them in it.

The same power (Greek, *dunamis*) which raised Jesus from the dead has raised up OUR NEW MAN. Resurrection power is what helps us to fight sin and walk as new men and women. We can only do this together with Christ.

Ephesians 3:20
20 Now unto him that is able to do exceeding abundantly above all that we ask or think, according to *the power [dunamis]* that worketh in us.

The best picture of us experiencing resurrection power and the faith OF Christ in the Bible is the famous story of Jesus coming to the disciples, walking on the water. As He approached their boat, He said:

Matthew 14:29–32

29 ...Come. And when Peter was come down out of the ship, he walked on the water, to go to Jesus.

30 But when he saw the wind boisterous, he was afraid; and beginning to sink, he cried, saying, Lord, save me.

31 And immediately Jesus stretched forth *his* hand, and caught him, and said unto him, O thou of little faith, wherefore didst thou doubt?

32 And when they were come into the ship, the wind ceased.

As long as Peter held Jesus's hand or gazed into His eyes, Peter could walk on water! Not by his own weak belief, but by the faith of Christ, which Jesus had given him. You are the same. The more moments you hold Jesus's hand throughout the day, being filled with the Spirit, the more power you have against sin. This means you can accomplish more powerful things that really matter in eternity!

The great mystery which Paul spoke of, which the O.T. prophets looked into as a glass darkly but could not understand, was Spirit Baptism. It is the idea of Christ in us.

Colossians 1:25–27

25 Whereof I [Paul] am made a minister, according to the dispensation of God which is given to me for you, to fulfil the word of God;

26 *Even* **the mystery** which hath been hid from ages and from generations, but now is made manifest to his saints:

27 To whom God would make known what *is* the riches of the glory of this mystery among the Gentiles; which is Christ in you, the hope of glory:

The only hope you have in this life, of bringing glory to God through the life you live, is "Christ in you, the hope of glory." The only reason you can please God is because you are in Christ and He in you. The only way you do anything truly good in a holy God's eyes is when you do it together with Him. None of this is possible without the miracle of *Spirit Baptism* which God performed upon you. The Holy Spirit is the Great Connector. Jesus meant it literally when He said:

John 15:5

5 I am the vine, ye *are* the branches: He that abideth in me, and I in him, the same bringeth forth much fruit: for *without me ye can do nothing.*

But, WITH Him, "all things are possible" (Matt. 19:26).

Spirit Baptism is the most important of the seven baptisms taught in the Bible. Now let's move to the next one, John's baptism.

2. John's Baptism—Baptism unto Repentance

John the Baptist was the forerunner of Christ. He announced Jesus to the world as "The true Lamb of God."

John 1:29

The next day John seeth Jesus coming unto him, and saith, Behold the Lamb of God, which taketh away the sin of the world.

The word "world" here in the Greek is quite different than the English word "world." It is *kŏsmŏs,* which means, God's orderly *arrangement of the creation.* Our English word Cosmos comes from it. Websters defines "cosmos" as: "an orderly harmonious systematic universe."

John said that Jesus had come to take away the sin of the *kosmos.*

This same word is used a little later in John, in the more famous John 3:16.

John 3:16
For God so loved the *world*, that he gave his only begotten Son, that whosoever believeth in him should not perish, but have everlasting life.

God so loved the *kosmos*, that He gave His only begotten Son…. God so loved His orderly, harmonious, systematic universe, that He gave His only begotten Son to die to restore it and remove the sin from it. It is about FAR more than just you and me—He died for the whole *kosmos*, to restore the original order to His universe.

John the Baptist knew exactly what the mission of the Messiah was, and he announced His arrival on the planet. He warned the Jews to get ready to receive Him.

John also proclaimed this about Christ:

Matthew 3:11–12

11 I indeed baptize you with water unto repentance: but he that cometh after me is mightier than I, whose shoes I am not worthy to bear: *he shall baptize you with the Holy Ghost, and with fire.*

12 Whose fan *is* in his hand, and he will throughly purge his floor, and *gather his wheat into the garner*; but he will *burn up the chaff with unquenchable fire.*

John the Baptist just introduced three different types of baptism! His own baptism, the baptism of John, who, (1) baptized with water unto repentance. He said Jesus would (2) baptize you with the Holy Ghost, and (3) baptize you with fire.

We have already studied Spirit Baptism, we shall study baptism by fire later, and for now let's look at John's water baptism unto repentance.

Matthew 3:1–6

1 In those days came John the Baptist, preaching in the wilderness of Judaea,

2 And saying, *Repent ye: for the kingdom of heaven is at hand.*

3 For this is he that was spoken of by the prophet Esaias, saying, The voice of one crying in the wilderness, Prepare ye the way of the Lord, make his paths straight.

4 And the same John had his raiment of camel's hair, and a leathern girdle about his loins; and his meat was locusts and wild honey.

5 Then went out to him Jerusalem, and all Judaea, and all the region round about Jordan,

6 And *were baptized of him in Jordan*, _confessing their sins._

John's message was *"repent for the Kingdom of God is at hand."* People from the surrounding area came out to be baptized by him in the Jordan river, *"confessing their sins."*

Therefore, John's baptism was more like the O.T. bathing of the priests' hands prior to offering sacrifices in the wilderness tabernacle, or later in the temple. The purifying water used in the bathing made possible the ceremonial cleansing of the body which was to be done only upon a priest who had a heart of repentance and confession of sin.

The High Priest would enter the Holy of Holies once per year on the Day of Atonement on the 10th of Tishri (September/October on the Gregorian calendar. It is the first month of the Jewish year, and seventh month according to the traditional biblical calendar), around the time of the autumnal equinox. He would enter and sprinkle the blood of the sin offering as an atonement (covering) for himself and the people. In preparing for this holy work, he would first cleanse himself with the water of purification.

In his scholarly work, *New Testament History*, F. F. Bruce gives us a glimpse at what this bathing might have looked like:

> To perform this solemn ceremony he had to be in a state of complete ritual purity, and in later times he was

isolated for the seven days preceding the Day of Atonement to guard against accidental contamination, and perhaps even sprinkled twice [on the third and seventh days] with purifying water during the period....[44]

Bruce goes on to explain where the water of purification came from:

Another, but more infrequent, ceremony which called for the presence and action of the high priest in person was the slaying of the red heifer, in accordance with the ritual prescribed in Numbers 19. When the red heifer was slaughtered, her body was completely incinerated; the *ashes were stored in a suitable place and used from time to time for the preparation of purifying water*, the sprinkling of which was necessary for the *removal of ceremonial defilement,* such as might be contracted through contact with a corpse. The ashes of one heifer would suffice for the preparation of purifying water for several years.... The ashes of the last red heifer to be killed [by Samaritan priests] were preserved for 250 years, until the end of the sixteenth century. According to the Mishnah, the last Jewish high priest to slay the red heifer was Ishae ben Phiabi (c. A.D. 58–60)....[45]

---

[44] F. F. Bruce, *New Testament History*, (Doubleday–Galilee edition: 1980), pp. 56–57.

[45] Ibid.

These ashes would have been the ones used in the water of purification for the High Priest who offered the last sacrifice on the same day at the same moment Jesus Christ was crucified. Bruce explains how John's baptism had some relation, though distant, to the cleansing with water that the priest performed upon themselves before the sin offerings were made.

> The baptism of John was a new thing in Israel, although it had antecedents in some degree. Cleansing lustrations, by means of the water of purification and otherwise, were prescribed in the Law....
>
> A further analogy to John's baptism may be sought in the practice of Jewish proselyte baptism. A Gentile who was converted to Judaism had to be circumcised (if he was a male) and to offer a special sacrifice in the Temple (while it stood), and also to undergo *a ceremonial bath....* [This was a *self-baptism*, the (origin) date of which is disputed...but must have gone back to the beginning of the Christian era....] But John's baptism was distinctive in that he administered it to others, and in its eschatological [end-times] significance.
>
> Ez. 36.25 promised that in the dawn of the new age, the God of Israel would purify his people from the defilement with the clean water and give them a new heart and a new spirit—his own spirit.
>
> Those who heeded John's call to repentance and accepted baptism at his hands would form the righteous remnant of the end-time, the "people prepared" whom John was charged "to make ready for the Lord" (Lk. 1:17). This is

probably the point of Josephus's statement that John called upon his hearers "to come together by baptism."...

Jesus accepted John's baptism as from God (Matt. 3:15).[46]

I have always been fascinated by John's baptism, and pondered what it was, what it meant, and how it could be contrasted with Christian water baptism. Christian water baptism is a picture of the Spirit Baptism which had already taken place in the life of the believer upon his spiritual birthday. What was John's baptism all about?

I think Bruce is getting warm. It seems likely that John the Baptist, being raised by his priestly father, Zecharias, would have learned of the water of purification in the priestly cleansing. He would have known about the self-baptism of proselyte Jews. He would have also been familiar with Ezekiel 36:25:

Ezekiel 36:24–28

24 For I will take you from among the heathen, and gather you out of all countries, and will bring you into your own land.

25 Then will I *sprinkle clean water upon you*, and ye shall be clean: from all your filthiness, and from all your idols, will I cleanse you.

26 *A new heart also will I give you, and a new spirit* will I put within you: and *I will take away the stony*

---

[46] Ibid. p. 159.

heart out of your flesh, and I will give you an heart of flesh.

27 And *I will put my spirit within you*, and cause you to walk in my statutes, and ye shall keep my judgments, and do *them*.

28 And ye shall dwell in the land that I gave to your fathers; and ye shall be my people, and I will be your God.

This is an O.T. prophecy of the born-again experience that Jesus Christ would make possible. "I will sprinkle clean water upon you and you shall be clean," together with the idea of the proselyte self-baptism, may have given John the idea of baptizing in the Jordan river, for outward ceremonial cleansing that accompanied the inward cleansing of repentance and confession of sin.

He would also have been familiar with the passage that spoke of the forerunner of the Messiah:

Malachi 4:5–6

5 Behold, I will send you Elijah the prophet Before the coming of the great and dreadful day of the Lord:

6 And he shall turn the heart of the fathers to the children, And the heart of the children to their fathers, Lest I come and smite the earth with a curse.

These were the last words recorded from Malachi, before the 406-year silent period prior to the first advent of Christ!

John the Baptist knew this was a reference to himself, because he had the *sign gift* of prophecy, as did his father. Here is John the Baptist's testimony that Jesus is the Christ.

John 1:19–36

19 And this is the record of John, when the Jews sent priests and Levites from Jerusalem to ask him, Who art thou?

20 And he confessed, and denied not; but confessed, I am not the Christ.

21 And they asked him, What then? Art thou Elias? And he saith, I am not. Art thou that prophet? And he answered, No.

22 Then said they unto him, Who art thou? that we may give an answer to them that sent us. What sayest thou of thyself?

23 He said, I *am* the voice of one crying in the wilderness, Make straight the way of the Lord, as said the prophet Esaias.

24 And they which were sent were of the Pharisees.

25 And they asked him, and said unto him, Why baptizest thou then, if thou be not that Christ, nor Elias, neither that prophet?

26 John answered them, saying, I baptize with water: but there standeth one among you, whom ye know not;

27 He it is, who coming after me is preferred before me, whose shoe's latchet I am not worthy to unloose.

28 These things were done in Bethabara beyond Jordan, where John was baptizing.

29 The next day John seeth Jesus coming unto him, and saith, ***Behold the Lamb of God***, which taketh away the sin of the world.

30 This is he of whom I said, After me cometh a man which is preferred before me: for he was before me.

31 And I knew him not: but that he should be made manifest to Israel, therefore am I come baptizing with water.

32 And John bare record, saying, I saw the Spirit descending from heaven like a dove, and it abode upon him.

33 And I knew him not: but he that sent me to baptize with water, the same said unto me, Upon whom thou shalt see the Spirit descending, and remaining on him, the same is he which baptizeth with the Holy Ghost.

34 And ***I saw, and bare record that this is the Son of God.***

35 Again the next day after John stood, and two of his disciples;

36 And looking upon Jesus as he walked, he saith, ***Behold the Lamb of God!***

John, the forerunner, prophesied by Malachi 406 years earlier, was preparing the Jews for their true sacrificial Lamb, Jesus Christ who was about to come on the scene and be offered as the true inward spiritual sacrifice which **REMOVED** sin, rather than just covering it. They needed their hearts ready to meet their Messiah.

John the Baptist preached as a prophet, with power bringing conviction of sin to the hearers. Many fathers repented from their sins and began to care for their children and be the spiritual leaders they should be, and many sons repented and had their hearts turned back to loving their parents and honouring them. In the end, most of the nation did not repent and turn to their Messiah; therefore, Malachi's prophecy of being smitten with a curse (4:6) came to pass in A.D. 70 when Titus and the Roman army destroyed Jerusalem, and again when Hitler killed six to eight million Jews during WWII.

The Jews sealed their fate when they responded to Pilate, who wished to release Jesus, an innocent man, with these words:

Matthew 27:24–26

24 When Pilate saw that he could prevail nothing, but *that* rather a tumult was made, he took water, and washed *his* hands before the multitude, saying, I am innocent of the blood of this just person: see ye *to it*.
25 Then answered all the people, and said, ***His blood be on us, and on our children.***
26 Then released he Barabbas unto them: and when he had scourged Jesus, he delivered *him* to be crucified.

Malachi prophesied the curse upon the Jews and onto their children, all the way out to Hitler, for killing Jesus. Of course, the Roman (Gentile) government contributed to His death also. (It ceased to exist as a nation several hundred years later. Its zenith of power was when Christ walked this earth, and its power went downhill from there.)

Yet, God turned this to the Jews favor, because the world felt so badly toward the Jews after WWII that they gave them a portion of their land in the Middle East to return to and have their own nation of Israel restored. This, too, was fulfillment of prophecy.

John's water baptism of repentance pictured the cleansing that comes from repentance and the proper sacrifice. We might ask, why was Jesus Himself baptized by John? Did He need cleansing? Did He need to repent?

Here is the account of Jesus's baptism. Jesus asked John to baptize Him, and John at first said, "No."

Matthew 3:14–17

14 But John forbad him, saying, I have need to be baptized of thee, and comest thou to me?

15 And Jesus answering said unto him, Suffer *it to be so* now: for thus it **becometh us to fulfil all righteousness**. Then he suffered [allowed] him.

16 And Jesus, when he was baptized, went up straightway out of the water: and, lo, the heavens were opened unto him, and he saw the Spirit of God descending like a dove, and lighting upon him:

17 And lo a voice from heaven, saying, This is my beloved Son, in whom I am well pleased.

Jesus's ministry began that day. Jesus said His own baptism had a different purpose than any other, for He was the only man who was "tempted in all points as we, and yet without sin." He was the only man who could fulfill the law of Moses in His life perfectly, and part of that was to be cleansed according to the Law of Moses before He began His priestly ministry on earth. The **baptism of John** fulfilled this requirement.

Leviticus 8:4–6

4 And Moses did as the Lord commanded him; and the assembly was gathered together unto the door of the tabernacle of the congregation.
5 And Moses said unto the congregation, This *is* the thing which the Lord commanded to be done.
6 And Moses brought Aaron and his sons, and ***washed them with water.***

Once the baptism was complete, the Holy Spirit descended from Heaven and indwelt Jesus, providing the added power He would need in His ministry, and the Father's voice was heard from heaven saying, "This is my beloved Son, in whom I am well pleased." ***He had begun to fulfil all righteousness*** in his baptismal cleansing, and He would complete this process by keeping the law perfectly, His whole life, without sin.

He was now ready to serve His people, to walk with and teach His disciples who would one day turn the world upside down (or perhaps right side up) with the gospel, and then ultimately to die on the cross as the perfect Lamb, without blemish, for the sins of God's people of every generation.

Acts 19:3–5

3 And he said unto them, Unto what then were ye baptized? And they said, Unto John's baptism.
4 Then said Paul, John verily ***baptized with the <u>baptism of repentance</u>, saying unto the people, that they should believe on him which should come after him, that is, on Christ Jesus.***
5 When they heard *this*, they were baptized in the name of the Lord Jesus.

John's baptism, a baptism which was a picture of the true repentance of the heart, therefore prepared the people of God and their Messiah to meet each other.

3. Baptism by Fire—the Day of the Lord

John the Baptist said:

> I indeed baptize you with water unto repentance: but he that cometh after me...he shall baptize you with the Holy Ghost, **and _with fire_.—*Matthew 3:11*

The next verse explains what this **baptism by fire** entails. It also shows that baptism is not just about water. It is about anything that engulfs you! In this case, fire.

> **12** Whose fan *is* in his hand, and he will throughly purge his floor, and **gather his wheat into the garner;** but he will **burn up the chaff with unquenchable fire.—Matthew 3:12**

Jesus is coming back again someday to raise the dead at the first resurrection, and after that to rapture His church, the Bride of Christ, and to destroy His and His people's enemies at the battle of Armageddon.

Jesus told a story about a man who planted a field. A bad man came in by night and sowed weed seeds in his field. The wheat and the tares came up together. Jesus's disciples asked Him to explain the story, and they asked Him, "Did you plant bad seed?"

First, He said, "No, I don't plant bad seed. I plant only the wheat." Jesus said, "The enemy who came by night is Satan—he planted the tares in the field," and the field pictured the world. Jesus said they would grow up together, and then, on the last day, the angels would separate the wheat from the tares. He would place the wheat in His father's barn (heaven); He would bind the tares in bundles and burn them (hell).

This is what John the Baptist was prophesying when he said:

> "Whose fan *is* in his hand, and he will throughly purge his floor, and **gather his wheat into the garner; but he will burn up the chaff with unquenchable fire**."
>
> **—Matthew 3:12**

The baptism of fire relates to all the events surrounding the second coming of Christ to the earth, and especially the resulting judgment.

Paul wrote:

1 Thessalonians 4:14–18

14 For if we believe that Jesus died and rose again, even so them also which sleep in Jesus will God bring with him.

15 For this we say unto you by the word of the Lord, that we which are alive *and* remain unto the coming of the Lord shall not prevent [Gk. precede] them which are asleep.

16 For the Lord himself shall descend from heaven with a shout, with the voice of the archangel, and with the trump of God: and the dead in Christ shall rise first: **17** Then we which are alive *and* remain shall be caught up together with them in the clouds, to meet the Lord in the air: and so shall we ever be with the Lord.
18 Wherefore comfort one another with these words.

The Lord will return at the second coming, the first resurrection will occur first, and then the rapture (which cannot precede the first resurrection that will occur at the end of the church age). The Lord divides the sheep/wheat from the goats/tares, destroys the enemies of God, and remaining Jews and Gentiles who receive Him will usher in the Millennial Kingdom, where Christ literally reigns from King David's throne in Jerusalem for 1,000 years.

The *baptism by fire*—the last three and one-half years of the seven-year tribulation period—will be devastating for unbelievers.

Revelation 6:13–17

13 And the stars of heaven fell unto the earth, even as a fig tree casteth her untimely figs, when she is shaken of a mighty wind.
14 And the heaven departed as a scroll when it is rolled together; and every mountain and island were moved out of their places.
15 And the kings of the earth, and the great men, and the rich men, and the chief captains, and the mighty men, and every bondman, and every free man, hid

themselves in the dens and in the rocks of the mountains;

16 And said to the mountains and rocks, Fall on us, and hide us from the face of him that sitteth on the throne, and from the wrath of the Lamb:

17 For the great day of his wrath is come; and who shall be able to stand?

Dear reader, if you have any doubt in your mind that you have received Jesus Christ as your personal Lord and Saviour, then please listen to the still, quiet voice of the Holy Spirit as He points you to the face of the Great Shepherd and gives you ears to hear Him say, "To as many as receive Him give I the power to become the sons of God, even to those who believe on His Name"—**John 1:12.**

If you desire the Lamb of God, then the Holy Spirit has already called you! Just respond as a bride to the Bridegroom and receive Him into your heart. Spirit Baptism, being in Christ, is the only protection from the ***baptism by fire*** that is coming. The forces of Armageddon are already lining up across the world; Jesus may be standing at the threshold of the door, preparing His return right now! Be ready!

The Apostle Paul warned:

1 Thessalonians 5:1–6

1 But of the times and the seasons, brethren, ye have no need that I write unto you.

2 For yourselves know perfectly that the day of the Lord so cometh as a thief in the night.

3 For when they shall say, Peace and safety; then sudden destruction cometh upon them, as travail upon a woman with child; and they shall not escape.

4 But ye, brethren, are not in darkness, that that day should overtake you as a thief.

5 Ye are all the children of light, and the children of the day: we are not of the night, nor of darkness.

6 Therefore let us not sleep, as *do* others; but let us watch and be sober.

2 Timothy 3:1–7

1 This know also, that in the last days perilous times shall come.

2 For men shall be lovers of their own selves, covetous, boasters, proud, blasphemers, disobedient to parents, unthankful, unholy,

3 Without natural affection, trucebreakers, false accusers, incontinent, fierce, despisers of those that are good,

4 Traitors, heady, highminded, lovers of pleasures more than lovers of God;

5 Having a form of godliness, but denying the power thereof: from such turn away.

6 For of this sort are they which creep into houses, and lead captive silly women laden with sins, led away with divers lusts,

7 Ever learning, and never able to come to the knowledge of the truth.

2 Thessalonians 2:8–13 (The Rise of the Antichrist)

8 And then shall that Wicked be revealed, whom the Lord shall consume with the spirit of his mouth, and shall destroy with the brightness of his coming:

9 *Even him*, whose coming is after the working of Satan with all power and signs and lying wonders,

10 And with all deceivableness of unrighteousness in them that perish; because they received not the love of the truth, that they might be saved.

11 And for this cause God shall send them strong delusion, that they should believe a lie:

12 That they all might be damned who believed not the truth, but had pleasure in unrighteousness.

13 But we are bound to give thanks alway to God for you, brethren beloved of the Lord, because God hath from the beginning chosen you to salvation through sanctification of the Spirit and belief of the truth:

4. Water Baptism

Matthew 28:18–20

18 And Jesus came and spake unto them, saying, All power is given unto me in heaven and in earth.

19 Go ye therefore, and teach all nations, *baptizing them in the name of the Father, and of the Son, and of the Holy Ghost:*

20 Teaching them to observe all things whatsoever I have commanded you: and, lo, I am with you alway, *even* unto the end of the world. Amen.

The great commission is for the church to witness to those the Holy Spirit leads her to. As people are regenerated and experience Spirit Baptism, being placed into the body of Christ spiritually, the first step of obedience is to be baptized in water. *Water baptism pictures the Spirit Baptism* which the believer has already experienced. After salvation, every believer should be baptized in water.

Here's why. When you step into the water, it pictures that you died with Christ (because your sins were in Him when He died). When you go under the water, it pictures that you were buried with Him, and when you rise out of the water it pictures that you are risen with Him unto NEW LIFE. It is a beautiful picture of the fact that THE NEW MAN WAS BORN when you came to know Christ personally. The old man was a slave to Satan and sin but is crucified now. The new man serves Christ as Lord. Water baptism, therefore, pictures the born-again experience and the spiritual resurrection of the new man. This speaks of the resurrection power that you have within you, to live your new life now.

2 Corinthians 5:17–18

17 Therefore if any man *be* in Christ, *he is* a new creature: old things are passed away; behold, all things are become new.

18 And all things *are* of God, who hath reconciled us to himself by Jesus Christ, and hath given to us the ministry of reconciliation.

Spirit Baptism is the Holy Spirit placing you into Christ. Once in Him, you instantly become a *new creation*. (God did not fix up your old man; He crucified him with Christ and birthed a NEW MAN in you.) Now your old self is passed away with his sin habits and worldly intentions. A new man, the real you, is born. All things become new as you have a personal relationship with God. Bible study is Him talking to you; prayer is you talking to Him. Over time your relationship grows, your desires change, and your goals in life are on a higher plane.

Water baptism is the first step of obedience for a new Christian, and it is a beautiful physical picture of what has happened to us spiritually. It is like "putting on Christ's uniform" and being proud of it and showing this publicly to everyone.

The Proper Mode of Water Baptism

The church has fought over the correct mode of baptism for thousands of years, whether to sprinkle, pour, or submerge under the water.

The Scriptures make the choice clear. This is a story of the Ethiopian eunuch who had been studying the Scriptures in Isaiah 53. He asked Philip about how to properly interpret the passage.

Acts 8:35–38
35 Then Philip opened his mouth, and began at the same scripture, and preached unto him Jesus.
36 And as they went on *their* way, they came unto a certain water: and the eunuch said, See, *here is* water; what doth hinder me to be baptized?

37 And Philip said, If thou believest with all thine heart, thou mayest. And he answered and said, I believe that Jesus Christ is the Son of God.

38 And he commanded the chariot to stand still: and they *went down both into the water*, both Philip and the eunuch; and he baptized him.

39 And when they were *come up out of the water*, the Spirit of the Lord caught away Philip, that the eunuch saw him no more: and he went on his way rejoicing.

The preacher and the convert both went down into the water and came up out of it. This is immersion—not pouring, not sprinkling.

The picture that water baptism paints can only be painted on the canvas of immersion under the water and rising up out of the water. Try picturing Jesus's death, burial, and resurrection with just a sprinkle!

What about sprinkling babies? I saw a fascinating gospel tract one time. On the outside it said, "Everything the Bible teaches about sprinkling babies!" When I opened it, the inside pages were blank white paper. I laughed and thought, *that's exactly right*. The Bible says nothing about it.

Is Water Baptism Necessary for Salvation?

Water baptism does not save you, nor is it necessary for salvation. It is a picture of the Spirit Baptism which has already occurred when you were called and regenerated by the Holy Spirit. Water baptism is administered AFTER salvation. *Spirit Baptism* is necessary for salvation, and water baptism pictures it perfectly.

I have many Church of Christ friends here in the South. I say "in the South" because northern Churches of Christ are different—they are more like Christian Churches in the South (TCU in Ft. Worth is one of the biggest colleges). The old-line southern Churches of Christ believe water baptism is required for salvation. Not only that, but it must be THEIR water, in their church building.

I cut my teeth as a new Christian knocking on doors and sitting on porches with elderly Church of Christ women—boy did they know their Scriptures. They believed you could lose your salvation, they believed you had to be baptized in their water to be saved, but they always made great citizens and businesspeople because they believed if they mistreated you, they could lose their salvation!

I have spent hours showing them scores and scores of eternal security passages which prove you cannot lose your salvation. Some would listen; others just quoted their one or two verses attempting to make the Bible say what they wanted it to say.

I would ask them, "If you have to be baptized in water to be saved, how did the thief on the cross beside Jesus enter Paradise with Him that very day? He died on the cross before dusk, and never had a chance to be baptized."

The honest ones would answer, "I don't know, maybe there was a special situation for him since Christ promised it." The dishonest ones would say, "That was in the O.T. economy. The church did not start until 50 days later at Pentecost."

Well, that sounds good, but the problems with it are legion. There are hundreds of Scriptures which teach salvation by grace through faith alone apart from the works of the law, and scores which teach eternal security of the believer, or many teaching Spirit Baptism. The bottom line is that maintaining a stance that it was easier for the thief on the cross to get into heaven under the O.T. economy (by having to keep every point of the law) than under the N.T. economy of salvation by grace, through the blood of Jesus plus nothing, would be subject to ridicule by anyone who actually knows their Bible.

This would mean that the thief that day would have it far better than a thief fifty days later, after Pentecost, in the church age. The O.T. thief could just waltz right into heaven without having offered the proper Levitical sacrifices, without having attended the feasts, with no grace, but all law, yet without having to be baptized in water! Yet, fifty days later the thief would not make it to Paradise, even if he were covered by the blood of Christ but never got dunked in Church of Christ water at a Church of Christ building! Their argument simply falls apart, as you can see.

And, what about a person who found a Bible in the desert, read it, believed, and received Christ, but could find no Church of Christ water to be baptized in? Or a person saved on their death bed, like my father-in-law, or others (which I have seen take place several times)? Would they all go to hell due to lack of Church of Christ water?

It is amazing what people will believe just to remain part of their social club. I don't mean to be unkind, for I have many Church of Christ friends, but when we grow up, we should all be willing to lay aside the wrong, unreasonable, and unbiblical things that our denominations teach. Much of it comes from the social clubs at the seminaries. Grown men and women are afraid they will be cast out if they question any unreasonable belief and ask for a plain answer. The peer pressure is worse than on a seventh-grade playground.

Churches that teach that water baptism is necessary for salvation base their entire belief system upon one or two verses, like v. 16 below.

Mark 16:15–16

15 And he said unto them, Go ye into all the world, and preach the gospel to every creature.

16 He that believeth *and is baptized* shall be saved; but he that believeth not shall be damned.

The problem is that their interpretation would contradict hundreds of verses in the Bible that teach salvation is by grace through faith alone, and not of works. Water baptism is a good work—the first good work that a saved person should do. If water baptism *DOES* the saving, then we are saved by works. Yet the Scriptures make it clear that we are NOT.

Titus 3:5

5 Not by works of righteousness which we have done, but according to his mercy he saved us, by the washing of regeneration, and renewing of the Holy Ghost.

We are saved NOT by works of righteousness (like water baptism, or anything else) but BY THE WASHING OF REGENERATION AND RENEWING OF THE HOLY GHOST! We are saved by regeneration, the born-again experience which occurs along with *Spirit Baptism (the "renewing of the Holy Ghost")*, not water baptism.

"He that believeth and is baptized shall be saved; but he that believeth not shall be damned." Let's think about this sentence structure.

Would it not also be true if we said:

He that believeth and is a *football player* shall be saved; but he that believeth not shall be damned.

Or, he that believeth and is a *trombone player* shall be saved; but he that believeth not shall be damned.

The key is that, "He that believeth not shall be damned."

This verse in 1 Peter makes it clear that *water baptism is a figure*, or type, to which *Spirit Baptism is the antitype*.

1 Peter 3:21
21 The *like figure* whereunto *even* baptism doth also now save us (not the putting away of the filth of the flesh, but the answer of a good conscience toward God,) by the resurrection of Jesus Christ.

The word *"figure"* in the GK is:

antitupŏn – which means, "antitype," i.e., a *representation.*

The verse makes it clear that we are not saved by putting away the filth of the flesh, but by the resurrection of Christ from the dead! It is HIS work that saves us.

So, Spirit Baptism (being immersed into or connected to the body of Christ in His death, burial, and resurrection) is the antitype (i.e., fulfillment); and water baptism is the type (or the picture of it).

Spirit Baptism by the Holy Spirit when He calls us is what saves us, and it is a purely spiritual event.

To put it more plainly, water baptism is a physical representation of the spiritual work God does on us when He regenerates us and places us into Christ through Spirit Baptism. Water baptism represents or pictures Spirit Baptism, or immersion into the body of Christ, spiritually. Therefore water baptism does not contribute to our salvation, for it is not a cause; it is an effect. We do it because we ARE saved and wish to please our Lord who has instructed us to be baptized in the name of the Father, Son, and Holy Spirit.

There are several verses that intimate that water baptism is not essential for salvation.

John 4:1–3
1 When therefore the Lord knew how the Pharisees had heard that Jesus made and baptized more disciples than John,
2 *(**Though Jesus himself baptized not**,* but his disciples,)
3 He left Judaea, and departed again into Galilee.

If water baptism were essential to salvation, why does Scripture teach that Jesus ***never*** baptized anyone?

And then there is the greatest Christian who ever lived, the Apostle Paul:

1 Corinthians 1:12–15
12 Now this I say, that every one of you saith, I am of Paul; and I of Apollos; and I of Cephas; and I of Christ.

13 Is Christ divided? was Paul crucified for you? or were ye baptized in the name of Paul?

14 *I thank God that I baptized none of you*, but Crispus and Gaius;

15 Lest any should say that I had baptized in mine own name.

17 For *Christ sent me not to baptize, but to preach the gospel:* not with wisdom of words, lest the cross of Christ should be made of none effect.

18 For the preaching of the cross is to them that perish foolishness; but unto *us which are saved it is the power of God.*

If water baptism is necessary for salvation, why did Paul neglect to baptize most of his converts, and why did he say, "Christ sent me not to baptize"? Why did Paul say it was the preaching of the cross that had the power of God unto salvation, not water baptism?

If Jesus did not baptize, and Paul baptized only a couple of people, then it must be the gospel message itself—the preaching of the cross—that is "the power of God unto salvation," and that alone!

The Apostle Paul would have a strong rebuke for works-oriented salvation teachings.

Romans 3:26–28

26 To declare, *I say*, at this time his righteousness: that he might be just, and the justifier of him which believeth in Jesus.

27 Where *is* boasting then? It is excluded. By what law? of works? Nay: but by the law of faith.

28 Therefore we conclude that a man is justified by faith without the deeds of the law.

Galatians 3:1–3

1 O foolish Galatians, who hath bewitched you, that ye should not obey the truth, before whose eyes Jesus Christ hath been evidently set forth, crucified among you?

2 This only would I learn of you, Received ye the Spirit by the works of the law, or by the hearing of faith?

3 Are ye so foolish? having begun in the Spirit, are ye now made perfect by the flesh?

Ephesians 2:8–9

8 For by grace are ye saved through faith; and that not of yourselves: *it is* the gift of God:

9 Not of works, lest any man should boast.

Works are the EFFECT of salvation, not its cause. The whole book of James speaks mostly of the effects of salvation, and rightly so, but where it speaks of the cause, James agrees 100% with Paul.

James 1:16–18, 21–22; 2:23

16 Do not err, my beloved brethren.

17 Every good gift and every perfect gift is from above, and cometh down from the Father of lights, with whom is no variableness, neither shadow of turning.

18 Of his own will begat he us with the word of truth, that we should be a kind of firstfruits of his creatures.

21 Wherefore lay apart all filthiness and superfluity of naughtiness, and receive with meekness the engrafted word, which is able to save your souls.

22 But be ye doers of the word, and not hearers only, deceiving your own selves.

2:23 And the scripture was fulfilled which saith, Abraham believed God, and it was imputed unto him for righteousness: and he was called the Friend of God.

Paul said the same thing:

Romans 4:9–10, 16, 18, 21–24

9 *Cometh* this blessedness then upon the circumcision [the Jew] *only*, or upon the uncircumcision [Gentile] also? for we say that faith was reckoned to Abraham for righteousness.

10 How was it then reckoned? when he was in circumcision, or in uncircumcision? Not in circumcision, but in uncircumcision [i.e., he was saved by faith before he was circumcised].

16 Therefore *it is* of faith, that *it might be* by grace; to the end the promise might be sure to all the seed; not to that only which is of the law, but to that also which is of the faith of Abraham; who is the father of us all,

18 Who against hope believed in hope, that he might become the father of many nations; according to that which was spoken, So shall thy seed be.

21 And being fully persuaded that, what he [God] had promised, he was able also to perform.

22 And therefore it was imputed to him [Abraham] for righteousness.

23 Now it was not written for his sake alone, that it was imputed to him;

24 But for us also, to whom it shall be imputed, if we believe on him that raised up Jesus our Lord from the dead.

James and Paul both teach that the *cause* of salvation is faith in Christ. The *effect* is good works. ***The effect cannot be the cause of the cause.*** That's a pure logical statement, so think about it.

Circumcision and water baptism are similar in that they are both physical symbols of spiritual truths. Circumcision pictures a new heart; baptism pictures the New Man. The picture does not DO the saving. It PICTURES the saving.

Water Baptism should be the First Step of Obedience for the New Christian.

Acts 2:38–41

38 Then Peter said unto them, Repent, and be baptized every one of you in the name of Jesus Christ for the remission of sins, and ye shall receive the gift of the Holy Ghost.

39 For the promise is unto you, and to your children, and to all that are afar off, *even **as many as the Lord our God shall call**.*

40 And with many other words did he testify and exhort, saying, Save yourselves from this untoward generation.

41 Then they that gladly received his word *were baptized*: and the same day there were added *unto them* about three thousand souls.

We see in this passage that we are to repent and be baptized in the name of Jesus for remission of sins. I have said countless times that Greek is like math. It settles many arguments.

In the verses above, the word "repent" is in the active voice in the Greek, which means it is something we do. Remember, however, from our earlier studies together that repentance is a gift from God—it must be given to us before we will do it, just like faith. It is true that all people who will be saved will have repented, i.e., changed their minds about who Christ is and who they are.

However, the phrase "be baptized" in the Greek is in the passive voice, which means this is something that someone bigger and stronger and outside of you does TO you. Obviously, it is the Holy Spirit—God Himself—who performs *Spirit Baptism*, the "operation of God," upon you, whereby God gives you a heart transplant! And it is a preacher who submerges you into the water, picturing your salvation, so baptism is never—whether Spirit Baptism or water baptism—something you do to yourself. *Therefore, it cannot be something YOU __DO__ TO GET SAVED.*

At the same time, *Spirit Baptism* is exactly what saves you—water baptism pictures it. Spirit Baptism is not something you DO; it is something DONE to you by God, as He births you into His family. He knew you as His own dear child before the foundation of the world (Ephesians 1, Romans 8, et. al.), and He gave birth to you on your spiritual birthday.

Verse 39 above indicates clearly that you must be "called." The promise is "to as many as the Lord God shall call." The calling is the operation of regeneration and Spirit Baptism performed by God on His people by the Holy Spirit, to bring them into His family. Just as in physical birth, the parents do all the work—so in spiritual birth, God performs the operation (new heart) and the birthing (the born-again experience).

The last verse shows the first step of obedience after having been called and saved by God.

"Then they that gladly received his word _**were baptized**_: and the same day there were added *unto them* about three thousand souls."—**Acts 2:41**

Water Baptism Must be Preceded by Belief.

Acts 8:36–37
36 And as they went on their way, they came unto a certain water: and the eunuch said, See, here is water; what doth hinder me to be baptized?
37 And Philip said, If thou believest with all thine heart, thou mayest. And he answered and said, I believe that Jesus Christ is the Son of God.

The Eunuch could not be baptized in water until after he had believed with all his heart. It was the believing that saved him.

In the following story, Gentiles heard the word of God preached, the gospel message, and as many as God had foreordained to eternal life, BELIEVED.

Acts 13:48–49
48 And when the Gentiles heard this, they were glad, and glorified the word of the Lord: and *as many as were ordained to eternal life believed*.
49 And the word of the Lord was published throughout all the region.

Jesus Himself said THIS is the way to be saved.

John 6:40
40 And this is the will of him that sent me, that every one which seeth [beholdeth] the Son, and **believeth on him**, may have everlasting life: and I will raise him up at the last day.

No mention of water baptism here. So genuine belief and regeneration must take place first, then water baptism has something to be a picture of.

And, then there is the story of the jailer after God freed Paul and Silas from prison. He feared death because they got freed on his watch. He was about to commit suicide.

Acts 16:29–33

29 Then he called for a light, and sprang in, and came trembling, and fell down before Paul and Silas,

30 And brought them out, and said, Sirs, *what must I do to be saved?*

31 And they said, *Believe on the Lord Jesus Christ, and thou shalt be saved, and thy house.*

32 And they *spake unto him the word of the Lord*, and to all that were in his house.

33 And he took them the same hour of the night, and washed *their* stripes; and *<u>was baptized</u>*, he and all his, straightway.

The process is clear. The jailer asked, "What must I do to be saved?" The answer was, "*<u>Believe</u>* on the Lord Jesus Christ, and thou shalt be saved." They spoke the Word, the gospel, and he believed and was saved! THEN *later* that evening he was *baptized in water*, picturing the salvation. This act of obedience was an effect of the salvation. The belief was the CAUSE.

The belief and Spirit Baptism must come first, then the water baptism. Salvation comes with the belief.

5. Baptism unto Moses

1 Corinthians 10:1–6

1 Moreover, brethren, I would not that ye should be ignorant, how that all our fathers were under the cloud, and all passed through the sea;

2 And were all baptized unto Moses in the cloud and in the sea;

3 And did all eat the same spiritual meat;

4 And did all drink the same spiritual drink: for they drank of that spiritual Rock that followed them: and that Rock was Christ.

5 But with many of them God was not well pleased: for they were overthrown in the wilderness.

6 Now these things were our examples, to the intent we should not lust after evil things, as they also lusted.

Paul writes of "baptism unto Moses." What could this be?

The text gives us the answer. The people of God were baptized unto Moses "in the cloud and in the sea." This is the cloud that followed them by day, and a fire by night.

We see this story in the O.T.

Exodus 13:21–22

21 And the Lord went before them by day in a pillar of a cloud, to lead them the way; and by night in a pillar of fire, to give them light; to go by day and night:

22 He took not away the pillar of the cloud by day, nor the pillar of fire by night, *from* before the people.

The people chose not to have a personal relationship with God, though it was offered. They insisted that Moses be their intercessor between them and God. So, Moses led them out of Egypt and toward the Red Sea. God provided a pillar of fire by night and a cloud by day which led Moses, who, in turn, led the people in the right direction.

The pillar of the cloud not only gave them God's direction, but it also separated them from the Egyptian army, which was coming after them, bringing certain destruction. This is a picture of spiritual warfare. Egypt is a symbol of the world system. Pharaoh pictures Satan. The people of God also struggled with the flesh in the wilderness. These are our three enemies today—the world, the flesh, and the devil!

Being baptized unto Moses, first, is to be immersed into Moses' protection and closeness to God. Second, they were baptized unto Moses, or connected with Moses in that they all "did eat the same spiritual meat, and drink of the spiritual Rock that followed them."

1 Cor. 10:3–4
3 And did all eat the same spiritual meat;
4 And did all drink the same spiritual drink: for they drank of that spiritual Rock that followed them: and that Rock was Christ.

The Israelites were connected to Moses who, due to his power with God, was able to see God provide them with manna from heaven when they needed food; and water from the Rock, which represented Jesus Christ, THE Rock, who followed them and was present with them as they trekked toward the Promised Land.

Because they were connected to Moses, they were connected to God, and God's provision and protection.

Baptism unto Moses is quite a type, or picture, of how you and I must experience Spirit Baptism. You were not close to God in the flesh while you were in your sins, and yet that is exactly the condition you were in prior to salvation. You never could have seen the power of God if you had not been connected to the Holy Spirit as He called you and indwelt you, Who in turn is connected to Christ and to the Father.

As Moses was their connector, the Holy Spirit is your connector to the Godhead.

The Scripture says this in the same context:

1 Corinthians 10:11
Now all these things happened unto them for ensamples: and they are written for our admonition, upon whom the ends of the world are come.

So, the entire O.T. is full of physical stories which teach you spiritual truths. It adds many additional colors of meaning and more depth to the N.T. doctrines you study. In this case, the baptism unto Moses teaches you that, just as the Israelites found it necessary to be attached to Moses, who was attached to God, you must be indwelt by the Holy Spirit—Who connects you to Christ, to the Father, and to every other Christian who has ever lived (even your loved ones in Heaven). There is no other way you could find the protection, guidance, provision, and joy the Lord intended you to have. As they followed Moses, we must follow the leadership of the Holy Spirit and the Word of God in everything we do if we are to find success.

6. Baptism for the Dead

The Mormons teach a false doctrine called "baptism for the dead." They get the idea by misunderstanding the proper interpretation of the following verses:

1 Corinthians 15:29–32
29 Else what shall they do ***which are baptized for the dead***, if the dead rise not at all? why are they then baptized for the dead?
30 And why stand we in jeopardy every hour?
31 I protest by your rejoicing which I have in Christ Jesus our Lord, I die daily.
32 If after the manner of men I have fought with beasts at Ephesus, what advantageth it me, if the dead rise not? let us eat and drink; for to morrow we die.

As I have said so many times, ***context is everything.***

If we read these verses from earlier in the same chapter, we see the subject of Paul's discussion.

1 Corinthians 15:12–14

12 Now if Christ be preached that he rose from the dead, how ***say some among you that there is no resurrection*** of the dead?
13 But if there be no resurrection of the dead, then is Christ not risen:
14 And if Christ be not risen, then *is* our preaching vain, and your faith *is* also vain.

There were some in the church in Paul's day saying that there is no such thing as the resurrection. They probably got the idea from Jewish people who were influenced by the Sadducees, who did not believe in miracles in general.

Paul was making an argument in favor of the resurrection.

Now if we know the world the Christians at Corinth lived in, it is helpful. John Walvoord of Dallas Theological Seminary wrote:

> Just north of Corinth was a city named Eleusis. This was the location of a pagan religion where ***baptism in the sea was practiced to guarantee a good afterlife.*** This religion was mentioned by Homer in Hymn to Demeter.... The Corinthians were known to be heavily influenced by other customs. After all, they were in a large economic area where a great many different people frequented. It is probable that the Corinthians were being influenced by the religious practices found at Eleusis where baptism for the dead was practiced.[47]

---

[47] Walvoord, John F., and Roy B. Zuck, *The Bible Knowledge Commentary*, Wheaton, IL: (Scripture Press Publications, 1985).

Paul had several arguments in favor of the resurrection, including a discussion of the practice of pagans in Corinth of "baptism for the dead." (And people from Corinth would understand it, especially.)

In the context just before his mention of "baptism for the dead" he argued:

1 Corinthians 15:13-14, 30-32

13 But if there be no resurrection of the dead, then is Christ not risen:

14 And if Christ be not risen, then *is* our preaching vain, and your faith *is* also vain.

The big reveal is this: ***if their faith is in vain, then they die in their sins!*** This is a very strong argument for any true Christian.

Then after his mention of "baptism for the dead" Paul argues:

30 And why stand we in jeopardy every hour?

31 I protest by your rejoicing which I have in Christ Jesus our Lord, I die daily.

32 If after the manner of men I have fought with beasts at Ephesus, what advantageth it me, if the dead rise not? let us eat and drink; for to morrow we die.

Paul argues, "Why would I suffer persecution all the time ('I die daily'), why would I fight beasts at Ephesus, what advantage would I have if there is no resurrection? We might as well eat, drink, and be merry, for tomorrow we cease to exist." These are strong arguments.

But amid these great points, he throws in another stout argument to bring real humiliation to those who believed the lie that there was no resurrection.

He said:

1 Corinthians 15:29

29 Else what shall they do which are baptized for the dead, if the dead rise not at all? why are they then baptized for the dead?

Paul now says, "Look, some of you Christians are saying there is no resurrection, but even the pagans know better! Why would they practice 'baptism for the dead' in their cult religion if THEY didn't believe in life in the hereafter? Why are they practicing that? Because even the pagans believe there is a resurrection—shame on you!"

Understanding the context, and a little about the customs in the area in the first century, is all it takes to avoid a false interpretation of this passage.

Of course, Joseph Smith, who founded the Mormon religion, didn't have access to Greek literature in his day, so he had no clue what Paul was talking about. His misinterpretation led to one of the strangest beliefs of the Mormon cult. They baptize people with the misplaced hope that it will cause their deceased loved ones to have a hope of heaven. Of course, that contradicts the whole Bible! But it came from a few words in one verse.

Always remember that there are no "stand-alone doctrines" in the Bible. God intertwines His truth here and there throughout the Scriptures, line by line across the breadth and depth of His Revealed Word. A true doctrine will always have another clear scripture to back it up and shed more light upon it. Cults arise from obscure verses taken out of context, which contradict other clear Scriptures.

It was a common practice for Paul to use tactics like the above arguments (speaking in terms they understand) when talking to groups of lost people, such as he did in Greece.

Acts 17:23–25
23 For as I passed by, and beheld your devotions, I found an altar with this inscription, TO THE UNKNOWN GOD. Whom therefore ye ignorantly worship, him declare I unto you.
24 God that made the world and all things therein, seeing that he is Lord of heaven and earth, dwelleth not in temples made with hands;
25 Neither is worshipped with men's hands, as though he needed any thing, seeing he giveth to all life, and breath, and all things;

He used their mythical religion to argue FOR the one true God!

1 Corinthians 9:22–23
22 To the weak became I as weak, that I might gain the weak: *I am made all things to all men,* that I might by all means save some.

23 And this I do for the gospel's sake, that I might be partaker thereof with *you.*

In biblical Christianity, there is no such thing as "baptism for the dead."

7. Baptism of Death

Matthew 20:21–23

21 And he said unto her, What wilt thou? She saith unto him, Grant that these my two sons may sit, the one on thy right hand, and the other on the left, in thy kingdom. **22** But Jesus answered and said, Ye know not what ye ask. Are ye able to drink of the cup that I shall drink of, and *to be baptized with the baptism that I am baptized with?* They say unto him, We are able. **23** And he saith unto them, *Ye shall drink indeed of my cup, and be baptized with the baptism that I am baptized with:* but to sit on my right hand, and on my left, is not mine to give, but *it shall be given to them* for whom it is prepared of my Father.

This baptism is a picture of the crucifixion of Christ, and the fact that His followers must bear their cross as well. The apostles may not have seen the fact coming that they all, except John, would be martyred for their faith in Christ.

Foxe's Book of Martyrs recounts the horrible deaths of thousands of Protestant Christians who were killed for their faith from the biblical times of Steven in the Book of Acts, to the reign of Bloody Mary in England.[48] It is a classic, life-changing book!

To be baptized into the death of the cross is really something that all Christians face, whether physical persecution or spiritual dying to the old self-life.

Luke 6:22–23

22 Blessed are ye, when men shall hate you, and when they shall separate you *from their company*, and shall reproach *you*, and cast out your name as evil, for the Son of man's sake.
23 Rejoice ye in that day, and leap for joy: for, behold, your reward *is* great in heaven: for in the like manner did their fathers unto the prophets.

Matthew 10:38–39

38 And he that taketh not his cross, and followeth after me, is not worthy of me.
39 He that findeth his life shall lose it: and he that loseth his life for my sake shall find it.

In the Greek, this actually says, "He that findeth SELF life shall lose it: and he that loseth SELF life for my sake shall find it." This is carrying one's cross as a Christian. Our old man lived exclusively for self. Our old man has now carried his cross to Golgotha, and

---

[48] John Foxe, William Byron Forbush, D.D., ed., **Foxe's Book of Martyrs** (1563), (Grand Rapids: Zondervan Publishing House, 1926).

been crucified together with Christ; now the new man lives for Christ and others, not self.

Galatians 2:20

20 I am crucified with Christ: nevertheless I live; yet not I, but Christ liveth in me: and the life which I now live in the flesh I live by the faith **of** the Son of God, who loved me, and gave himself for me.

Since you are "in Christ" after your Spirit Baptism, then you died a co-death together with Him. This death of your old man is the best reality to contemplate (it is your current position: old man dead, new man alive) to help you avoid the sin habits of your youth. This is a death to the old carnal mind.

The Scriptures renew our new man's mind day by day. There are no more practical passages of Scripture for learning how to *Walk Tall and Stand Straight in a Crooked World* than these:

Romans 6:9–14

9 Knowing that Christ being raised from the dead dieth no more; death hath no more dominion over him.

10 For in that he died, he died unto sin once: but in that he liveth, he liveth unto God.

11 *Likewise reckon ye also yourselves to be dead indeed unto sin, but alive unto God through Jesus Christ our Lord.*

12 Let not sin therefore reign in your mortal body, that ye should obey it in the lusts thereof.

13 Neither yield ye your members *as* instruments of unrighteousness unto sin: but yield yourselves unto

God, as those that are alive from the dead, and your members *as* instruments of righteousness unto God.

14 For sin shall not have dominion over you: for ye are not under the law, but under grace.

Romans 6:1–3

1 What shall we say then? Shall we continue in sin, that grace may abound?

2 God forbid. How shall we, that are dead to sin, live any longer therein?

3 Know ye not, that so many of us as were baptized into Jesus Christ were baptized into his death?

Not only has your old man died together with Christ, but the Holy Spirit now indwells your body and lives as one with your new man, leading you to serve God in this human body, in this life, as long as you hold Jesus's hand as you walk. Jesus paid the Ransom Price to set you free, so now you are free indeed—live like it!

1 Corinthians 6:19–20

19 What? know ye not that your body is the temple of the Holy Ghost *which is* in you, which ye have of God, and ye are not your own?

20 For ye are bought with a price: therefore glorify God in your body, and in your spirit, which are God's.

This baptism of death is a beautiful baptism because once the old man loses his clutch upon you and you learn to walk in the new man with Christ, you will find joy that passes all understanding. This only comes through the death of the old man—counting him as crucified.

Philippians 4:1, 4, 7

1 Therefore, my brethren dearly beloved and longed for, my joy and crown, so stand fast in the Lord, *my* dearly beloved.

4 Rejoice in the Lord alway: *and* again I say, Rejoice.

7 And the peace of God, which passeth all understanding, shall keep your hearts and minds through Christ Jesus.

We have God's four-dimensional love in our three-dimensional world.

Ephesians 3:18–21

18 [That you] May be able to comprehend with all saints what *is* the **breadth**, and **length**, and **depth**, and **height**;

19 And to know the love of Christ, which passeth knowledge, that ye might be filled with all the fulness of God.

20 Now unto him that is able to do exceeding abundantly above all that we ask or think, according to the power that worketh in us,

21 Unto him *be* glory in the church by Christ Jesus throughout all ages, world without end. Amen.

The baptism of death is a way of thinking right. It is a way of living right. Your true position is one of having been bought with a price, the blood of Christ, and set free from the slave market of sin. In Christ, you can remember that you not only died when He died (a co-death), and you were buried when He was buried (a co-burial), but you arose to new life together with Him (a co-resurrection).

Ephesians 2:5–6

5 Even when we were dead in sins, hath quickened [brought from death unto life] us together with Christ, (by grace ye are saved;)

God quickened you TOGETHER with Christ. In God the Father's mind, 2000 years ago you were already risen with Christ to live a life of victory, free from the old man who was crucified 2000 years ago as well!

6 And hath raised *us* up together, and made *us* sit together in heavenly *places* in Christ Jesus:

Yes, if you are saved, you have been baptized into His death! But now you are risen and still in Christ due to your Spirit Baptism by the Holy Spirit, Who is sealed with you.

Where is Christ now? He has ascended and is seated on the right hand of God! ***You are with Him still***, "made to sit together in heavenly places IN Christ Jesus!"

The next time you feel down and defeated, or sad and grieving, look up and realize you not only died with Him and were buried with Him and rose with Him, but you are also ascended with Him. You are positionally seated WITH CHRIST (spiritually) in the heavenlies right now!

Raise up your head and smell the unsullied, celestial air! Look around and see the glorious Son of God seated at the right hand of Majesty Whose resplendent Light glows and pulsates above the throne of God in the Third Heaven. Listen to the angels and creatures cry, "Holy, Holy, Holy." Sing with them now (I'm thinking of Steffany Frizzell Gretzinger's song, *Lamb of God*—what a Powerful song! What will the music sound like in heaven? (And we'll have ears to hear…*better!)*

We are seated in the heavenlies, high above the world system; high above the legalizers and their law that kills; high above the troubles of this life; above death, and pain, and suffering; spiritually seated in the heavenlies with the One Who Loved us before the Foundation of the World! Vitally connected to Him, and to the Father by the Holy Spirit Who lives within us right here and now. Able to boldly come before the throne of grace.

Is someone treating you badly, perhaps someone in your own family, or one you thought was a true friend? Remember this:

Hebrews 4:13–16

13 Neither is there any creature that is not manifest in his sight: but all things *are* naked and opened unto the eyes of him with whom we have to do.

14 Seeing then that we have a great high priest, that is passed into the heavens, Jesus the Son of God, let us hold fast *our* profession.

15 For we have not an high priest which cannot be touched with the feeling of our infirmities; but was in all points tempted like as *we are, yet* without sin.

16 Let us therefore come boldly unto the throne of grace, that we may obtain mercy, and find grace to help in time of need.

Chapter 14

The Doctrine of the Laying On of Hands—
INTRODUCTION

*"Therefore leaving the principles
of the doctrine of Christ,
let us go on unto perfection; not laying again the
foundation of repentance from dead works, and of
faith toward God.
Of the doctrine of baptisms,
and <u>of laying on of hands</u>...."*
—Hebrews 6:1–2

The practice of "laying on of hands" is our fifth Core Doctrine. In the early N.T. times this practice was often associated with utilizing *sign gifts* such as healing and raising the dead or imparting the Holy Spirit to people who had received Christ. There was one case of laying on of hands that was not connected with sign gifts, and that was the ordaining of various church officers. We see all this activity in the N.T. book of Acts and other N.T. books describing life in the early church.

In these two chapters (and in the first six chapters in Volume 2) we will be asking the following questions: What are the "sign gifts" associated with laying on of hands? What was their purpose? Are any of these still bestowed upon God's people in the church age today and energized by the Holy Spirit? And how are sign gifts different from the other gifts of the Holy Spirit listed in the N.T.? Finally, we will talk about how laying on of hands is utilized properly in the church today.

I wish to begin by saying to a large number of my friends in the world who are of the Pentecostal or charismatic faith, I desire to provide information for you to consider which, to the best of my ability and with a pure heart before the Lord, is accurate and truthful, but information with which you may not initially agree— information you may have never seen or considered. My intent is never to offend you, but only to inform you in love, and always to defend the truth.

Many of you are in the Word as much as I, so I know it would be a hefty task to persuade you to change your mind about very many things, though hopefully a few truths. But I am not called by our Lord to change your mind; rather, to share with you why I believe that which I believe, in good conscience before the Lord, so that is what I will do.

1 Peter 3:15–16
15 But sanctify the Lord God in your hearts: and *be ready always to give an answer* to every man that *asketh you a reason* of the hope that is in you with meekness and fear:
16 Having a good conscience....

Please, never think that my ardency is a spirit of strife or variance. It issues from the sheer joy of sharing truth from the Word of God, as I see it, while utilizing the rules of proper Bible interpretation.

I know some of you will disagree with a few of my propositions, I can only ask you to hear them, contemplate them, and study to prove them right or wrong with the same joy I have as I study. If you do that, I am happy.

Now, please take a deep breath, ask the Holy Spirit to be your teacher, and realize that I am on your side. I am a born-again believer, saved in my car in the spring of 1978 during the 40-mile drive from Baylor grad school to my office, where I managed our family oil business. I had a degree in business and was a week away from receiving my second degree, an MBA. I was 24 years old when the Holy Spirit called me, awakened me, and changed my life forever. I was called to preach at Evangelist Lester Roloff's funeral four years later. I have been a business-man preacher ever since.

I continued to run our family oil business while studying systematic theology under Dr. Irwin Freeman, who suggested that I not attend seminary because I had to run the business—being an only child, and, in his words, "the seminaries are too liberal; at your age, they will suck the faith right out of you." Dr. Freeman became my "seminary" and my seminary professor. When he went to heaven years later, his wife Pat gave me his library, and I am self-taught. I've spent 45 years in ministry, and after 33 years, I am still the Sr. Pastor of Park Meadows Church in Corsicana, Texas, which Charlotte and I co-founded.

I don't live in any seminary's "God-box" or under any denomination's wing. Charlotte and I left the denomination we grew up in, the Southern Baptists, three years after my salvation, and determined to keep the good they had taught us (and there was much) and—to the best of our abilities—throw out everything else that was not biblical.

You and I are on the same team in a world that literally despises us. (And now, with the murder and martyrdom of the amazing Charlie Kirk, we as Christians in America are actually beginning to *believe* Jesus when He said, "If the world hate you, ye know that it hated me before *it hated* you"—**John 15:18**.) So, we are tied together by the very Holy Spirit Who connects us to Jesus and our Father in Heaven and each other. We will not, and need not, agree on everything, but can love each other and even walk together. When the tribulation begins, we will not care about our denominational labels. We will **know** we are on the same team.

I'm going to assume we agree that we are saved by the efficacy of the blood of Jesus plus nothing, and through personally receiving the Lord Jesus Christ as our Lord and Saviour. So, we're on the same team, fighting against this world and the invisible forces of darkness. We must not allow the enemy to bring even more division into God's army.

Here is something I have learned by experience, having lived this out, and I'll share the principle with a story.

If you'll remember, earlier I told you the story of an older gentleman and his wife who walked into our church one Sunday in 1997—Otis and Bea Fisher. Hundreds of thousands of people across the country have heard me tell "Bro. Otis" stories through TRADEway, on radio, and through my podcast, "The Word on Investing," since then.

Very early in our friendship we co-authored a document called "The Ten Rules of Bible Interpretation," which we gleaned from theologians from many different denominations. We shook hands and agreed to live by these principles, and never cheat on them to win a theological argument. *(For a copy of "The Ten Rules of Bible Interpretation," visit ChristianPosture.com.)*

When we met, we had about eight to ten things we disagreed on. He was an older gentleman but had the openness and curiosity of a 21-year-old. He would change a doctrine he had taught for 50 years if you showed him in the Bible that it was not right—and he would change on a dime. All he cared about was the truth.

Through the years, he changed my mind on several doctrinal points as well, and we both threw out probably fifty words and/or phrases we had heard other preachers say—and which we had taught—which we found were not biblical.

Through studying this way together, with honest hearts, seeking only the truth, never cheating on the rules of proper Bible interpretation just to win a debate, by the time I preached Bro. Otis's funeral, we had complete unity in our doctrinal beliefs.

We had only one small thing we disagreed on. I thought people in heaven could see us, and he did not. I believe today he is looking down and watching me write this book—so I'm right, and I am sure he knows it! (I smile every time I tell this story.)

Our views had, over time, merged and become almost identical. This was made possible through studying the Bible together, keeping the rules of context, grammar, word definitions, and making everything fit with the whole of the Bible, etc. We had complete love, trust, and friendship the entire thirteen years we worked together. In the end, we had one mind.

I suggest that if you and I do the same, we will get similar results, but it takes time. Now, while you are sitting there, relaxed, breathing calmly, and being assured *we are on the same team*, let me begin a very important line of thinking for you to consider.

"…Try the spirits whether they are of God."–John 4:1

Allow me to ask: "Do you believe in speaking in tongues? Do you believe that God still provides Apostles to the church today? Do you believe men or women can lay hands on people and impart the Holy Spirit, or heal them, or raise them from the dead (it is the same apostolic gift)?"

If so, let me humbly suggest that many of you (as many of my friends have done in person) might say something like this: "You cannot tell me that speaking in tongues is not real because I have done it myself." Or, "You cannot say that faith-healing is not real, because I have seen it happen right before my eyes (or seen someone do it in the very room in which I was standing)."

I would answer, "I am not saying speaking in tongues or faith-healing (by laying on of hands, etc.), is not real. I am just asking you to *consider the source of the power*. Is it *dunamis* from God, or could it be something else?" Now, please don't drop out here. Take a deep breath, let the adrenaline drop, and just think with me.

I want to ask you to imagine yourself standing, 2000 years ago, on a street corner in Philippi, one of the chief cities of Macedonia (in Eastern Greece). It's around 10 am. You see the Apostle Paul, the N.T. prophet Silas, the young preacher Timothy, and the evangelist Luke (a physician) walking toward you, on their way to prayer down by the river.

A naturally pretty, somewhat earthy young woman, possessing a very spiritual aura, is following after them. (You would have heard of Paul because he has been in town for several days and his reputation preceded him.)

As Paul and the men pass by, the young woman cries out in an excited, authoritative fashion, words you cannot at first discern. The second time she raises her voice, you are startled by the loud, high-pitched vibrato in her voice, as she shouts, *"These men are the servants of the most high God, which shew unto us the way of salvation."* You see Paul turn to her and say something quietly but firmly, with a very serious face, but you cannot make out the words.

Now, you know these men have been known to preach "the Way" of salvation through Jesus Christ, the Nazarene. They have also been known to do miraculous things, and many have believed their message because of the miracles. You're thinking they must be of God, and the miracles seem to indicate that the message *IS* of God, though it is very different than the Law of Moses, and the gods of the Greeks with which you are somewhat familiar.

As you hear this young woman, she seems to be speaking the truth about these men, for surely, they *ARE* showing the way of Salvation, and you think, *"She must be filled with the Holy Spirit and doing good works for God."*

My question is, could you be sure that just because someone is saying the right things and walking among God's servants, that the *source* of their power and their words is the Holy Spirit?

You feel confident, though, because most other people around you on the streets feel the same way you do. "Look at her, she is a very vibrant and animated servant of God with an enthusiastic message! I know she is of God because I heard her speak the truth and glorify God and I saw her supporting God's men and showing the way of salvation!"

But not everything is as it seems.

It might not have been enough to say, "I know she was filled with the Holy Spirit because I was there. I observed first-hand her enthusiasm and heard her praising God and saw her supporting God's men. I saw it with my own eyes, so I know this is real."

However, the question is never, "Is it real." The right question is, "What is the source of the power?"

The Bible tells us:

"Beloved, *believe not every spirit, but try the spirits* whether they are of God: because many false prophets are gone out into the world."—**1 John 4:1**

You may not have discerned the reality correctly. Why?

Because it does not matter what ***experience*** you may have had or seen—what matters is the ***source of the power***. It may be God, or it may be Satan. It may be the Holy Spirit, or it may be ***an unclean spirit mimicking the Holy Spirit*** for Satan's purpose, perhaps to bring embarrassment, shame, and mockery to the gospel message and to the messenger.

The only way you can discern is to have wisdom from having been in the Word, rightly dividing it. (We will soon study together what it means to "rightly divide the Word of God.")

Here is the eyewitness account, and now you may see behind the scenes:

Acts 16:16–18

16 And it came to pass, as we went to prayer, a certain damsel…met us….

17 The same followed Paul and us, and cried, saying, These men are the servants of the most high God, which shew unto us the way of salvation.

18 And this did she many days. But Paul, being grieved, turned and said to the *spirit*, I command thee in the name of Jesus Christ to *come out of her*. And he came out the same hour.

She was exhibiting the ability to prophesy the future. *People had SEEN AND HEARD HER DO IT! But was it the Holy Spirit providing the power?* Would you have known for sure the source of the power? Paul did, because he was walking closely with the Lord. She was performing works "for God" by the power of an *unclean spirit* within her!

Just a few verses above this passage, in the context, we see who this young woman *really* was. She was not what she appeared to be.

Acts 16:16–17

16 And it came to pass, as we went to prayer, a certain damsel *possessed with a spirit of divination* met us, which brought her masters much gain by soothsaying. [The O.T. teaches us it is against God's law to utilize fortune tellers, calling upon familiar spirits!]
17 The same followed Paul and us, and cried, saying, These men are the servants of the most high God, which shew unto us the way of salvation.

All the right words! She had the look. She had the voice of a prophetess! But…her source of power was NOT the Holy Spirit—it was an unclean spirit *mimicking* the Holy Spirit.

Sometimes your EXPERIENCE can lead you away from truth, rather than toward it.

I find it sad, and troubling, that through the years quite a number of my friends have listened and changed their views, but many of my friends that I share evidences with—such as I will share in these chapters—set them aside simply by saying, "You cannot tell me tongues are not for today, because I have spoken in tongues." Or, "I know a certain faith-healer is real because I've been to her services and seen people healed. ***The spirit*** *was all over that room!"*

Yet in that room all manner of false doctrine was taught, and often, historically, by people of suspect morality. It is always interesting they often ***don't*** say, *"**THE** Holy Spirit* was in the room." Sure enough, it is sometimes not ***The*** Holy Spirit, but ***a*** *spirit* of divination.

So, my friends, experiences are not enough!

One should not, and cannot, place the authority of his or her *experience* higher than the authority of *the Word of God.*

Please do not mistake my passion for ill will. If there is any dislike in my heart for people, it would only be toward those teachers and preachers whose fruit (their life and their doctrine) I believe reveals that they are false prophets and beguiling teachers of bad doctrine.

The only fault I find with the sweet, kind people who listen to these apparent "ministers of righteousness," who are really "wolves in sheep's clothing," is that they have not learned the rules of proper Bible interpretation, and/or they cheat on them to try and win an argument. They do not understand that there are genuine dispensational considerations that affect the correct interpretation and application of Bible passages (which we will discuss below).

But then, the reason you may not know these things is because the wolves do not WANT you to, so again, *my problem is not with you, but with the false teachers.* My love is with you, sincerely— even if you find it difficult to agree with me on some things. We do not have to agree on everything. My goal is to get YOU to study to prove me right or wrong.

When teachers play loosely with Biblical truth, as these imperious false teachers do, they are *taking freedom away* from God's people and directing them away from God's better gifts; at the same time, they are causing the lost to run away from the Gospel as fast as they can!

These *false teachers, false apostles, and false prophets* are described adeptly by the Apostle Peter:

> **2 Peter 2:14–19**
>
> **14** Having *eyes full of adultery*, and that cannot cease from sin; beguiling unstable souls: an heart they have exercised with covetous practices; cursed children:
>
> **15** Which have forsaken the right way…
>
> **17** These [false preachers] are wells without water, clouds that are carried with a tempest; to whom the mist of darkness is reserved for ever.
>
> **18** For when they speak great swelling *words* of vanity, they allure through the lusts of the flesh, *through much* wantonness, those that were clean escaped from them who live in error.
>
> **19** While *they promise them liberty*, they themselves are the *servants of corruption*: for of whom a man is overcome, of the same is he brought in bondage.

The false teachers work every day and fly their jets to every part of the world to spread their bad doctrine, so *there is much ground to cover.* The following will not be a full discussion of the topic related to *sign gifts* in the early church and whether they are still energized by the Holy Spirit today, but I have a book coming out on the subject soon. We will just touch on these topics here.

These particular false teachings bring mockery to Jesus Christ and His message, just as the young woman did who was following the Apostle Paul and his men around, saying, "These men are the servants of the Most High God, which show us the way of salvation!" She was bringing attention to the man of God in an inappropriate way. While everyone around assumed she was filled with the Holy Spirit and lifting up God's message, Paul knew better. The apostle finally got tired of it and cast the unclean spirit out of her!

Now, most bystanders thought she was of God from her good *words*. But Paul, discerning that her *actions* brought a mockery to him and made it less likely people would listen to his *life-and-death message of salvation*, rebuked the demon and cast him out of her.

Please do not miss this! It was *not* the Holy Spirit causing her to say what seemed to be good things, "These men are the servants of God, listen to them...." It was a demon *mimicking* the Holy Spirit, but this did not fool the man of God. He would not allow her to make a mockery of his message. Many of the so-called manifestations of the Holy Spirit in modern churches are just like this. Demonic entities are *mimicking* the Holy Spirit and bringing mockery to the church and the gospel.

Paul recognized this mimicking going on even in the early church, and he admonished the Corinthians to cease and desist:

1 Corinthians 14:11–12, 23
11 Therefore if I know not the meaning of the voice, I shall be unto him that speaketh *a barbarian*, and he that speaketh *shall be a barbarian* unto me.
12 Even so ye, forasmuch as ye are zealous of spiritual *gifts*, seek that ye may excel to the *edifying* of the church.
23 If therefore the whole church be come together into one place, and all speak with tongues, and there come

in *those that are* unlearned, or unbelievers, *will they not say that ye are mad*?

So, even in the early church during the Apostolic age, Paul rebuked the carnal Corinthian church for abusing the ***sign gifts*** and bringing mockery to the gospel message! He explained to them that tongues were NOT a sign for believers, but ***for unbelievers.*** They were for the ***Jews, not Gentiles***.

1 Corinthians 14:22
22 Wherefore tongues are for a sign, ***not to them that believe***, but to them that believe not....

1 Corinthians 1:22
22 For the ***Jews require a sign***, and the Greeks [Gentiles] seek after wisdom [i.e., Bible Study].

So, my question is, why are modern churches allowing so-called tongue speaking in predominately Gentile (not Jewish) churches full of believers (not unbelievers)?

Abusing ***sign gifts*** was not the only damage caused by false teachers in the early church (and today); they also ***scout out our liberty and take it away from us***—the liberty to serve the Lord in the most important areas, which edify other people rather than ourselves!

Galatians 2:4–5
4 And that because of false brethren unawares brought in, who came in privily ***to spy out our liberty*** which we

have in Christ Jesus, that they might *bring us into bondage*:

5 <u>To whom we gave place by subjection, no, not for an hour</u>; that the truth of the gospel might continue with you.

There are many things about the Bible that we can agree to disagree on, but some things are so glaringly wrong when held up honestly beside the testimony of church history and Scripture, in proper context, that they should be expunged for the truth of the gospel's sake.

In some cases, well-meaning people (who themselves have been fooled) teach these false doctrines; in some cases, they are taught by those who utilize "sleight of men, and cunning craftiness, to deceive," knowingly. We do not always know which, but both should be avoided and corrected.

Titus 1:11

11 Whose *mouths must be stopped*, who subvert whole houses, teaching things which they ought not, for filthy lucre's sake.

So, here we go. This is a large but important task. We must all have a solid biblical grounding in this information concerning laying on of hands. Why? Because the Bible says:

"That we henceforth be no more children, tossed to and fro, and carried about with every wind of doctrine, by the sleight of men, and cunning craftiness, whereby they lie in wait to deceive."—**Ephesians 4:14**

The Book of Acts is a transitional book taking us from the O.T. economy into the N.T. economy, and therefore, generally, is not a good book to model church doctrine and practice after.

Many church groups use the Book of Acts as a model for their church's practice and doctrinal positions. I have always found this to be troubling because the book of Acts is a transitional book. It moves from the O.T. economy into the N.T. church-age economy; from law to grace; and from a substantially Jewish church (the church at Jerusalem) to a more Gentile church (the church at Antioch and most of the other early churches).

As we begin, let's define a few terms:

"Canon" means the entire O.T. and N.T. of the Bible, completed. The *canon of Scripture* was completed between A.D. 85–90.

"Economy" is a theological term for the "way of walking with God, as He reveals His will within a given dispensation."

"Dispensation" is a biblical term that means a *change* in how we are to walk with our Lord, during a given epoch or age, based upon new revelation from God.

"An Epistle" is a letter. Example: the books of the N.T. that Paul wrote were letters written to churches.

A *dispensational* change can affect how God's people live, act, worship, and teach doctrine. The book of *Acts, because of its transitional nature,* is not the best book of the Bible, in most cases, for making application to how we live, act, worship, and the doctrines we teach within the mature, mostly-Gentile, church age. There are some exceptions, of course, and we will discuss these. Nevertheless, we need to be very careful if we are going to employ methods of living from this book into our lives today.

Reading the Gospels (Matthew, Mark, Luke, and John) and the book of Acts is *like moving through a dispensational change in real time*—from the O.T. economy (Gospels and Acts Ch. 1), through the Apostolic Age (the Book of Acts after Ch. 1, Paul's epistles and other N.T. books written *prior to* A.D. 60), to the mature N.T. church age (Paul's epistles and other N.T. books written *after* A.D. 60).

As the book of Acts ends, and the Apostle Paul's ministry nears its end, we see the early church moving from mostly Jewish to the beginning of the predominately Gentile church. First, we see Paul preaching to the Jewish leaders:

Acts 28:17, 22–24

17 And it came to pass, that after three days Paul called the chief of the Jews together: and when they were come together, [they said]....

22 But we desire to hear of thee what thou thinkest: for as concerning this sect [Jewish believers in Christ], we know that every where it is spoken against.

23 And when they had appointed him a day, there came many to him into *his* lodging [Paul was under house arrest in Rome]; to whom he expounded and testified the kingdom of God, persuading them concerning Jesus, both out of the law of Moses, and *out of* the prophets, from morning till evening.

24 And some believed the things which were spoken, and some believed not.

The beginning of the TRANSITION from a predominately Jewish church to a mostly Gentile church:

Here we have a pronounced change in the direction of the N.T. church, as the book of Acts comes to a close—having begun with the history of a mostly Jewish church in Jerusalem, then Paul's missionary journeys to Gentile lands, and then finally the progression into a mostly Gentile church as it is today. As the passage in Acts 28 continues, we see the turning point in the history of the early church, and really, the entire 2000+ years of the church age:

Acts 28:25 And when they agreed not among themselves, they departed, after that Paul had spoken one word, Well spake the Holy Ghost by Esaias the prophet unto our fathers,

26 Saying, Go unto this people, and say, Hearing ye shall hear, and shall not understand; and seeing ye shall see, and not perceive:

27 For the heart of this people is waxed gross, and their ears are dull of hearing, and their eyes have they closed; lest they should see with their eyes, and hear with their ears, and understand with their heart, and should be converted, and I should heal them.

Paul was quoting directly from a passage these Jews knew well, and *they came under great conviction*, which brought with it great anger, because their minds were closed to the truth.

"And he said, Go, and tell this people, Hear ye indeed, but understand not; And see ye indeed, but perceive not. Make the heart of this people fat, And make their ears heavy, and shut their eyes; Lest they see with their eyes, and hear with their ears, And understand with their heart, and convert, and be healed."—**Isaiah 6:9–10**

After Paul quoted this passage, we see the *turning point* in church history:

Acts 28:28 Be it known therefore unto you, that the salvation of God is <u>sent unto the Gentiles</u>, and that <u>they will hear it</u>.
29 And when he had said these words, the Jews departed, and had great reasoning among themselves.
30 And Paul dwelt two whole years in his own hired house, and received all that came in unto him,
31 Preaching the kingdom of God, and teaching those things which concern the Lord Jesus Christ, with all confidence, no man forbidding him.

Paul prophesied that the N.T. church would soon be primarily a Gentile church. This transpired quickly (v. 28) and has remained this way throughout the church age. The Gentile church also began to grow rapidly, even halfway through the book of Acts.

Acts 12:24
24 But the word of God grew and multiplied.

Acts 14:1
1 And it came to pass in Iconium…that a great multitude both of the Jews and also of the Greeks [Gentiles] believed.

Some of the more Jewish practices—such as laying on of hands by apostles to impart the indwelling of the Holy Spirit—were no longer practiced in the more Gentile-oriented churches later in the book of Acts. However, laying on of hands was utilized for other purposes such as ordaining officers of the church, and it continues today as a symbolic gesture confirming that the church recognizes God's calling on an individual.

The pastoral epistles, First and Second Timothy and Titus, and all the epistles of Paul written after A.D. 60, provide the best light on how the N.T. church should look today, and of course, what she should teach.

As we move through these chapters on "Laying on of Hands," we will see why churches often get wrong ideas about life and doctrine for the church during today's church age by focusing on the transitional book of Acts and other N.T. books written prior to A.D. 60, which record the history of the Apostolic age.

We will suggest a more proper interpretation of the magnificent book of Acts and make suggestions for gaining a better understanding of **the laying on of hands** and several of the phenomena often associated with it in the early church, and we will discuss the practical use of all this now in the mature church age in which we live.

As you read this, please remember that my desire is that you **not read into** the Bible what men may have **told you they think** it means. Do you remember our discussion on the Jewish targums in Chapter 2? Here is an example of why that is dangerous.

For at least 200 years of the 406 "silent years" before Christ was born, the Jews heard their rabbis teach from the **targums**, which were **paraphrases** teaching what their rabbis **thought** the Scriptures meant—the people were not being allowed to read the actual Hebrew Scriptures, which is the Old Testament. What if their teachers, who morphed into the Pharisees during those years, were wrong? (We know now they were. They crucified Jesus!) Most of the Jews missed their Messiah because of this.

Rather than trying to force the Bible to fit some preacher's or denomination's ideas (their **paraphrases** of the Bible), please let the Bible say to YOU what it actually *MEANS* by using the rules of proper Bible interpretation. No man's teachings (mine included) should be placed above the inspired, written Word of God, properly interpreted.

Just be honest and desire to know the truth more than you wish to defend these false teachers' positions. They are not your interpretations anyway—you borrowed them! Seek the truth for yourself in the Bible. Don't worry about the peer pressure from your church, denomination, or seminary. Just seek truth with an honest heart. God, ultimately, is the only one we need to worry about answering to concerning our viewpoints (1 John 2:27).

False teachers and preachers in a serpentine way *paraphrase* the Bible, changing it slightly or using it out of context, or misemploying a passage from one dispensation that does not apply to another, *just as the Pharisees did*. Don't study from their *paraphrase*—please go straight to the Scriptures yourself.

Would you consider allowing the Scriptures to have more authority than the books you've read *about* the Bible (someone else's idea about what certain passages or doctrines mean)?

Be wary of topical sermons, where a verse or two are cited, but the context is left out. In this book, my goal is to teach you the "best practices" for the proper way to interpret the Bible, considering the dispensations, the immediate context, word studies, rules of grammar, and holding the passage up against the whole of the Bible. Then YOU can decide for yourself what the Bible means by what it says, provided you study with the help of the Holy Spirit, and with an honest heart.

It is a funny thing how, when people teach us what *they think* the Bible means, then if we are impressed by them, we *personalize* their doctrines and then we feel like *we own them*. From that point our minds are closed, at least for a while, and we are unteachable and unchangeable. Now these become *OUR doctrines,* and we argue for them and get emotionally attached to them; and often we cheat on the rules of proper Bible interpretation to uphold them and become offended if others disagree with us. I am merely desiring that you never cheat on the rules to prove a point. Just allow the Bible to say what it means.

Let's admit that some of the things all of us have been taught by our denominations, pastors, and teachers (or by YouTube Bible gurus) could be wrong. (The Lord knows I've laid aside many words, phrases, and ideas I had been taught earlier in my Christian walk.)

Let's honestly seek truth together. I believe it would be far better to learn what *YOU* think the Bible means, after prayer and meditation, without putting the Scripture through the sieve of someone else's doctrinal position that you may have adopted.

Lose the sieve. Read the Bible plainly, and let it speak to you. Ask the Holy Spirit to help you understand it as God meant it when He said it.

Now, this is hard to do if we have personalized a doctrine. It takes sincere prayer to literally let go of preconceived impressions and seek truth. But this is what mature Christians must do to find truth and grow in knowledge of the Lord.

What is the "Full Gospel"?

The "full gospel" folks think (because they have been taught) that *they* believe the "full gospel" and *the rest of us do not*. Their definition of this is that they believe ALL the book of Acts. They also define a "full gospel" church as one which believes that all the manifestations of *sign gifts* in books of the N.T. written *prior to* A.D. 60 should still be applied today, and they think we do not believe their idea of "full gospel."

That's really only half-true. We do believe all the book of Acts, and all of the Bible—every word, every jot and tittle—and we employ the things that are applicable today.

However, we also believe one must read and make application while using the rules of proper Bible interpretation, in context, and *understanding that dispensational changes in the Bible affect interpretations and applications.*

What are the rules? Basically, the rules of Bible interpretation are about the same as rules anyone would learn in basic English literature class about how to interpret any literary work. You read it plainly, understanding that the context will tell you when allegories or other figures of speech are being used. These rules in various formats are agreed upon by most conservative scholars (i.e., people who believe in verbal plenary inspiration, as we do).[49]

I wish we could agree together not to cheat by violating rules of Bible interpretation just to believe what we want to believe, or make the Bible say what we want it to say. That is unfair and never leads to the truth.

What is the truth? It is the Word of God, allowed to say what it *means.* I do NOT ask you to agree with everything I say. Get angry if you wish, or inquisitive (I hope), but I ask that you *study the Bible* to prove me right or wrong. Dig in with an honest desire for truth and have fun studying. If I can get you to do that, that's all a true teacher wants.

---

[49] For a copy of "The Ten Rules of Bible Interpretation" by David Mitchell, go to: ChristianPosture.com

Chapter 15

The Doctrine of the Laying on of Hands—
THE EARLY CHURCH

In the passage below, we have an example of ***laying on of hands*** in one of the early churches at Antioch. This was a large city and had a substantial Jewish community. The church there consisted of Jews and Gentiles (mostly Gentiles) who spoke Greek (the language of commerce in that day). This is what we know about Antioch.

> "After the stoning of Stephen in 35 AD, some *Greek*-speaking Jewish believers travel to Antioch in Syria to spread the Good News to the Jews living there. Other believers from Cyprus and Cyrene (in modern-day Libya) also arrive in Antioch and preach to the *Greek*-speaking Gentiles living there…. The believers are called "Christians" for the first time in Antioch."[50]

---

[50] Chris and Jenifer Taylor, ***The Bible Journey***, West Midlands (UK), https://www.thebiblejourney.org/biblejourney1/7–journeys–of–jesuss–followers/the–gentile–church–at–antioch/. The author recommends this website—very nice.

It is good to let our minds travel back in time and examine life in the church at Antioch in the book of Acts and here is the backstory:

Acts 11:19–24

19 Now they [Christians from the church at Jerusalem] which were scattered abroad upon the persecution that arose about Stephen travelled as far as Phenice, and Cyprus, *and Antioch*, preaching the word to none but unto the Jews only [at first, i.e., the gospel was usually taken to the Jews first, and then to the Gentiles].

20 And some of them were men of Cyprus and Cyrene, which, when they were come to Antioch, spake unto the Grecians, preaching the Lord Jesus [now the gospel goes to the Gentiles].

21 And the hand of the Lord was with them: and a great number believed, and turned unto the Lord [the predominately Gentile church grew rapidly].

22 Then tidings of these things came unto the ears of the church which was in Jerusalem [the "mother" church]: and they sent forth Barnabas, that he should go as far as *Antioch*.

23 Who, when he came, and had seen the grace of God, was glad, and exhorted them all, that with purpose of heart they would cleave unto the Lord.

24 For he was a good man, and full of the Holy Ghost and of faith: and *much people was added unto the Lord.*

Acts 11:25-30

25 Then departed Barnabas to Tarsus, for to seek Saul [the Apostle Paul]:

26 And when he had found him, he ***brought him unto Antioch.*** And it came to pass, that <u>a whole year</u> they assembled themselves with the church, and taught much people. And the disciples were ***called Christians first in Antioch.***

27 And in these days came ***prophets from Jerusalem*** unto Antioch.

28 And there stood up one of them named Agabus, and signified by the spirit that there should be great dearth throughout all the world: <u>which came to pass</u> in the days of Claudius Caesar.

29 Then the disciples, every man according to his ability, determined to send relief unto the brethren which dwelt in Judaea:

30 Which also they did, and sent it to the elders by the hands of Barnabas and Saul.

Acts 12:1-7

1 Now about that time Herod the king stretched forth *his* hands to vex certain of the church.

2 And he killed James the brother of John with the sword.

3 And because he saw it pleased the Jews, he proceeded further to take Peter also. (Then were the days of unleavened bread.)

4 And when he had apprehended him, he put *him* in prison, and delivered *him* to four quaternions of soldiers to keep him; intending after Easter [lit. Gk., Passover] to bring him forth to the people.

5 Peter therefore was kept in prison: but prayer was made without ceasing of the church unto God for him.

7 And, behold, the angel of the Lord came upon *him*, and a light shined in the prison: and he smote Peter on the side, and raised him up, saying, Arise up quickly. And his chains fell off from his hands.

In Acts Chapters 11 and 12, God answered prayers for Peter to miraculously escape prison. Then we see that the persecution of the Christians in Jerusalem was turned for good by God, and as the people fled the persecution, the church spread far and wide.

The gospel was preached to the Jew first, and then to the Gentiles, and the church at Antioch grew explosively and became primarily a Gentile church.

We see the operation of the *sign gift* of *prophecy* occurring at the church at Antioch, with Agabus predicting a drought, which came to pass. (He later, in Ch. 21, prophesied that Paul would be imprisoned, which he was.)

The *sign gift* of prophecy in the early church was initiated in a person by the *laying on of hands*, thus imparting the Holy Spirit to that person to empower the gift of prophecy which God had given.

It is important to note that in the Bible, if a person claimed to be a prophet, and his prophecy was not fulfilled, he was to be put to death (Deut. 18:20-22). I wonder what would happen if this were applied today to those who claim to be "prophets" or "apostles?" Of course, we know it is not supposed to be applied today because we live under grace, not law. However, it is something to ponder, considering how seriously God takes it when people lie about being a prophet.

(Pentecostal friends have told me, "Well things are different today. Prophets can make mistakes." I always answer, "Where in the Bible does it say prophets today can make mistakes? If, by definition, a prophet speaks the words of God, how can a genuine prophet make a mistake in his prophecy?")

This drought led to those who had money or lands sending financial relief to the poor church at Jerusalem to buy food for the saints there.

We also see that constant persecution continued, especially in Jerusalem, with James being martyred at the hand of Herod. Christians would suffer for Christ, giving their blood as a testimony of their faith, for the next 2 ½ centuries of the early church.

These passages in the book of Acts provide meaningful details about the history of the early church some 2,000 years ago.

In this chapter, and the six which follow in Vol. 2, I will discuss the laying on of hands and associated *sign gifts*, as well as the *offices* of the *N.T. prophets and teachers* we see in the passages.

In the story about the church at Antioch, a group of N.T. prophets and teachers are listed. Barnabas is the best known, for he traveled with Paul and preached throughout the Bible lands in this, Paul's first missionary journey (Acts Chs. 12, 13). He vouched for Paul before the other apostles when he first went to Jerusalem. Paul, formerly Saul, had been an enemy of the church (Acts 9:26–27). Barnabas's name was Joseph, but the Apostles nick-named him Barnabas, which means "son of consolation." He brought great comfort to the early church, including selling some of his lands and giving to the poor saints at Jerusalem (Acts Ch. 4).

Barnabas was a powerful preacher. He embarked with Paul on their first missionary effort. Their journey began from this church at Antioch, as we saw in the passage above. We see that the leaders of the church, the prophets and teachers, *laid hands on* Paul and Barnabas, and "sent them" after prayer and fasting for their success. This type of laying on of hands was, in part, a symbolic human gesture (which continues today), recognizing the previous call of God on the lives of these two men for a specific mission (or ministry). It was Jewish in nature, coming from practices in the O.T. However, it was more than just symbolic in the early church. During the Apostolic Age, the gift of prophecy was imparted by the laying on of hands of an apostle, as the Holy Spirit energized the gift.

This is also an early view of church government. It was not congregational but led by the apostles, prophets, and teachers (and within a few years, elders were ordained, and they led, as they do today).

We know the church soon had elder rule from Acts Chapter 14:21–23: "And when they had preached the gospel to that city, and had taught many, they returned again to Lystra, and *to* Iconium, *and Antioch*...And when *they had ordained them elders in every church, and had prayed with fasting, they commended them to the Lord, on whom they believed*."

There is a very nice website called "The Bible Journey," which gives a great biblical rendition of this journey, step by step. I would suggest you take some time and enjoy it.[51] I have been to Israel twice but never followed Paul's journey in this part of the world. After

---

[51] Ibid. https://www.thebiblejourney.org/biblejourney1/9–pauls–journey–to–cyprus–pamphylia–galatia–/paul–starts–his–1st–missionary–journey/.

spending about an hour on this site, it made me wish to travel to the places Paul travelled, on a future journey of my own.[52]

Many know the story of Saul, who was the destroyer of Christians before his conversion on the road to Damascus, where he was renamed Paul (Acts 9:3–19). He became the greatest of the apostles and was perhaps the most magnificent Christian who ever lived from then until now. He penned most of the N.T. under the inspiration of the Holy Spirit; the Apostle Peter claimed that Paul's writings were Scripture, and they certainly are! (2 Peter 3:16)

The epistles of Paul are perhaps the richest words of the entire Bible. It is an understatement to say that the church at Antioch was a strong church. His letter to this church, along with all the churches to which Paul wrote his epistles, together with the book of Acts, gives us a very good view of the early church and its doctrines and practices.

Now, let's get back to *laying on of hands* in the early church, and the *gifts of prophecy and teaching*.

The original uses of laying on of hands, and the sign gifts often associated with it in the Early Church:

How was the practice of "laying on of hands" used? We see the following practices in the Early Church prior to A.D. 60.

1. Laying on of hands to anoint men for a specific ministry.

---

[52] Ibid.

The first use, as we saw above, was to ordain men and confirm them for a specific ministry and to send them to do the work of God. This was not unlike the prophets of the O.T. laying on hands to anoint kings or sons of the prophets. The laying on of hands was a Jewish practice brought into the early church.

Acts 13:2–3:
2 As they ministered to the Lord, and fasted, the Holy Ghost said, Separate me Barnabas and Saul for the work whereunto I have called them.
3 And when they had fasted and prayed, *and laid their hands on them,* they sent them away.

The Holy Spirit had called these men, Barnabas and Paul, as missionaries to the Gentiles, and the leaders of the church laid hands on them. This was done during the ordination of these men for this ministry, confirming that they were in fact called by the Holy Spirit to this end, and officially sending them forth with the church's blessings and support. Ordaining men for specific ministries and sending them forth with blessings was an important purpose of laying on of hands in the Early Church. Here we see the first deacons to be ordained in the Early Church.

Acts 6:5–7
5 And the saying pleased the whole multitude: and they chose Stephen, a man full of faith and of the Holy Ghost, and Philip, and Prochorus, and Nicanor, and Timon, and Parmenas, and Nicolas a proselyte of Antioch:

6 Whom they set before the apostles: and when they had prayed, ***they laid their hands on them.***
7 And the word of God increased; and the number of the disciples multiplied in Jerusalem greatly; and a great company of the priests were obedient to the faith.

We see, here, a method still correctly used in modern churches following this pattern. The early church chose deacons and brought them to the apostles to lay hands on them and confirm them for the office. The result was that the church multiplied greatly, and many Jewish priests became saved.

Today, there being no apostles in the mature church (see the Bible qualifications of an apostle below), elders lay hands on men as they are ordained to be deacons. While the church chooses the deacons, the elders themselves choose additional elders and lay hands on them during their ordination services.

2. Laying on of hands for healing and raising the dead.

Jesus Christ and those with ***apostolic sign gifts*** in the early church often imparted healing power through laying on of hands. Remember, Jesus and the apostles were still living in the O.T. economy (the church age did not begin until Pentecost, ten days after Christ ascended into heaven after his resurrection). It was the practice in the O.T. among the Jewish prophets and sons of prophets (their apprentices) to lay hands on people for healing when the Lord led them to. They could also raise the dead (which is actually the same apostolic or prophetic gift—the gift of healing). They also laid on hands to ordain new prophets or kings, after God had chosen them.

This O.T. pattern of laying on of hands for healing continued into the early history of the church, as we see from the earliest books of the New Testament (written before A.D. 60) with Jesus, the apostles, and N.T. prophets sometimes being given the *sign gift* of healing by the Holy Spirit, for God's sovereign purposes (which we discuss below).

The Apostle Paul and other apostles *laid hands on* people to impart healing power from God. We saw this in Paul's first missionary journey which we discussed earlier.

Acts 14:3

3 Long time therefore abode they speaking boldly in the Lord, which *gave testimony unto the word of his grace, and granted signs and wonders* to be done by their hands.

Before we continue, please notice that the PURPOSE of sign gifts, again and again in the N.T., is said to be *to authenticate the new message of grace* (as opposed to the law) *and to authenticate the messenger*. Here we see in verse 3 above that the Lord "gave testimony unto the word of His grace" by "granting signs and wonders to be done by their hands." The signs and wonders made people believe that these messengers were genuinely from God and that their new message of grace must also be from God. Without the signs and wonders, no one (especially among the Jews) would have accepted the message or the messengers! Once the message of grace was spread throughout the known world of the Roman Empire, it no longer needed to be authenticated. After the apostles died and the N.T. canon was completed, the signs and wonders became fewer until they ceased, as we will discuss here and in later chapters.

Notice that God, through His sovereign will, granted these powers to certain men and women for a specific purpose, at a specific time.

Acts 14:8, 10-11, 21-23

8 And there sat a certain man at Lystra, impotent in his feet, being *a cripple from his mother's womb, who never had walked:*

10 Said with a loud voice, Stand upright on thy feet. And he leaped and walked.

11 And when the people saw what Paul had done, they lifted up their voices, saying in the speech of Lycaonia, *The gods are come down to us* in the likeness of men.

21 And when they had preached the gospel to that city, and had taught many, they returned again to Lystra, and to Iconium, and Antioch,

22 Confirming the souls of the disciples, and exhorting them to continue in the faith, and that we must through much tribulation enter into the kingdom of God.

23 And when they had <u>ordained them elders</u> in every church, and had prayed with fasting, they commended them to the Lord, on whom they believed.

When the Gentiles saw the miraculous healings that Paul performed in his role as apostle, they thought him to be a god! They were barely constrained from worshipping him and Barnabas! Paul and Barnabas rebuked this action and turned the glory back to God. Nonetheless, the *miracle authenticated Paul's message* of salvation by the blood of Jesus Christ, and many listened to his preaching and were saved.

The Gentiles loved the preaching, but the Jews were jealous, and they began to hate the message and the messengers. Their anger rose up so hot that they took Paul and stoned him to death, dragging him out of the city, and leaving him in a ditch. He miraculously came back to life in the presence of other disciples of Christ, as they stood around his body praying.

These **sign gifts** were not performed in a church or hidden in a corner, **but they took place in public on the streets of the cities in front of the world!** The effect was profound with people seeing that **God had affirmed the message of these men**, by giving them the power to perform **signs and wonders**.

Here is another occasion where the Apostle Paul utilized the power of a **sign gift** and **raised a young boy from the dead**, just as Elisha had in the O.T. book of 2 Kings Ch. 4!

Acts 20:9–12

9 And there sat in a window a certain young man named Eutychus, being fallen into a deep sleep: and as Paul was long preaching, he sunk down with sleep, and fell down from the third loft, and was taken up dead.

10 *And Paul went down, and fell on him, and embracing him said, Trouble not yourselves; for his life is in him.*

11 When he therefore was come up again, and had broken bread, and eaten, and talked a long while, even till break of day, so he departed.

12 And they brought the young man alive, and *were not a little comforted.*

"Were not a little comforted" is old English KJV language for "THEY WERE HUGELY COMFORTED!" I love the KJV; it is written like we Texans talk—it speaks of eating *victuals*, wearing *breeches*, being *affrighted*, being *astonied*, a *comely woman*, to *holden* someone up, to *holpen* them when in need, to *staunch* the leak, I *strowed* the seeds, I was *anhungered* before breakfast, I was *astonied* when I heard the thunder, I asked for the *eyesalve*, I said not to *fret* about the disappointment, I wore my *leathern* jacket, I *lopped off* the snake's head, *whilst* I went to town, etc. The King James is not only the most accurate English version of the Bible, it speaks Texan! (Of course, hearing me say this from the pulpit in my Texas accent helps. Okay, end of rabbit trail and now, back to the actual point...)

We often also see *Jesus laying His hands on people* to impart miraculous healing upon them.

Mark 8:24–25

24 And he looked up, and said, I see men as trees, walking.
25 After that he [Jesus] *put his hands again upon his eyes,* and made him look up: and *he was restored,* and saw every man clearly.

3. Laying on of hands by (only) an apostle was used to impart the Holy Spirit upon regeneration for a short season.

Acts 19:5–6

5 When they heard *this*, they were baptized in the name of the Lord Jesus.

6 And when ***Paul had laid his hands upon them, the Holy Ghost came on them;*** and they spake with tongues, and prophesied.

However, soon the Holy Spirit just fell upon people, especially Gentiles, as they were saved, without the laying on of hands.

Please make note of the fact that the ***baptism of the Holy Spirit,*** which was indicated by the ***sign gift*** of speaking in foreign languages (in the early church)—languages that they had not learned in school, and this occurred due to their salvation experience. As we have covered extensively in this book, the indwelling of the Holy Spirit occurs once and for all when a person is regenerated.

These were Jewish disciples of John the Baptist who had believed Jesus was the Messiah, but Paul and Barnabas gave them the gospel more clearly, and explained the mystery of the indwelling Holy Spirit which their prophets of old had looked into but not understood. As soon as they heard and believed, they were indwelt, and the miracle of languages proved they were saved, as the Jews in Jerusalem had been after Pentecost.

The ***sign gifts*** were important at this stage, because people became convinced by them that the Comforter had in fact been sent by Christ to indwell every born-again person, even a Gentile!

4. Laying on of hands was _not_ utilized for casting out demons and other *sign gifts* such as recovering from poison and recovering from snake bites. Rather, these ***sign gifts*** were usually performed by ***_speaking_*** with apostolic authority.

Jesus cast out demons quite often with His Word.

Luke 4:31–39

31 And came down to Capernaum, a city of Galilee, and taught them on the sabbath days.

32 And they were astonished at his doctrine: *for his word was with power.*

33 And in the synagogue there was a man, which had a spirit of an *unclean devil*, and cried out with a loud voice,

34 Saying, Let *us* alone; what have we to do with thee, *thou* Jesus of Nazareth? art thou come to destroy us? I know thee who thou art; the Holy One of God.

[Isn't it troubling that the Jews, for the most part, did not believe Jesus was their Messiah, but the demons knew exactly who He was!]

35 And Jesus rebuked him, saying, Hold thy peace, and come out of him. And when the devil had thrown him in the midst, *he came out of him*, and hurt him not.

36 And they were all amazed, and spake among themselves, saying, What a word is this! for with authority and power he commandeth the unclean spirits, and they come out.

37 And the fame of him went out into every place of the country round about.

38 And he arose out of the synagogue, and entered into Simon's house. And Simon's wife's mother was taken with a great fever; and they besought him for her.

39 And he stood over her, and *rebuked the fever*; and it left her: and immediately she arose and ministered unto them.

Again, most of these miracles were performed on the street with many witnesses, both unbelievers and believers, and the people were astonished. Jesus's message was authenticated by the miracles. This was very different from modern "faith-healing" services, usually done in buildings or tents where everyone has been conditioned to desire to see a "miracle." The performance of the genuine *sign gifts* of the Apostolic Age cannot be compared, honestly, to the feigned acts of the modern tongues/faith-healing movement. The two are different in procedure, power, purpose, and probity.

PROPHECY and TEACHING were two gifts mentioned in Acts 13:1 above, together with Apostolic HEALING

The *Office of the Prophet* existed in the O.T. During the prophetic era in particular, they possessed the ability to perform *sign miracles and wonders*. This did not occur often even in the O.T. (with sometimes an average of 400 years passing between groups of miraculous events). They happened from time to time, usually introducing a new dispensation and authenticating the new messengers of it.

Upon the advent of the Messiah, a flurry of *sign gifts* occurred to validate the new message of Jesus and His apostles, especially to the Jews. Also, they were still living in the O.T. economy, and there were still prophets. We call them N.T. prophets because they are written about in the early N.T. books, but we must remember they still lived in the O.T. economy.

They were just like O.T. prophets, and there had been 406 *silent years* with no prophesy and no "open visions" prior to this! The "silent years" before the time of Christ and the apostles were much like the time before the prophet/priest, Samuel, in the O.T., and much like the time from the end of the Apostolic Age until now.

God's people walk by faith, not by sight, during the times between outpourings of miracles, because during these times, the sign gifts temporarily cease, and this has been true throughout biblical history.

When God is introducing a new dispensation, or manner with which He is going to deal with His people, these dispensational changes are accompanied by sign gifts, which authenticate the new era. There had been a long silent period of hundreds of years, and then God raised up Samuel, the prophet....

1 Samuel 3:1
1 And the child Samuel ministered unto the Lord before Eli. And the word of the Lord was precious in those days; *there was* **no** *open vision.*

After this prophetic period, there was another long period of silence. This cycle has repeated throughout Bible history.

As we get more into the later books of the N.T., we begin to see that the *sign gifts* which accompanied the ministries of the apostles and N.T. prophets begin to become less frequent, and the Apostle Paul prophesied that they would cease.

1 Corinthians 13:8

8 Charity never faileth: but whether *there be* prophecies, they shall fail; whether *there be* tongues, ***they shall cease***; whether *there be* knowledge, it shall vanish away.

This cessation of sign gifts has been the case from the death of the last apostle, John, in the first century, until now. However, the sign gifts will be reinstated by God during the last 3 ½ years of the tribulation period in our future, when "our sons and daughters shall prophecy" (Joel 2:28). The ***sign gifts*** have been paused by God's sovereign will since the Apostolic Age, but will be reenergized by the Holy Spirit during the Great Tribulation.

Below, in the N.T. book of Romans, (written prior to A.D. 60), we see that the following gifts were still operating in the Early Church:

Romans 12:6–7

6 Having then gifts differing according to the grace that is given to us, whether ***prophecy, let us prophesy*** according to the proportion of faith;

7 Or ministry, let us wait on our ministering: or he that teacheth, on ***teaching.***

In the early church, prior to the death of the last apostle, ***sign gifts***—including the gifts of prophecy, "words of knowledge," and "words of wisdom"—still existed. Today, prophecies have ceased, according to the Bible and the testimony of church history, but people still are given the gifts of ministering, teaching, and others found in other passages of Scripture.

Here are examples of prophetic *sign gifts* being practiced in the Early Church and also the gift of teaching, which is a *non-sign gift*:

- **Prophesying**

  In **Acts 21:8–12** we see the example of the four virgin daughters of Philip the evangelist prophesying. So did the prophet Agabus, who predicted Paul would be arrested.

- **Teaching**

  In **Acts 18:24–26** Apollos, "an eloquent man, mighty in the Scriptures, spoke and *taught* diligently the things of the Lord."

Aquila and Priscilla "took Apollos and expounded unto him the way of God more perfectly." The gift of teaching is still operating in the modern church because this was *not a sign gift*. It is a gift that has remained throughout the 2000+ year church age.

Dr. Irwin (Rocky) Freeman, Bro. Otis Fisher, and Dr. Myron Golden are three of the best examples in my lifetime of people with the gift of teaching who have blessed my life immeasurably.

Bill Nichols was an elder in our church, a physics professor, and one of our adult Sunday School teachers who took over Bro. Otis Fisher's class when he went to heaven. Bill taught in a very anointed manner for exactly the same number of years as Bro. Otis—13 years—and then he went to heaven.

Before these amazing people, there were other teachers. In my teen years through my young adult years, I remember Sue Riddle, another highly gifted Bible teacher that blessed and influenced my life in a powerful way even as a teenager. And there was Gary Plumlee, who discipled me for a brief time in my early twenties (he had a brilliant mind), and then Frank and Patty Ford who taught the young couples' class when Charlotte and I were first married, who we have been life-long friends with. Charlotte and I still have talks with them about the deeper things of God.

Now, in our church, two young men astound me every week, as they teach the adult Sunday School class that was originally Bro. Otis's class, my son Ben Mitchell, who is an elder in our church, and my new son (that is what Charlotte and I call sons-in-law) Dave Huber (married to my second-born daughter, Katie). These guys have the gift. And last of all, and best of all, is my wife, Charlotte, who is a gifted teacher. She is a perfect pastor's wife and teaches me things she has learned about the Lord many days each week. She teaches the best class of all at our church, the children (my youngest grandbabies' ages). We are blessed with great teachers in our church.

When the gift of teaching is present, you will see it because Jesus said the good teacher would teach both something new and something old. A great teacher will teach you doctrines you already know but need to be reminded of, and will teach you something you never thought of before. This keeps things interesting for the students.

Matthew 13:51–52

51 Jesus saith unto them, Have ye understood all these things? They say unto him, Yea, Lord.

52 Then said he unto them, Therefore every scribe *which is* instructed unto the kingdom of heaven is like unto a man *that is* an householder, which **bringeth forth out of his treasure things new and old.**

There have been many teachers in my life, but you get the idea, the **gift of teaching** is very important in today's church, as it was in the early church.

- **Apostolic Healing and other *sign gifts***

1 Corinthians 12:8–11

8 For to one is given by the Spirit the word of wisdom; to another the word of knowledge by the same Spirit;

9 To another faith [not saving faith, here, but faith to do miracles] by the same Spirit; to another the **gifts of healing** by the same Spirit;

10 To another the **working of miracles**; to another prophecy; to another discerning of spirits; to another divers kinds of tongues; to another the interpretation of tongues:

11 But all these worketh that one and the selfsame Spirit, **dividing to every man severally as _he_ will.**

Verse 11 makes it clear that these gifts were not given to everyone but were divided among men **according to GOD'S SOVEREIGN WILL.**

There are two groups of spiritual gifts in the Bible. One group includes **sign gifts** (like the ones above); the second group includes **non-sign gifts** (like teaching, administration, giving, etc. [1 Cor. 12:27–28]).

Most of these **sign gifts** listed in the above passage continued only until near the end of the Apostolic Age (approx. A.D. 100) because their job of authenticating the messengers of the N.T. Gospel at the beginning of the N.T. dispensation was completed.

Some **sign gifts,** which provided Scriptural knowledge to the Early Churches before they possessed all the N.T. books, passed away later, only after the churches had the complete canon of Scripture. Let's look at an example of this below:

"Words of Knowledge," "Words of Wisdom"

Acts 13:1, 3
1 Now there were in the church that was at Antioch certain **prophets and teachers**;
3 And when they had fasted and prayed, and laid their hands on them, they sent them away.

The verse mentions that these men were "prophets and teachers." They ministered before the Lord during the brief **Apostolic Age**, which we have discussed. As we will continue to say a number of times, so that you never forget this principle—**No Jew would have believed the new Gospel message without the signs and wonders which accompanied these messengers.** How do we know this? Because the Bible says:

1 Corinthians 1:22

22 For the ***Jews require a sign,*** and the Greeks seek after wisdom.

The life they had lived under the law for thousands of years was vastly different from the dispensation of Grace which Jesus and His apostles introduced to the world. Clearly, the Jews needed a sign to believe the new Gospel message.

Prophetic words of knowledge and words of wisdom (1 Cor. 12:8, above) were necessary in the Early Church, prior to the completion of the canon, because no local church had all the N.T. truths revealed to them yet. If they needed certain truths, then a person with the **sign gift** of "a word of knowledge" would speak the truth to the congregation, which the Lord had revealed to them individually, earlier. This passage teaches that there were people whom God would reveal things to in private, which they would then share with the congregation publicly, and there was a proper order for doing it.

When it says in verse 32, below, "And the spirits of the prophets are subject to the prophets," this is very important. It means that if someone prophesied something that contradicted any passage, or even a verse of Scripture, properly interpreted, then that prophet's words would be ignored. Also, women were not allowed to prophesy in the church services. This is because often the prophecies were actually Scriptural principles that would later be within the completed canon, and women were not allowed to preach or teach men in the assemblies of the church (1 Timothy 2:12, 13).

1 Corinthians 14:29–34

29 Let the prophets speak two or three, and let the other judge.

30 If *any thing* be revealed to another that sitteth by, let the first hold his peace.

31 For ye may all prophesy one by one, that all may learn, and all may be comforted.

32 And the spirits of the prophets are subject to the prophets.

33 For God is not the author of confusion, but of peace, as in all churches of the saints.

34 Let your women keep silence in the churches: for it is not permitted unto them to speak; but they are commanded to be under obedience, as also saith the law.

GOD'S PURPOSE for giving the sign gifts, according to the Bible:

Jesus, before leaving this earth, told His disciples that they would have power to lay hands on the sick and heal them. But people miss a very important part—one of the main PURPOSES of these *sign gifts* is revealed at the end of the passage below.

Mark 16:17, 20

17 And these signs shall follow them that believe; In my name shall they cast out devils; they shall speak with new tongues.

But look at the last verse in the context:

20 And they went forth, and preached every where, the Lord working with them, and <u>*confirming the word* with signs following</u>. Amen.

The word "**confirming**" in Greek is:

bĕbaiŏō, to *make stable:*—confirm, establish.

The word "**following**" in the Greek is:

ĕpakŏlŏuthĕō, to accompany.

I really believe most people who teach this passage or study it, get the "emphasis on the wrong syllable." The most important information is at the end of the passage, but most people focus on the sign gifts listed in the middle.

Jesus is saying that when He ascends into heaven and sends the Comforter (in 10 days, on Pentecost), the disciples will have power to witness to the world. Their job would be to take this NEW gospel message of grace to a world consumed with Law and paganism, and not inclined to receive the message or the messengers. Therefore, the Lord Himself will go with them, working with them, and CONFIRMING THE WORD *with signs that accompanied the Word*.

The signs and wonders were that which *confirmed, established, and vouched for the truth* of the WORDS—the *new* message they accompanied! The words, as Jesus said, "were spirit and life." The gospel message of salvation by grace through faith, without the works of the law, began to turn the world upside down. Without the sign gifts, which accompanied the words, no one would have listened.

In the context of this passage, the signs had a purpose to *authenticate the new message of salvation*. Once the canon was completed (A.D. 85–90) and people had observed the miracles, once the message had been authenticated, the signs subsided.

Now, please remember, at the time Jesus taught this, the words which were being confirmed were the apostles and disciples teaching a gospel that was very different from the O.T. law. Jews would have never believed this new "word" without the *signs which accompanied the message and the messengers. This is no longer needed today, for the Scriptures have been completed and accepted as God's Word for 2000 years!*

It is very important to understand the dispensational changes that took place when moving from the early, mostly Jewish, Apostolic Age, to the more mature, Gentile, church age. The *signs* were paused for 2000 years when their purpose was fulfilled. They will be reinstated when there is a new purpose—to herald the second coming of Christ!

If you are never taught the biblical purpose of sign gifts in the first place, you miss the truth of the completion of their purpose, and their resulting pause.

The above passage in Mark said that the disciples which Jesus sent forth would have the power to survive poison. In the early apostolic age, the Apostle Paul had the power to survive a snake bite, as Jesus had prophesied that His followers would be able to do.

These signs and wonders authenticated their message as they took the gospel from Jerusalem to all Judaea, to Samaria, and to the uttermost part of the world (Acts 1:8).

Look how the sign gift of surviving poison affected the people observing the Apostle Paul.

> **Acts 28:3–6**
>
> **3** And when Paul had gathered a bundle of sticks, and laid *them* on the fire, there came a viper out of the heat, and fastened on his hand.
>
> **4** And when the barbarians saw the venomous beast hang on his hand, they said among themselves, No doubt this man is a murderer, whom, though he hath escaped the sea, yet vengeance suffereth not to live.
>
> **5** And he shook off the beast into the fire, and felt no harm.
>
> **6** Howbeit they looked when he should have swollen, or fallen down dead suddenly: but after they had looked a great while, and saw no harm come to him, ***they changed their minds, and said that he was a god.***

In the passage above, we see the profound effect upon these pagans—they concluded that Paul and Barnabas ***must be gods***. These were powerful, life-changing miracles unlike the feigned "miracles" of today by so-called faith-healers. These miracles were irrefutable and were done in the presence of antagonistic people, often on the streets of the cities. Often, when the Jews would see these, they would attempt to do bodily harm to the Apostles.

The same gifts that allowed speaking in tongues and healing also allowed saints to drink poison and not die, or to be bitten by poisonous snakes and survive. We have not observed today's "faith-healers" drinking poison and surviving snake bites. Why not? If they truly had *sign gifts*, they could.

So-called snake-handlers in Pentecostal churches in Kentucky and Tennessee regularly die from being bitten by the snakes they are handling in church services. I remember, through the past 45 years, hearing of such deaths in the news from time to time. Here is an example from a 2014 CNN report on a Pentecostal snake handler on a reality TV show!

> Jamie Coots died Saturday evening after refusing to be treated, Middlesboro police said.
>
> On "Snake Salvation," the ardent Pentecostal believer said that he believed that a passage in the Bible suggests poisonous snakebites will not harm believers as long as they are anointed by God. The practice is illegal in most states, but still goes on, primarily in the rural South.[53]

Unfortunately, they do not realize, until it is too late, that these *sign gifts have been placed on hold by God*, and that the perpetrators are *not legitimate apostles* (see the qualification of an apostle, below).

---

[53] Ashley Fantz, *Reality show snake-handling preacher dies of snakebite*, CNN, (Updated 8:29 AM EST, Tue. February 18, 2014), https://www.cnn.com/2014/02/16/us/snake–salvation–pastor–bite/index.html.

I think I should pause, and deal with the criticism that could come at this point. Some might attempt to label me as a "cessationist." I really think name calling is a subtle form of the *ad hominem* fallacy, in logic. If you are afraid you cannot win in a fair debate on the facts, you call the other party a name and try to get the audience on your side.

I am not a cessationist, but rather, I am a *"LAPSATIONIST."* I don't believe the sign gifts ceased forever. I believe they were *temporarily laid aside by our Sovereign God* because *all HIS purposes for them had been fulfilled* until the end of the church age when they will be reinstated by Him.

I know and believe that God can do what He wants, when He wishes, and I believe these gifts will *return to full operation* during the last portion of the Great Tribulation period. So, *they have not permanently ceased; they have been paused by God*, who controls them according to His Will.

We see that the laying on of hands was practiced in the early church, and *sign gifts* often accompanied this practice in O.T. and early N.T. history, *but they began to wane even before the death of the Apostles.*

Four Purposes of First Century Sign Gifts

Sign gifts were given to the apostles and people closely associated with them. We have just seen one of the most important purposes of the sign gifts, in the Bible: (1) To authenticate the NEW message of the gospel of grace, and the messengers thereof (mainly for the sake of the Jews, who require a *sign*).

Other purposes are: (2) To prove Gentiles could be saved; (3) To provide Scriptural truths before the churches had the entire N.T. (as by "words of wisdom" and "words of knowledge"); (4) To warn Israel of impending judgement (which happened in A.D. 70 when Titus and the Roman legions destroyed Jerusalem). Once these purposes were fulfilled, the *sign gifts* abated.

Let's discuss the purposes in more detail:

(1) To authenticate the NEW message of the gospel of grace

We have already cited many Scriptures, above, providing examples of sign gifts authenticating the messengers of the new gospel message before the Jews first, and also the Gentiles. The effect was profound and powerful, and it changed the belief system of the Roman Empire in just a few short years (5–7 years) as word spread of the miracles, signs, and wonders done by Jesus and then the apostles and prophets, along with the disciples of Christ. This is what we learn:

**This idea of authentication of the message
by a miracle is not just a theological idea
but rather, a <u>Scriptural fact</u>.**

This scriptural fact that *sign gifts authenticate* the *messengers of new dispensational revelation from God,* is true of Jesus, and His apostles and early church Christians; and it was true of Noah and the Ark; Jonah and the whale; Moses and the rod of God; Daniel in the lion's den; Joseph and his dream interpretation; and Elijah and fire from heaven.

It is true from Genesis to Revelation, for all 6,000 years of human history from the creation until now. Those who would disagree can never cover up the truth of Scripture or Church history, for the truth speaks too loudly and too pervasively.

In the verses below, we see Jesus speaking and He says that they would believe Him *only because the sign miracles* He would do *vouched for His authenticity* as the Son of God, the Messiah. The signs and miracles attested to His message of grace.

- *Jesus's message* was authenticated by signs and wonders.

John 10:37–38, 42

37 If I *do not* the works of my Father, *believe me not.*
38 But *if I do*, though ye believe not me, *believe the works*: that ye may know, and believe, that the Father *is* in me, and I in him.
42 And many believed on him there.

John 4:39
39 And many of the Samaritans of that city believed on him for [because of] the saying of the woman, which testified, *He told me all that ever I did.*

John 20:24–26
24 But Thomas, one of the twelve, called Didymus, was not with them when Jesus came.

25 The other disciples therefore said unto him, We have seen the Lord. But he said unto them, *Except I shall see in his hands the print of the nails,* and put my finger into the print of the nails, and thrust my hand into his side, *I will not believe.*

26 And after eight days again his disciples were within, and Thomas with them: *then came Jesus, the doors being shut, and stood in the midst,* and said, Peace *be* unto you.

If you want to talk about a ***sign miracle***, after His resurrection, Jesus passed right through the walls of the room, the door being closed, and appeared to Thomas and the rest. He turned "doubting Thomas" into believing Thomas, utilizing a miraculous entry into the room!

John 20:27 Then saith he to Thomas, Reach hither thy finger, and behold my hands; and reach hither thy hand, and thrust *it* into my side: and be not faithless, but believing.

The sign here was attesting that this was in fact Jesus, and He was RISEN FROM THE DEAD! Jesus told doubting Thomas, "Because of this sign, believe." The sign authenticated Jesus's message that "I am risen."

John 20:28, 30
28 And Thomas answered and said unto him, My Lord and my God.

30 And many other signs truly did Jesus in the presence of his disciples, which are not written in this book:

And the last verse in the passage defines the very reason for sign gifts of miracles and wonders…

> **John 20:31** But these are written, [why?] *that ye might believe* that Jesus is the Christ, the Son of God; and that believing ye might have life through his name.

At the time these Jews lived, including Jesus's disciples, they *could never have conceived of gaining eternal life through believing in the name of Jesus.*

Jesus found it necessary to *affirm* this message from God, through miracles, signs, and wonders, *in order that men might believe HIM.* If this were true of the Saviour, imagine how the apostles needed to be authenticated, and so they were. God granted them the ability to perform *sign gifts* for a season.

Therefore, according to Scripture, the gifts were to be the *authentication of a new message in a new dispensation.*

> **Hebrews 2:4** God also *bearing them witness*, both *with signs and wonders*, and with divers miracles, and gifts of the Holy Ghost, *according to his own will.*

> **Acts 2:22** Ye men of Israel, hear these words; Jesus of Nazareth, a man *approved of God among you by*

miracles and wonders and signs, which God did by him in the midst of you, as ye yourselves also know.

This is not a theological idea; this is not my idea. The Holy Spirit wrote this: "***God also bearing them witness, both with signs and wonders***, and with *divers miracles*, and *gifts of the Holy Ghost*, according to ***his own will***."

God established the ***purpose of sign gifts***. ***He*** said HE was "bearing them witness"! And PLEASE notice that the sign gifts were given to certain people at a certain time for this purpose, "according to God's own will." Men do not get to choose which gifts they have—God disburses them according to His will! They are not taught; they are received as a gift.

Don't let your preacher establish new purposes for so-called modern sign gifts. Stick with the Bible. Don't pass the Word of God through *anyone else's sieve*. Let it speak clearly to you, as God meant it. The truth will set you free.

We have seen then that Jesus and His message were authenticated by *signs and wonders*. So were other messengers:

- ***The Apostle Peter's message*** was authenticated by signs and wonders.

The Apostle Peter's message of salvation by Jesus Christ was only received because *his sign gift of healing* (which was *also a gift of raising people from the dead*) authenticated his message.

Acts 9:40–42

40 But Peter put them all forth, and kneeled down, and prayed; and turning *him* to the body said, Tabitha, arise. And she opened her eyes: and when she saw Peter, she sat up.

41 And he gave her *his* hand, and lifted her up, and when he had called the saints and widows, presented her alive.

42 And *it was known* throughout all Joppa; and *many believed in the Lord.*

See the result of the sign gift? Many believed the Lord. This is the purpose!

- *The Apostle Paul's message* was authenticated by signs and wonders.

The Apostle Paul's gospel message preached to Sergius Paulus, the deputy of Salamis, in Cyprus, was believed *because his words were authenticated by a sign miracle.*

Acts 13:8–12

8 But Elymas the sorcerer (for so is his name by interpretation) withstood them, seeking to turn away the deputy from the faith.

9 Then Saul, (who also *is called* Paul,) filled with the Holy Ghost, set his eyes on him,

10 And said, O full of all subtilty and all mischief, *thou* child of the devil, *thou* enemy of all righteousness, wilt thou not cease to pervert the right ways of the Lord?

11 And now, behold, the hand of the Lord *is* upon thee, and thou shalt be blind, not seeing the sun for a season.

And immediately there fell on him a mist and a darkness; and he went about seeking some to lead him by the hand. **12** Then the deputy, when he saw what was done, <u>believed,</u> being astonished at the doctrine of the Lord.

Why was he astonished at the doctrine (the message)? Because of the miracle that accompanied it and affirmed it.

- ***The rest of the apostles' and disciples' message*** was authenticated by signs and wonders, for a season.

The believers who took the gospel to the whole known world immediately after Jesus ascended into heaven exhibited ***sign gifts*** for a season which ***authenticated their message.***

Mark 16:15–20

15 And he said unto them, Go ye into all the world, and preach the gospel to every creature.

20 And they went forth, and preached every where, the ***Lord working with them, and <u>confirming</u> the word with signs following.*** Amen.

Don't miss that last verse! The *PURPOSE* of the signs and wonders was to "***confirm the word with signs that followed.***"

Once the message had been verified and proven factual, the sign gifts were suspended.

I could quote many more passages like these, but many times throughout Bible history, from Noah to Jesus and the apostles, we see that *sign gifts from God* were for a certain purpose—to authenticate the *NEW dispensational message* being brought by God's messengers in a particular time-period, and then once the message is authenticated and received by the people, the miracles ceased for an average of 400 years. Then, when God presented new revelation, they appear again for a short season. You will see proof of this in detail in Vol. 2, Chapter 18.

(2) To prove Gentiles could be saved

Acts 10:44–48

44 While Peter yet spake these words, the Holy Ghost fell on all them which heard the word.

45 And they of the circumcision which believed were astonished, as many as came with Peter, because that *on the Gentiles also was poured out the gift of the Holy Ghost.*

46 For they heard them speak with tongues, and magnify God. Then answered Peter,

47 Can any man forbid water, that these should not be baptized, *which have received the Holy Ghost as well as we?*

48 And he commanded them to be baptized in the name of the Lord. Then prayed they him to tarry certain days.

It is clear the Jews were astonished when the Gentiles were saved and spoke in tongues. Do you believe the Jews would have ever believed God would save a Gentile if He had not attested to the fact by granting the *sign gift* of speaking in unlearned languages to these new Gentile converts, the same way He had confirmed the Jewish converts earlier? The N.T. makes it clear that the Jews did not want to believe God would even save a Gentile!

(3) To provide Scriptural truths before the churches had the entire N.T.

Let's explore a third reason sign gifts were necessary prior to the completion of the canon.

Before the N.T. canon was completed, when the early churches only had perhaps one copy of the Old Testament Scriptures, and one or two books of the N.T. (if any), there was a need for New Testament prophets—for "words of wisdom" and "words of knowledge" to be spoken to congregations. This also required those with the gift of discernment and interpretation to confirm these words, for otherwise they were totally subjective (whereas the written Word is objective).

For example, the church at Antioch was founded just after Steven was martyred and the disciples were scattered abroad, most likely in A.D. 34–35. *If this church did not yet have a copy of Paul's letter to the Ephesians*, which it could not have since it was written in A.D. 64,[54] then there is *no way that local church could*

---

[54] SCOFIELD REFERENCE NOTES, Old Scofield, (1917 Edition). The chronological order of Paul's Epistles is believed to be as follows: 1 and 2 Thessalonians, 1 and 2 Corinthians, Galatians, Romans, Philemon, Colossians, Ephesians, Philippians, 1 Timothy,

have understood the amazing knowledge that we gain from Ephesians 2:8–9:

Ephesians 2:8–9

8 For by grace are ye saved through faith; and that not of yourselves: *it is* the gift of God:

9 Not of works, lest any man should boast.

That is, UNLESS…they had a New Testament prophet among them!

That person could stand, and under the influence of the Holy Spirit, provide a *"word of knowledge"* to the church at Antioch, and tell them one Sunday morning, "The Lord has spoken to me, and He said, 'We are saved by grace through faith which is a gift from God—not something we can do for ourselves, not of our own good works, lest any of us should boast.'" Another man or woman would stand and say, "Yes, this is from the Lord," and the congregation would say, "Amen."

The Apostolic Age continued from the ministry of Jesus, until the death of the last apostle, John. There were apostles and New Testament prophets in the early church until that time. They were *"the Foundation of the church,"* which we will discuss in detail Vol. 2, Chapter 17.

Titus, 2 Timothy. The Epistles written by Paul from Rome, commonly called the Prison Epistles, [are] Ephesians, Philippians, [and] Colossians…. Ephesians was written from Rome in A.D. 64. It is the first in order of the Prison Epistles.

(4) To warn Israel of impending judgement

This last purpose for sign gifts in the early church is one of the most important and least known of all. It is highly important because this is the first mention of the use of tongue speaking in the Bible, and therefore it sets the tone for everything that follows. Here, we find the Apostle Paul speaking, and he will quote from the O.T.

1 Corinthians 14:19–22

19 Yet in the church I had rather speak five words with my understanding, that by my voice I might teach others also, than ten thousand words in an unknown tongue [foreign language].

20 Brethren, be not children in understanding…

Now this is very important. Paul is calling them "children in understanding" if they do not know about the *first purpose of tongue speaking taught in their Scriptures* (i.e., the O.T.)—i.e., a warning of impending judgment (which certainly the Jewish believers in the church should have already known). The passage continues:

21 In the law it is written, With ***men of other tongues*** and other lips will I speak unto this people; and yet for all that will they not hear me, saith the Lord.

22 Wherefore ***tongues are for a sign***, ***not to them that believe***, ***but to them that believe not***: but prophesying [speaking forth God's Word, either from the Scripture, or in the early church, by prophetic utterance] serveth not for them that believe not, but for them which believe.

Here, Paul clearly teaches that tongue speaking was for unbelievers (not Christians), and prophesying was for believers. If this had been taught clearly in American churches before 1901, there would be no Pentecostal or charismatic churches anywhere on the planet today! (See Vol. 2, Chapter 21.) Think about this, it is a little known, and sad fact.

1 Corinthians 14:23 If therefore the whole church be come together into one place, and all speak with tongues, and there come in *those that are unlearned*, or *unbelievers, will they not say that ye are mad?*
24 But if all prophesy, and there come in one that believeth not, or *one* unlearned, he is convinced of all, he is judged of all.
26 How is it then, brethren? when ye come together, every one of you hath a psalm, hath a doctrine, hath a tongue, hath a revelation, hath an interpretation. *Let all things be done unto edifying.*

When Paul wrote this, the *sign gift* of "languages" was still operative in the early church, (until A.D. 60). However, Paul teaches several things here that totally dismantle the modern tongues movement.

(1) He says praying and singing in the spirit with languages that are unknown to the crowd *does not edify the crowd*, and therefore should be done less and less (not increasingly) (vv. 15–19).

(2) Paul said that tongues *were NOT for believers*, but for "unbelievers." (Verse 22 above—so, why would we have genuine tongues in churches filled with saved people?)

(3) He says, "*Jews require a sign*, and the Greeks [Gentiles] seek after wisdom [Bible study]." (1 Cor. 1:22—so, again, why in the modern Gentile church?)

(4) Paul says that the people of the carnal Corinthian congregation were like children, abusing these gifts, because they did not understand that the *first mention of tongues* in the Bible indicates that the gift was to be given for a primary PURPOSE, and that purpose was *to warn Israel of impending judgment* (which would happen in their future, in A.D. 70 when Titus and the Roman legions would invade Jerusalem). Those who received Paul's preaching that day and let their loved ones and friends in Jerusalem know, allowing them to prepare, and leave the city and survive. Nearly 100% of those who did not heed this warning and remained in the city, perished.

> "Brethren, be not children in understanding…. In the law it is written, With *men of* other tongues and other lips will I speak unto this people; and yet for all that will they not hear me, saith the Lord."—**1 Cor.14:20–21**

Paul, here, is quoting from passages in the O.T. which provide the original purpose of tongues in the Bible.

The Ancient Prophecies that Tongues would Appear As a Warning to Israel of Impending Judgement:

Deuteronomy 28:49 The LORD shall bring a nation against thee from far, from the end of the earth, as swift as the eagle flieth; a nation *whose __tongue__ thou shalt not understand;*
50 A nation of fierce countenance, which shall not regard the person of the old, nor show favour to the young.

The following O.T. prophecies of tongues dealt with the Assyrian language, which sounded like stammering lips to the Jews, and this was prior to the Babylonian captivity (600 B.C.). The primary purpose of tongues, then, was in fact *to warn Israel of impending judgment by God*, as you will see below:

Jeremiah 5:15–20
15 Lo, I will bring a nation upon you from far, O house of Israel, saith the LORD: it is a mighty nation, it is an ancient nation, a nation whose language thou knowest not, neither understandest what they say.
16 Their quiver is as an open sepulchre, they are all mighty men.
17 And they shall eat up thine harvest, and thy bread, which thy sons and thy daughters should eat…. They shall impoverish thy fenced cities, wherein thou trustedst, with the sword.
18 Nevertheless in those days, saith the LORD, I will not make a full end with you.

19 And it shall come to pass, when ye shall say, Wherefore doeth the LORD our God all these things unto us? then shalt thou answer them, Like as ye have forsaken me, and served strange gods in your land, so shall ye serve strangers in a land that is not yours.

20 Declare this in the house of Jacob, and publish it in Judah....

Prophecies usually have a ***near fulfillment and a far fulfillment.*** The near was the destruction of Israel by the Babylonians. The far was the Destruction of Jerusalem in A.D. 70, by the Romans.

Isaiah 28:10–11, 16–17

10 For precept must be upon precept, precept upon precept; line upon line, line upon line; here a little, and there a little:

11 For with stammering lips and another tongue will he speak to this people.

16 Therefore thus saith the Lord GOD, Behold, I lay in Zion for a foundation a stone, a tried stone, a precious corner stone, a sure foundation: he that believeth shall not make haste.

17 Judgment also will I lay to the line, and righteousness to the plummet: and the hail shall sweep away the refuge of lies, and the waters shall overflow the hiding place.

Now we have seen all four purposes God had in granting the ***sign gifts*** to exactly whom He wished, ***when*** He wished during the Apostolic Age.

Once the N.T. gospel message of grace, and its messengers, had been authenticated; and the Jews saw that God would actually save the Gentiles (because they too spoke in tongues); and the Early Church finally had all the books of the N.T. canon (A.D. 85–90); and the Jews had been warned of impending judgement for their sins, and for rejecting their Messiah; all God's purposes for the *apostolic sign gifts* had been fulfilled, and they faded away.

But God did not pause them permanently. There has been a *lapse*, or interval of time, between when they were no longer energized by the Holy Spirit, due to the Father's will, and when they will be *reinstated during the last 3 ½ years* of the *tribulation period.*

When they are reinstated, they will have virtually identical purposes: to authenticate the new message of the new Gospel of the Kingdom (slightly different than the gospel of the church age, suited for preparing for the Kingdom of God); perhaps to provide words of knowledge to those who no longer can find a Bible (and who knows, maybe by then Gentiles will believe God would save a Jew!); and finally, to warn the Jews of impending judgement during the remainder of the tribulation period. They will need to be warned to listen to the two prophets, to the angel circling the earth and witnessing, and to the 144,000 Jewish evangelists preaching the soon return of the Messiah found in the Book of Revelation!

Why I Need Volume II

SYNOPSIS OF VOL. I AND INTRO TO VOL. II

We have come to the conclusion of Volume 1, having studied the first five of eight core doctrines of the Bible, which must be mastered before moving on to the deeper things of God.

The Doctrine of Christ was the all-important starting point, which gives structure and meaning to all the other doctrines. Once we know exactly Who Jesus is, and then we come to know Him personally, then we benefit from everything else in the Bible, for He is "God seen."

The Doctrine of The Foundation of Repentance from Dead Works is very important because it teaches us what true repentance is (the changing of one's mind), and what it is not (stop smoking, stop cursing, etc.). It also teaches us what we are changing our minds about. For example, works of the flesh, or religious works cannot save us, and they cannot take our sins away. Also, God is God, and we are not—we cannot save ourselves. Jesus is a better Lord of our lives than we are! Only the finished work of Christ, His blood given as payment of our sin debt, can accomplish salvation.

We now understand that most Christians in modern churches do not really have a clear understanding of what true repentance is, or how the gospel works to bring salvation.

The Doctrine of The Foundation of Faith Toward God is important because it is different than faith "in" Jesus, or the faith "of" Jesus, though vitally related. If we put God's kingdom first, and His imputed righteousness, all the worldly THINGS we need will be provided by Him. We no longer need to fret about these things. The teaching brings a very important aspect of the Christian faith into full view as expressed in the following verse:

1 Timothy 5:8

8 But if any provide not for his own, and specially for those of his own house, he hath denied the faith, and is worse than an infidel.

We are held responsible to create enough wealth to provide for our children and grandchildren, but we can only do this by seeking God's Kingdom first! We must keep the eyes of our faith looking toward God as we walk in this life. We must rely upon God for our well-being, not upon money (or any other person or thing).

In our lesson on *The Doctrine of Baptisms* we learned that there are seven different types of baptism taught in the Bible. The most important principle learned is that water baptism is a picture, or type, of Spirit Baptism, and Spirit Baptism occurs at the moment of our salvation when we are indwelt by the Holy Spirit once and for all. Having a clear understanding of this, and the difference between the indwelling and the filling of the Spirit, can save one from a world of false doctrine.

IMPORTANT INFORMATION IN VOL. II

The Doctrine of the Laying On of Hands and things associated with this N.T. practice were introduced in Volume 1. In Vol. 2, Chapters 16–21, there is much more detailed information on sign gifts associated with ***Laying on of Hands in the early church***. This includes important information from the Scriptures and from church history on when these gifts were paused by God, and when they will be reinstated, and why this knowledge is imperative for the joy and success of Christian people in the mature church age.

Chapter 22 is an important study on the core ***Doctrine of the Resurrection of the Dead,*** which is key in understanding the timing of the Second Coming and the Rapture of the church.

How many resurrections are there? When do they occur? What other things are associated with these resurrections? The answer to all these questions are found in Vol. 2. A misunderstanding of the resurrections may lead to a false belief in the chronology of the end-times. ***This could be devastating to the family which is not prepared for the tribulation that is to come.*** Vol. 2 therefore, is indispensable to the Christian with regard to preparing for the "Day of the Lord."

Chapter 23 clarifies what the Bible teaches about the core ***Doctrine of Eternal Judgment***, including hades and hell, the Judgment seat of Christ, and the Great White Throne Judgment. It also discusses why God is just in judging a fallen race, and also just in saving a remnant.

It answers the question, "Why would a loving God doom any human to hell for eternity?"

Volume 2, therefore, is indispensable in equipping us to be able to humbly explain the dangers of not personally knowing Jesus Christ. It motivates us to tell the gospel to loved ones and friends, and it motivates them to listen!

Chapter 24 is the most important core doctrine of all—*The Eternal Security of the believer*. Of all the core doctrines in this book, this one is the *most essential for the mental and spiritual well-being of new Christians and mature Christians alike*; this doctrine must be mastered by all Christians before they may have a joyful and peaceful life, and then also move on to the deeper things of God.

Do you have friends who believe they could lose their salvation after being born again? Do you have the answers for why you believe they are incorrect? You'll find all the answers in Volume 2!

It is my prayer that Volume 1 of *Christian Posture* has been a help and a blessing to you. More than anything, it is my desire for you to STUDY the Word of God for yourself, for there is nothing in this world more powerful or important than the truth found in its pages.

Now, please enjoy *Volume 2—Christian Posture: Walk Tall, Stand Straight in a Crooked World–Eight Core Doctrines.*

Appendix 1, Vol. I
Bibles and Study Helps

If you can locate a copy of ***The New Scofield Study Bible, KJV*** at a used book store or online, grab it. (Make sure it is not a regular Scofield, but NEW Scofield Study Bible, and please make certain it is KJV.) The KJV has the correct underlying Greek, and virtually all modern versions do not, including the NIV and the NAS Bibles, for example. All modern versions of the English Bible are interpreted from the Westcott/Hort Greek which is perverted. Certain YouTube hosts speak of lies about these two men, but you must go back to the scholars of the 1800s, such as Dean John Burgon and F.H.P. Scrivener who wrote against Westcott and Hort to find the truth of their serious errors. Their bad underlying Greek manuscripts make the modern versions unreliable, unfortunately.

Some say the KJV is difficult to read (even though for much of the history of our nation, children were taught to read from the Book of John in the KJV). However, the New Scofield not only comes from the proper Greek line of manuscripts, it also ***removes archaic English words*** and replaces them with modern English, ***making it easy to read.*** It has the integrity to show you where these changes are made, placing the original KJV word in the margin. My amazing mentor, Dr. Irwin (Rocky) Freeman used this Bible in his preaching around the world, and I have used it many times. Many of our TRADEway friends across the nation have located these Bibles on **eBay** or from other sources for used books. (You may wish to pick up a used copy of the ***Unger's Bible Dictionary*** as well, published in the late 1900s and very early 2000s—the newer versions are not as good.)

To connect with me, please visit parkmeadowschurch.com where you will find a treasure trove of sermons, lessons, and resources to help you grow as a Christian (including our weekly live church services). You may also email me at info@christianposture.com. Or for more information on our family business, you may visit tradeway.com.

To get a FREE copy of "The Ten Rules of Bible Interpretation," go to ChristianPosture.com.

Appendix 2, Vol. I
The Doctrine of Christ (Summarized)

1. First Old Testament prophecy: The Messiah would be born of a virgin. He would be fully God and fully man.

2. Second Old Testament prophecy: The Messiah would be born in a specific town. This infers once again that He would be fully God and fully man.

3. Third Old Testament prophecy: The Messiah would be born at a specific time.

4. Fourth Old Testament prophecy: Tells WHO the Messiah IS—the God-man. The New Testament Confirms He is fully God and fully man, and His name is Jesus Christ.

5. Fifth Old Testament prophecy: The Messiah would be crucified (predicted 440 years before crucifixion was invented).

   a. Jesus said the very words that the Psalms predicted the Messiah would say while on the cross.

   b. The people around the cross despised Him and He was a reproach of men. They laughed at him, and said, "He trusted on the Lord *that* he would deliver him: Let him deliver him, seeing he delighted in him."

   c. It was prophesied that the Messiah's "strength is dried up like a potsherd; And my tongue cleaveth to my jaws, And thou hast brought me into the dust of death" (Psalm 22:15).

    d. It was prophesied, "For dogs have compassed me: The assembly of the wicked have inclosed me: They pierced my hands and my feet" (Psalm 22:16).

    e. It was prophesied, "They look *and* stare upon me" (Psalm 22:17b).

6. Sixth Old Testament prophecy: The Roman guards would cast lots for Jesus's clothing.

7. Seventh Old Testament prophecy: The Messiah's bones would not be broken on the cross.

8. Eighth Old Testament prophecy: The Messiah, the Son of God, would be called out of Egypt.

9. In the Old Testament book of Exodus, God calls Himself "I AM." The man Jesus Christ claimed to be the "I AM."

10. Jesus Christ claimed to be God to the Apostle Thomas.

11. Jesus claimed to be God to Philip, the Apostle.

12. Jesus claimed to be the BREAD of life, who gives everlasting life to all who partake of Him by faith.

13. Jesus claimed to be the WATER of life.

14. Jesus claimed to be the only DOOR to heaven. All other ways to heaven are false, and all others who claim to be the way are thieves and robbers who come only to steal and to kill and to destroy (i.e., false teachers; false Messiahs).

15. Jesus claimed He was the ONLY way to heaven, the ONLY truth, and the ONLY life, and that _no_ man comes to the Father except by Jesus Christ. He also said, "If you've seen me, you have seen the Father."

16. Jesus said of Himself that no other had ever seen the Father except Himself, adding, "He that believes in me

HAS everlasting life," and, "I am the light of the world… if you follow me you shall have the light of life."

17. Jesus claimed that He was the Good Shepherd who laid down His life for the sheep. He also claimed He would be resurrected. He is the risen Saviour.

18. Jesus claimed that He would go to Heaven and prepare a place for us and come again (the Second Coming of Christ) to take us there.

19. Jesus claimed that after He went to heaven, He would send the Holy Spirit to indwell every believer and be our Comforter.

20. Jesus claimed He would die and raise Himself up in three days.

21. Jesus claimed He came to seek and to save that which was lost.

22. Jesus prayed for His own sheep.

23. Jesus claimed He would come again, just as He went into Heaven.

24. Jesus claimed He would raise the dead at the first resurrection.

25. Jesus claimed He would separate the sheep from the goats, the wheat from the tares; that He would send the wheat/sheep (believers) to heaven; and bind the tares into bundles and burn them, i.e., send the tares/goats (unbelievers) to hell.

26. John the Baptist testified that Jesus Christ was the Son of God, the Lamb of God who would die for the sins of God's people.

27. The Apostle Paul says Jesus Christ is "all of the fullness of the Godhead in a body." He is God in the flesh.

28. Jesus is the Author and Finisher of our Faith, according to the author of Hebrews.
29. Jesus is our Intercessor, our Advocate with the Father, and our High Priest.
30. The Apostle Peter preached a sermon in the book of Acts and said that Jesus Christ was the <u>ONLY name</u> given under heaven among men, whereby we must be saved.
31. The Great Apostle Paul says that Jesus is declared to be the Son of God with power by His resurrection and that over 500 people who were still alive in Paul's day saw the resurrected Saviour.
32. Paul also made it clear that salvation is by the FAITH OF Christ on the cross and not by works of righteousness which we could try to do. Righteousness comes to us only as we have the faith of Christ.
33. Paul teaches that Christ died for us before we even knew we wanted Him! He died in our place. This is known as the substitutionary death of Christ.
34. Paul says our salvation in Christ is a FREE GIFT. As such, we cannot lose it because we did not earn it and because Jesus's love for His sheep is eternal.
35. The Scriptures teach that Jesus's death was the RANSOM paid to set us free.
36. The Scriptures teach that Jesus's death propitiated Holy God's justice and hatred of sin.
37. Jesus says all true Christians bear fruit, and also He ascended to heaven and gave gifts to men.
38. Jesus made us righteous by giving us HIS righteousness. This is called <u>positional</u> righteousness. This righteousness comes because of the great <u>Doctrine of Imputation</u>.

39. Perhaps the greatest testimony of all is God the Father's. He said exactly Who Jesus is.

40. Jesus's LOVE for us caused Him to become our SUBSTITUTE (He died in our place).

41. Jesus's DEATH Reconciled us to God.

42. Jesus's finished work Justified us.

43. Jesus gave His blood to Redeem us.

44. Because we experienced a co-resurrection with Christ, we are FORGIVEN all our trespasses—PAST, PRESENT, AND FUTURE.

www.ingramcontent.com/pod-product-compliance
Lightning Source LLC
Chambersburg PA
CBHW051129120626
46547CB00012B/725